# *Updated Teaching*

# *Encounters with Gurdjieff*

*(Now in a simpler and generally accessible form, an introduction to Gurdjieff's personal/ spiritual development teaching, including crucial new material previously unavailable.)*

*David Hughes*
*(M.A., M.Ed.)*

Balboa Press books may be ordered through booksellers or by contacting:

Balboa Press
A Division of Hay House
1663 Liberty Drive
Bloomington, IN 47403
www.balboapress.com.au
1 (877) 407-4847



Print information available on the last page.

ISBN: 978-1-5043-0546-4 (sc)
ISBN: 978-1-5043-0547-1 (e)

Balboa Press rev. date: 12/22/2016

Why should we think that,
a mystical/spiritual teacher like Gurdjieff,
who sought to show his students the path to
personal mastery and immortality,
could not find a way after passing over,
to fulfil the mission he was unable to
complete satisfactorily while here,
to give his teaching simply to those who
could use it,
when the time was right for its acceptance?

Remember, Gurdjieff once said that "many things" were possible when asked if we could have communication with those who had died. (See Ouspensky's In Search of the Miraculous, p. 31.)

# Contents

# Who Was Gurdjieff?

In the early 1920s a powerful and unusual spiritual teacher 'arrived' in the West. It was George Ivanovich Gurdjieff (1867-1949), known universally just as "Gurdjieff". (Pronouncing his name as "gur-dee-eff" is fine.)

He is sometimes grouped with Aleister Crowley and Rasputin as one of the three most important 'occult' figures of the era. While he displayed fewer powers of the magician than the other two, his understanding of the path to personal development and masterhood was greater. He also constantly sought to teach those who came to him.

He was born of a Greek father and Armenian mother into a comfortable 'peasant' family in the Caucasus region of what later became the USSR. Some unusual childhood and adolescent experiences projected him into a life-long quest to understand the mystery of human existence. He followed various clues in a highly individual way, and this method proved as integral as what he discovered for unlocking the potential we all have.

As a young man he travelled widely into various countries to collect ancient and surviving teachings. Mystical, spiritual, philosophical, religious, psychological, anthropological and practical inputs were all gathered. He had a genius for working in practical and resourceful ways, to get to the essence of matters. It eventually gave him the keys for how a person could attain higher states of consciousness. He told people to "work on themselves", "remember themselves", and seek what was "real".

He began organised teaching in Russia around 1908-10, where he transmitted methods for personal development. Groups were conducted around Russia until he moved south in the aftermath of the First World War, and the spread of the Russian Revolution. He was forced to move to Turkey, and then set his sights on the Western World, shifting first to Germany and then to France. His Paris Institute was set up in 1922.

He impacted the Western cosmopolitan scene, and

attracted many notable students. There were also a number of trips to the U.S., and groups were set up there. After a serious car crash in 1924 he began his own series of enigmatic writings. His teaching and 'presence' had a profound effect on hundreds, or thousands, of people who met him. He also organised groups to protect and transmit his writings, containing his veiled teachings, after his death.

He was extremely disappointed that the timing was always against him for his planned general awakening of people. He never stopped looking forward to a time when the full impact of what he knew could be released into the world

# Foreword (Gurdjieff's)

(The teaching in this book was inspired and guided by "channelled" messages. That is explained in my following Preface. I had always hoped Gurdjieff would provide an introductory preamble to this book which he had asked me to write. Then, in August 2012, his intention to provide a foreword to the book was conveyed to me. Several statements and claims were made for that purpose. He said that he could only directly write the foreword if it was read out loud to a group of people, so he could assess their responses. [That was how he composed his major work, Beelzebub.] Not possible in this case, he left it to me to pass on his 'ideas' as they were communicated to me.)

He said his message through the various (current) Gurdjieff groups "has been lost". This is because, as generally with this kind of teaching, as generations go on, people start bringing in too much of their own personalities. This imports imperfect understandings into the system.

He affirmed that when he 'anointed' Fritz Peters (as his successor), it was "a profound decision". He said Peters was, in fact, the "only fully independent functioning adult there". And, he had got the message (to anoint Peters) "intrinsically".

He said: "Look at Peters and how he lived. He wasn't a group member. He was just living his own life." And he said that Peters' book, Balanced Man, is "a crucially important book for the teaching".

He went on to say the (current) groups have "faded" because no-one in them intrinsically understands his teaching. They have become "delusional" and "inward-looking".

In his early life, he had travelled widely to collect and put together teaching based on an amalgam of ancient teachings. The central concern and theme of them was "lifting the veil of illusion".

He affirmed that his childhood experience had been crucial for him. But the Russian experience, as he fled amid the chaos (of the aftermath of war and revolution), consolidated his sense of the danger of man acting on false beliefs.

He said if he was born today, he wouldn't spend much time with the "groups". But he would "venture out, trying to find what they'd lost".

He saw this present book as "the start of trying to get people re-engaged in that journey". This book, he said, "does have within it...the very strong basic understanding of the material at the introductory level". But, claimed, within this book there are a "couple of blind alleys". (He wouldn't tell me where they were. But obviously he had allowed that, or led me into including them.) He said they "were put there for a reason". "Nothing easy", he said. (In other words, we must all work to make the teaching our own.)

It is important while people read this book, when they are confronted or challenged by something there, that they "must turn the mirror back on themselves". They should identify the issue, and then trace back the source of their belief. Then they should consider "what is the carrot of that belief?"

People have become too accepting of the 'traditions' of the Gurdjieff groups. They cling to the notion of the "unbroken oral tradition". The impression is given of "secrets being held". But, he said, there's nothing to them. If (people in the groups) held something of importance, they'd have "written 60 books about it by now".

Finally, he once said (while living) that he was the equivalent of Christ. What he meant when he said that was, <u>everyone</u> (including himself) had that equivalence. But now, he said, people in the groups don't even aspire to be him, far less Christ. So we need to find or recover our sense of wonder or aspiration, so we have the vision to rise to such a level.

# Preface (The Writer's)

Many may want to know how and why this book came to be written. It will no doubt be seen by those in the Gurdjieff traditions as "coming out of left field". The teaching proper starts in the following chapter, but the background information given here gives the context of the whole enterprise and contains much of interest.

An unusual collaboration began in 1984 when Gurdjieff addressed me through a trance medium. He asked me to write a book correcting and extending aspects of his available teaching.

I had not sought to contact him, far less obtain teaching from him. It didn't even occur to me that he might be available for that. A series of unusual events had been pushing my life in new directions at the time. I was lecturing in philosophy at a regional college. But my long-standing interest in psychic and spiritual things had been steadily quickening into more direct personal experience.

So I was surprised, and also delighted, by his 'appearance'. I was very interested in what he might have to say. At the time I barely understood why he might ask and expect <u>me</u> to advance his teaching. Over time, however, he expressed confidence in my "feeling perception" of things. This was apparently the element crucially lacking in those who sought his teaching earlier last century. The transmission of his teaching in those times had become impossibly convoluted and 'intellectual' as he sought to bridge that gap.

I was also, of course, wary of what such a task might involve. But he assured me he would assist me through the process, and was happy to proceed.

## Updating Gurdjieff's Teaching

So, what exactly did he want me to write this book about? Initially he said it was, "what he was about while he was here". Only, he had often been "misquoted", or what he actually said was "never quoted properly". Much of what he told people had been missed, or misunderstood, or misconstrued. There were important things he just couldn't get through to those who sought his teaching. In that situation there was much that couldn't be effectively said.

(He later said to me: "If you told people what they wanted to hear, they would listen. But when you told them something they didn't want to hear, they wouldn't. They would just ignore it.")

Everything had become so "knotted-up", for a variety of reasons. It had taken a long time to be able to stand back from that. But, now he wanted his essential message restated simply. He said it was becoming possible now to effectively pass on a number of things which couldn't be said before.

He wanted to inform a new generation, who would be ready for his message. He was especially concerned about genuine seekers, and what they needed to find their way. He didn't want them confused and led astray through old, misunderstood versions of his teaching.

Of course, I knew the teaching he left behind had been incomplete. It had involved and intrigued so many people. But it seemed to only take them to a certain point, where they were unsure about how to continue further. So I was eager to hear what more he had to say.

I asked him how he wanted me to present this teaching. I was wondering, amongst other things, how far people would be open to hear Gurdjieff messages "from the other side". But he said I was to "express fully and frankly", and that I "must tell it directly, as it is". So much of it would be just correcting and making sense of what he was reported as saying when he was here. Or, he needed to point out how things he said had not been understood properly. So I was happy to proceed on that basis.

It concerned me somewhat that "restating Gurdjieff simply" could be an almost impossible task. There were times when I struggled long and hard with it, even with his calculated inputs. This is where "feeling-perception" and grasping the essence of things had to come to the fore. I had to practice restating some of the ideas in his long and involved teaching just in their barest essentials. I had to work at the same time on modifying the philosophical style I had been trained in, to cut back the big words and long, involved sentences.

The results sometimes seemed too simple and obvious, hardly justifying the effort to get there. But he reassured me, "The simpler the better". However, everything of substance still had to be included.

**The Channelled Messages**

In all, there were seven months of channelled communication, spread through 21 trance sessions. So much of it was illuminating and heartening as it was given, but it was all in pieces. I had the task, after a specified interval of time, of fitting them together with the recognised teaching from a variety of published sources. There were reasons for that. The timing had to be right. It had to engage me, or my 'feeling perception', in the understanding and expression of it. It needed to "make sense" to me in the way I put it together. Once when I asked for further clarification of something, Gurdjieff just said: "You're the philosopher. That's your job."

Sometimes he just expected me to simplify sections of his previously given teaching where no special revision was called for. He wanted me to produce a simplified account of his basic teaching. (He'd emphasised, "simple, not simplistic".) This had not been possible, for a number of reasons, during his lifetime. I note that he had asked Ouspensky to perform this task back in the 1920s and 1930s. He asked him to rewrite the teaching in a form that would be intelligible, or accessible, to all. But it was something Ouspensky could not bring himself to do. He was too locked into the great intellectual adventure which had caught his imagination. So he ran with what he had – the initial talks given in 1915-7 to attract the attention of Western thinkers. But what Gurdjieff wanted then, to further advance his mission, was a way to make what he knew accessible to a wider range of people.

We see in his book, Life is real only then, when "I am" [p. 6], how he was troubled by this in 1934. After substantially writing his first two books, he was still wrestling with the need to make his ideas readily available to everyone. He was concerned that he could not achieve a peaceful conclusion to his life if that task was not completed.

In talking to me, he clarified an enormous number of things about his lifetime and previous teaching. He added much that was new or not previously revealed. (Including some of his 'secrets'.) At last I could see basically what he was trying to do with and for people during his lifetime. No-one with him at that time got the full picture. Anyone previously acquainted with the Gurdjieff material will find much of interest here. Those who haven't encountered him before will find an invaluable guide for their personal development.

## My Involvement

Initially I sought some clarification of why he was asking me to write this book. I told him I was honoured by his request of me. But he sidestepped any question of 'why', simply saying that it wasn't a question of honour. He just said drily that he was no longer in a position to write the book himself.

It subsequently became clear I had the same (inner) essence as him. (That is the essence of "Mercury", to be explained later.) He would by choice have looked for someone with the same essence, to match his own orientation. And presumably my "feeling perception" indicated growth in essence. Beyond that I had no further indication. But I suppose I was willing to persevere, to complete the task.

In terms of my situation, Gurdjieff 'arrived' just as I completed the thesis for my second Masters degree in the philosophical area. I was in my late 30s, having lectured in philosophy and education for 9 years. I had been pursuing a wide range of spiritual and psychic interests for some time.

Beyond that was an on-going desire to find the truth about, and connect with, the "otherness" that must lie behind everyday life. In that respect I was a "seeker". My quest had been fed by the wonderful explosion of cheap psychic/ spiritual books which became available from the late 1960s. During the 1980s a constant chain of coincidences led me into the realms of spiritualism and contact with those of similar interests.

Perhaps it was my philosophical training on the one hand, and my openness to psychic/spiritual matters on the other, which interested him. I had learnt how to be critical and discerning without buying into the self-assured sterile scepticism of so many academics. I knew there were "far more things in heaven and earth" than the average person manages to encounter in a few years at university.

I had been impressed when I read P.D.Ouspensky's <u>In Search of the Miraculous</u> (hereafter <u>ISOTM</u>) in 1972. I thought I had found someone in Gurdjieff who "actually knew something". It felt like the basis for a reliable explanation of the deeper things of life. I devoured what was there, and bought a few more books by and about him. But it wasn't clear how to advance much further in that direction. So I took "remembering oneself", "not identifying with outer life", and a new inner sense of self, and moved on. 1972 saw me change direction and head into the education area where job opportunities were then opening-up. I put my post-graduate philosophical work on hold, and abandoned some extra-curricula religious studies. By 1974 I was into Transcendental Meditation, and gained my lecturing job in 1975

The 1980s opened up areas of personal experience for me beyond the ordinary and everyday. I had longed for that for years. ("If there's more there, I want to experience it.") I learnt to balance dealing with different realities in their own terms at the same time. In my 20s I had struggled with the question of what was real, and how one knows it to be so. I wanted to contact dimensions beyond the everyday one, which were always enticing. But I was up against sceptical arguments, and the doubts they generate. Maybe what I wanted was not there, or couldn't be reliably accessed if it was there.

But by the 1980s I was directly experiencing things beyond the everyday world, which left no doubt. So I could relax in that knowledge and just address whatever reality presented itself at any time. I came to see the state (or being) of people in themselves governed what realities they were open to. Beyond that, it was pointless trying to argue them into or out of anything.

By 1983/4 I was sitting in spiritualist development circles. I was told there that I could contribute more by working with the messages from mediums rather than becoming one myself. That was all background for what was to follow.

## Context of the Gurdjieff Offer

Further 'coincidences' led me into working with someone whose clairvoyant and mediumship abilities opened-up after we met. We began weekly trance sessions. Before long, a number of other people heard about this, and asked to be included in a group with us.

This had barely got going, with the trance sessions on Mondays and the group meetings on Thursdays, when Gurdjieff 'arrived'. A night or two before one of our trance sessions, I had the strangest feeling as I drifted between waking and sleep. I 'felt' that Gurdjieff – who I had not even read anything about for years – was with me. Could it be that he might have a role to play in our trance and group work? When I explained this to the medium at our next session, she said: "That's right! He's here with us now, laughing like a drain-pipe. And he says he's ready to proceed!"

There were a few preliminaries at this first session. Gurdjieff put his offer to me as a *quid pro quo*. He said: "I help you with your group. Then you help me with the book." He was apparently still burdened by the fact that he'd left many things obscure and incomplete when he died. He said it was inhibiting his ability to go on. He hadn't found anyone during his lifetime that he was able to pass the rest of his teaching on to. But he apparently saw the opportunity with us to do something about that.

He said he would guide me through the whole process. He wanted to directly impress his thoughts on me while having the medium convey his words. This would confirm the sense and meaning of the messages as they were given. Often enough I anticipated the very things the medium was about to say from him. This was to avoid misunderstanding and misconstruction, which hampered his teaching in the past. It would also accustom me to his presence and influence while working on the material later by myself.

I was somewhat amused, but reassured, to see some of the characteristic behaviours he displayed. With typical autocratic gusto, he spoke abruptly to the medium: "You, woman – you say exactly what I say! Change nothing!" (She told me this later, It wasn't said out loud.) He seriously wanted the transmission to be accurate. It wasn't to be spoilt by the medium relying on her own ideas, or trying to correct anything that seemed 'odd' to her. Obviously she was peeved by his manner, and asked me: "Has he got a Messiah complex or something?" But it was just the way he normally operated, and he always gave people such 'jolts' for a reason. (And yes, he did have a kind of Messianic sense – a profound commitment to his 'mission'. But then again, who else knew what he did? If he couldn't pass it on, it would be lost.) He also didn't want the medium reading anything about him or his teaching while our sessions progressed, to avoid preconceptions.

Then, including the medium and myself, we realised our group had exactly seven members. This was set-up before he 'arrived'. Obviously it was all pre-planned at some level, where our conscious participation was the last piece to fall into place. Then, as he elucidated the seven essences, or inner natures, we saw our group had precisely one of each. It was far more than coincidence. It was as if everything in our lives for years had been pre-planned, or pre-agreed, for us to arrive simultaneously at that point.

## After-Death Communication

There might be a problem for some long-term followers of Gurdjieff to accept the reality of after-death communication from him. They might also be wary of the authenticity of what I received. Despite the amazing coincidences which led me into this work, I was always very mindful of establishing its trustworthiness. As a philosopher, my training had been in assessing evidence and its reliability. Gurdjieff had also told his followers to satisfy themselves about the truth of anything they were told, and to accept nothing without that.

Something immediately struck me as incongruous when the medium first confirmed Gurdjieff's presence to me. Like, this wasn't the way one expected to work with him and his teaching! (But then again, what other way is there to communicate with someone who has passed over?)

Anyway, I asked him to square his communicating with me in this way with what he taught during his life. (He had reflected the Sufi stance that we might or might not survive death.) I knew he had told his students to work to attain the possibility of a soul and immortality. That was a powerful motivation to get them working. He immediately took my question on board, and gave me seven reasons for teaching what he did, while here, when he knew somewhat otherwise.

Basically, he said people won't work to attain something they think they already have. (Yet, most people aren't in touch with the soul-aspect of themselves.) He also wanted to steer off intellectual curiosity in this area, and put peoples' attention on achieving important things more at hand. One of the 'reasons' he gave me was simply a long laugh. (I can't be more specific here. I wasn't using a tape-recorder at this first session, and lost some of the details. But I've given basically what he said.)

## It was All Known to Him

Gurdjieff, of course, knew all about trances, mediums and spiritualistic communications. He boasts in Herald of Coming Good of his unusually extensive knowledge of such supernatural "sciences". These included occultism, theosophy and spiritualism. He even claimed he was adept in bringing about 'tricks' in these domains. He had started his organised teaching at Tashkent around 1910 as a professed instructor in these supernatural areas.

Later, when he adopted a different, more "scientific", teaching strategy he just bundled those things under the heading of a "specific psychosis". He was protecting the credibility of the more 'scientific' presentation of his teaching, in the face of the rising scientific attitude of the Western mind. By that time he had determined his impact had to be in the Western world. So the teaching had to be adapted to that in its presentation.

He had also been concerned that the spiritualist-type circles he had originally set up in eastern Russia were only attracting certain 'types'. The method was wrong for drawing-in the full range of human types he needed for later work. Even in Moscow there still weren't enough types. So he had to consider working in Germany, England or France. Finally in Paris he found the most cosmopolitan mix of people. But the Western intelligentsia he attracted there in the 1920s weren't going to buy the 'supernatural' elements. So he pooh-poohed them and put them to the side.

While I was asking him how to present this teaching, he said to drop the scientific trappings. ("I tried it, and it didn't work.") It <u>had</u> worked for disseminating so much of his teaching in the West. But it didn't work for getting it all out properly, or for inducting people into advanced stages of working on themselves. He said to me: "Just tell it like it is", "make it simple", and "don't negate the spiritual" elements. People would be ready for that by the time this book came to be published. Readers of his previously published teachings may find it strange to see him talking freely to me about "old souls", "karma", "chakras" and so forth in his messages through the medium.

## Gurdjieff's Spiritual Guardian

An even bigger surprise may come for some when I say that Gurdjieff was in constant, direct contact with his attendant spiritual guardian. The "guardian" is the overseer from the other side which numerous spiritual traditions claim we all have during each earthly life. Not many people are aware of their guardians, and very few indeed have direct contact with them.

Gurdjieff heard the messages and promptings from his guardian in early childhood – as many do – but also later for most of his adult life. He even passed on much of the advice he received from there *verbatim* to others. He had a "trick" for doing this in a 'scientific' way. He simply attributed the words to that legendary character who he said embodied the popular wisdom of Asia – the Mullah Nassr Eddin! Apparently Gurdjieff could "do tricks" in the scientific as well as the supernatural areas!

Gurdjieff talks about the Mullah in Beelzebub's Tales to His Grandson, attributing dozens of sayings to him throughout the book. He claims that although people in Europe and America may have heard little or nothing of this personage, he is recognised throughout the East. He likens him to "Uncle Sam" in America or "Till Eulenspiegel" in Germany.

But clearly it wasn't that straightforward. Virtually everyone in the U.S. has heard of "Uncle Sam", and knows who or what is being referred to in this kind of reference. But when researchers began looking for Gurdjieff's Mullah in Asia, no trace of such a person or personage could be found! R.Zuber (in Who Are You Monsieur Gurdjieff?) registers his despair over this. Gurdjieff had claimed the Mullah and his sayings were his "guide". Yet Zuber found him to be non-locatable - someone that simply couldn't be traced anywhere in Eastern manuscripts or libraries.

You might think that people should have woken up to something strange going on here. But typically, they seem to have concluded that either Gurdjieff's Asian 'guide' was locked somewhere in cloistered secrecy, or maybe was as fictional as Beelzebub. Zuber thought the former, and assumed Gurdjieff had just covered-up his tracks very well. But what he was essentially saying here was, in the East people acknowledge their guardians, while in the West virtually no-one does!

It seems to have been imagined that Gurdjieff maintained contact with a secret school or teacher in another country, from which he received periodic communications and directions. It was simple, but the perfect cover. So he could go on dropping his pearls of wisdom from "a mysterious teacher in a secret place", as it were, and people were willing to accept that in an external sense. But they wouldn't have accepted that Gurdjieff's guardian was talking directly to him. The 1920s Paris *avant-garde* would've choked on the simple truth.

## Communication from the Other Side

Gurdjieff himself worked constantly with this "communication from the other side" then. And in Beelzebub he clearly describes the use of trance mediums. They were called "Pythias" or "pythonesses" in ancient Greek times, where they communicated messages from the 'gods' at famous temples like Delphi and Dodona.

Gurdjieff dubs them "Tiklunias" in his contrived 'Beelzebub-talk'. He talks about himself training and using such a female medium to obtain information. Some women have the subconscious ability to perform this role. They can be prompted externally to pick up or see things that have happened previously.

There is a valuable clue in the name Tiklunia here. The 'lunar' allusion tells us these women are Moon essence types. That is their subconscious gift, or part of it. (I'll say more about this later when I explain the seven essences.)

Everything thus far gels with Gurdjieff's extensive knowledge of these things, and his ability to convey his after-death messages to me. It is just a different mode of transmission.

## And, Constantly Checking

Of course, it is wise to be wary of any advice given to us from any source. It must be assessed for its reliability. Most people in the everyday world just accept whatever is told them by 'authorities'. The beauty and great advantage of the Gurdjieff teaching is that it shows us how to inwardly assess whatever one is told. Once one is working with the subconscious, there is an inner truth-sense. You still use your wits, and proceed with your eyes wide open to all available data. But there is a 'feel' to things which transcends mere sense data impressions.

So, obviously, I proceeded by constantly checking whatever I could. I was always assessing how far the new trance messages "fitted" with existing facts and published teaching. I was also constantly checking within myself the feeling of what I was being told. I deliberately asked questions intended to elucidate problems and difficulties apparent in what we already knew about Gurdjieff. If the messages were genuine, then he could convincingly answer those questions. He did.

I went on to research ancient sources for some of his teaching. I tested the soundness of his accounts of the essences and human types in both myself and others. It opened up more understanding of human behaviour than any other typology I could find. I have constantly used and depended upon it for reading things about people for over 25 years now. It all checked out very well, with no obvious contradictions or flaws. I wouldn't have proceeded otherwise.

## The Writing of the Book

I must emphasise that the content of this book wasn't delivered to me on a platter. It wasn't like the entity Seth dictating his teaching through Jane Roberts for Robert Butts to directly transcribe. Just direct channelled dictation is no good for Gurdjieff's type of teaching. He always made people work to understand him and the insights he dropped. People have to make things their own by using their inner abilities to put them together. The subconscious has to be roused and engaged in each person's case to get their faculties working properly. Otherwise, it can be just people collecting information in their sleep which doesn't actually change much.

So I was given an uneven bundle of information, claims and clues. (He called them "fragments".) Mostly, it would be when my questioning solicited it. But he sometimes gave prompts, put things in my mind, or dangled things in front of me. This was spread over the twenty-one trance sessions, with the explicit warning from the outset:

> *It is going to look like a mess for a long, long time... (3/Dec/84)*

Included in that "mess" were Gurdjieff's claims about having been misquoted. There was a good deal to be corrected or modified in how he has been depicted. He gave me a number of explanations and definitive pronouncements not given or published before. There were some important changes of mind or realisations he had come to after death. He gave me a franker assessment of himself than one is likely to find anywhere else.

He graphically portrayed some important events and episodes integral to his life and understanding. He disclosed two important exercises he had used productively himself. I was, however, given a comprehensive run-down of the "essences and types" - not without having done much of the work myself at his instigation. He now wanted a clear explanation of them given to the world. And he had me running to identify the "seven salient points" in his major work Beelzebub, which are the keys to understanding it. Then there was the final key to the whole book. He spelt it out clearly and precisely, and then said: "This is terribly important".

As our trance sessions progressed, he told me he wanted a simpler account of his teaching produced for a new generation of people. He had set-up various "groups" before his death. They were indispensable for protecting and transmitting his writings for future generations. These groups were given some things not available to the general public. But he was also planning for a future time when at last the full effect of what he knew could be birthed into the world. He had looked forward to that since the early 1920s. But the 'timing' was always against him. Those who came to him as students simply weren't ready to move decisively.

Even in 1984/5 he told me my book would "gather dust" for a few years. He projected a time "closer to 2000" when the readiness would be there for public acceptance. So I left it on the back burner for many years, after having done my best to research the necessary background for it. Other events turned my life upside-down in the meantime, and I was taken off into many new areas of spiritual interest.

### The "Groups"

I have never belonged to a "Gurdjieff group". Perhaps I might have if one had been available and known to me. But he told me in 1984/5 not to bother with that. He said the groups had lost most of their meaning, and there were "a lot of head-trips going on". (This was always the problem when the "head people" took up his teaching. They ignored or negated the feeling/subconscious side which was integral to it, and intellectualised the message.) But he did tell me that, in Australia, there were two middle-aged men in an Adelaide group who had an implicit grasp of his teaching. I had no occasion to follow that up.

### The Passage of Time

My interest was sparked in 1998 with the appearance of Susan Zannos' book, Human Types: Essence and the Enneagram. I had been working on many other things for years. There had been a succession of channellers I worked with, whose abilities in the main opened-up after we met. That had taken me off into many new areas. But by 1998 all that had fallen away, and I then just had the internet for pursuing my interests.

The Zannos book seemed like a reminder that it was time for me to write up the Gurdjieff material. It was then "nearer to 2000", which was the original timetable I'd been given. There were some heartening things about the Zannos treatment. She focused attention on Gurdjieff's incomplete teaching about the "types". And she complemented what he'd told me by using planetary names for them. She even talked about the "combined types", which he explained to me. But her understanding beyond that differed markedly from mine.

Since Zannos was a kind of Gurdjieff group 'insider', it gave me some idea of the kinds of claims and clues that had been passed down in the various groups after his death. It was suggestive, but incomplete. I could see the cobbling together of various elements, with the attempt to produce a coherent account of the types. But Gurdjieff hadn't said enough for it to be reassembled that way, even with laudable insight and ingenuity. And there was always the inevitable misunderstanding which took people off in wrong directions. It was clear I still had a task to perform in explaining the types.

**Work on My Book**

I immediately set to work to prepare my material for publication. But it was very hard going. Very little would flow. I worked for months, with little to show for it. I seemed to run into brick-wall after brick-wall. He had warned me in 1984 that there would be "head-banging" when I started the "real work" of trying to put it all together.

Eventually I put it aside. Another attempt in 2005/6 still wouldn't work.

My constant research on "what was happening" spiritually told me everything was in flux. Much of the older guidance that people had been receiving had dropped away in the 1990s. New things were possible after the year 2000, but there was no definite consensus, for some reason. It was like the future was "still open", and decisions still had to be made about what would be part of it. Through this period I had no word or indication from Gurdjieff, and previous channels were no longer available for me. I wondered seriously if the project had been abandoned, or superseded by new energy currents after 2000. All I could do was keep an open mind, and wait.

**The Energy of 2012**

Then, early in 2012, there was a breakthrough. It always concerned me that I hadn't completed the task I had agreed in 1984/5 to perform. I deliberately asked out loud, "Do I need to write this book, or not?" I directed the question to any and every spiritual presence around me.

By coincidence – if you believe in that – I had my answer in six days. Someone I'd known decades previously rang me. They said: "You won't believe this, but last night I had an incredibly vivid dream. It had both you and Gurdjieff in it, and it was in your lounge room." This person had no previous channelling experience.

Also coincidentally, I'd had computer problems for weeks, until my existing computer died. A series of strange events then gave me three working computers, up and running the day before I got the phone call. Suddenly I had ample means to get on with any writing.

I knew then that "the game was on". My long-lost friend had more vivid dreams. Gurdjieff said this new kind of contact was only possible because of the completed results of our 1980s group work, specifically in my lounge room. He then passed on some exercises for stirring the subconscious, and serious work began on the book. Beginning was hard, but in a few weeks it started to flow. Within 6 months I'd written over half of it.

**Other Channellers?**

I often wondered if others, as well, had received channelled messages from Gurdjieff as I had. Quite early I found four pages of "Seth material" in volume 2 of S.M.Watkins' Conversations with Seth which talked about him. E.Nyland had taken some of his Gurdjieff students to a Seth channelling in 1973. Seth talked insightfully about Gurdjieff and his 'work', which was useful. But there was no direct message from Gurdjieff himself.

Interestingly, Seth talked about Gurdjieff having the vitality and joyfulness of the "grasshopper". This was the same characterisation the medium had (independently) given me in 1985. She described his manoeuvres in writing Beelzebub as "like your grasshopper doing acrobats". This reflected his 'fun' in writing it. Though, it incorporated a mischievous glee, since the book is incomprehensible to most people.

My internet searches revealed virtually nothing about other attempts to channel Gurdjieff. While I found one or two claims which talked of channelling him, there was nothing I could see which in any sense rivalled the quality of the material I had been given.

## Extending His Own Teaching

In general, many internet sites display a kind of solemn duty in restating and expounding material from very old sources. I am aware that groups and foundations were established to protect what had been received from the man himself prior to his death. That is important. Beyond that, some attempts are made to reinterpret the Gurdjieff teaching, and for the most part I find them rather unconvincing. There remains a kind of impasse between what was given prior to 1950, and any credible attempt to go beyond that.

I have found no one else who can rival Gurdjieff's depth and breadth of understanding, or restate his teaching in a way that takes us forward. I once said to the medium, during a 1985 trance session, that Gurdjieff was without rival in his lifetime. He quickly picked this up and barked at her: "I still am!" What is needed to breach the impasse then, is a further input from him, albeit from the "other side". There is no-one who can explain and extend his teaching as well as himself.

I have now completed the task I was charged with in 1984/5. At least, I've written the book. From recent communications, Gurdjieff seems happier with it than I am. He said I'd put more in the book than I realised. The emphasis on the subconscious and the essence will assist many who wish to actively pursue their own growth, to find and express their own true selves.

# CHAPTER ONE

# The Conscious And The Subconscious

Gurdjieff was emphatic. I should start with "the conscious and subconscious". Quite early he said to me:

> *At the very beginning of the very text that you'll be writing (make it)..the conscious and subconscious. [trance session, 3/Jan/85]*

This was, in fact, his starting-point for <u>all</u> his teaching, not just this book. It <u>had</u> to be the starting-point. It was the pathway into everything else.

## It All Starts with...

We find it stated with unmistakable clarity at the very middle of his long-winded introduction ("The Arousing of Thought") to his major work, <u>Beelzebub</u>.

(That was the major part of <u>All and Everything</u>, which he gave the particular title <u>Beelzebub's Tales to His Grandson</u>. Hereafter it will be called just <u>Beelzebub</u>.)

On page 25 of <u>Beelzebub</u> Gurdjieff tells us that we all have <u>two</u> consciousnesses. They are equally present within us, and function self-sufficiently of each other. As well as the consciousness we all use in everyday life, which we know as our conscious mind, there is also the subconscious.

The centrality and importance of the 'two consciousnesses' claim is underlined by his introducing it on the previous page specifically as the entrance to everything else he wrote.

His pivotal claim applies to <u>every</u> person. We <u>all</u> have these <u>two</u> consciousnesses. And they're <u>disconnected</u>, and they operate <u>independently</u> of each other.

Of course, we all know we have an everyday

consciousness in our waking state. It's what you are now using to read this. But not everyone knows they have a subconscious. Or, if you accept that you do, it is almost certainly just a general acknowledgement. Very few people have a working relationship with it. (Since the two minds are disconnected, you would have to know how to reconnect them.)

This is the first step on the path to personal awareness and development. The existence of the subconscious is a precondition for everything that follows here.

Surrounding his initial claim, and elsewhere, Gurdjieff adds some further statements. Our everyday waking consciousness, formed after birth, and entirely from the influences of the everyday world, is full of false and fictitious beliefs. They are oriented to living in the everyday world as it exists, but not to how things are in the reality behind it. To move beyond that, and get a grip on the reality behind appearances, we need to start using the subconscious.

In the typical person, their "inner life" (inner thought life) – such as it is – normally operates without reference to the subconscious. It is chiefly a reflection and internalisation of features we've acquired from "outer life".

But nevertheless, in the few – perhaps – there is a sensing of "something else". In older souls, and sometimes even younger souls, a dissatisfaction starts to develop with 'life in the world'. This would not begin unless there was some 'bleed through' and an awareness, at some level, of the second consciousness within us. When it does so, typically, the way 'outer life' is lived is felt to lack meaning, reality, fairness, or what is needed for personal fulfilment. We start to think, "There must be a better way", or "There must be something else".

This can't begin unless we have started to sense a different input, from inside us somewhere, from what is in fact the subconscious.

**Two Consciousnesses**

Who else has ever told us we have two consciousnesses, much less thrown it directly at us like this? And, why insist on "two minds", rather than say, two aspects of the one consciousness? It is precisely because of the disconnection between the two, and their independent operation, that it is both true and needs to be stated as Gurdjieff did.

While it is obvious enough what this everyday waking consciousness is, the subconscious is something of a mystery. That's where we need to work, to understand what there is to it.

Over time there have been many published sources commenting on and expounding Gurdjieff's teaching. But in this area, where clarification is sought of the conscious/subconscious distinction, comment is curiously lacking. How could such a crucial and important feature of his teaching be glossed over?

Even when we look for academic treatments of the subconscious, there is little of value. You will typically be told that not much can be said about the subconscious, because, academics don't have an agreed definition of it yet! Or, you may be treated to the kind of quibble that 'subconscious' should be used as an adjective and not a noun. (As if, we can talk of "the subconscious mind", but shouldn't just call it "the subconscious".) And why is that? Well, simply because that's how Freud used the word! No-one appears game to say anything substantial or step outside of old arbitrary conventions!

So, here we are, about eighty years after Gurdjieff committed his "two consciousnesses" pronouncement to writing, and no-one else seems to know much about it. It is basically avoided. One notable exception is the pioneer psychologist Carl Jung, who chose to explore the subconscious in himself. Unlike Freud, who basically just scared people off by claiming there were "dark forces" there, Jung ignored the short-sighted warning and ventured productively into it himself.

## Approaching the Subconscious

What is distinctive of the subconscious – as opposed to what people might call the "unconscious" in general – is that it exists either at, or just below, the threshold of conscious awareness in us. (Thus, sub-conscious.) We CAN be vaguely aware of it, at least at times. And we can work to bring what is in it to our conscious attention. Jung did. It is just below the level of awareness we use in everyday living, and is easily ignored when we are strongly focused in everyday reality. But in times of quiet reflection, when we are by ourselves, and free of the immediate demands of 'outer life', some contact can be made.

The existence of the subconscious has been a kind of "cultural fact" for almost two hundred years now. That is long enough for us to recognise the notion, even when we have no direct personal experience of it. We owe that to the work of Franz Anton Mesmer (1734-1815) and the discovery of hypnotism. The subconscious had to exist for the phenomenon of hypnotism to be possible, and to be explained.

Still, general acknowledgement of the fact is one thing. And, it is quite another for an individual to actually contact their own subconscious. Gurdjieff reviews the work of Mesmer in Beelzebub, and marks it as the time when people, at last, began to notice the subconscious in themselves. He says that Mesmer had reached the point of recognising the dual nature of human consciousness. But he didn't get as far as comprehending the reason for it.

So Mesmer 'found' the subconscious, and used it in trance and healing work. Jung came upon it in himself, and uncovered a rich vein of cultural and symbolic meanings there. He went far beyond Freud's reluctance and scaremongering to see it as an essentially creative force. He used it in his analytical psychological work, to steer people towards personal and spiritual wholeness.

Gurdjieff said neither of these pioneering thinkers went far enough. (He reviewed Mesmer's work in Beelzebub. And he made comments to me about Jung in February 1985.) They did not get the fuller picture that Gurdjieff had, even though they did invaluable work in bringing the subconscious to public attention. I could see then that trying to find important background to this topic from others would not get me very far. The "expert" on the subconscious was

Gurdjieff himself. Though, we still await public recognition of that. People aren't going to 'see' it until they start taking his teaching seriously and get into it for themselves. What we need to do then, is note and follow what he himself said about it.

J.G.Bennett reached a similar conclusion after talking to Gurdjieff about hypnotism through the 1920s to 40s. (Gurdjieff: A Very Great Enigma, pp. 66ff.) Bennett was a hypnotist himself, having trained under and spoken with many of the current 'experts' in the field. But he said Gurdjieff knew far more about it than anyone else he had met.

## The Second Consciousness

So Gurdjieff tells us we have two separate and independent consciousnesses. Until we register that fact, we don't start to look for the second one, far less try to engage with it. There is a second, independent consciousness in each of us – an "inner" source of knowing, distinct from what we use all the time in everyday life. And it can be accessed directly from where we are, if we were interested and chose to do so. Most people aren't, and don't.

The subconscious is not simply "unconscious", but sits in a quiet corner waiting, as it were, to be noticed and talked to. A certain focus of our attention or awareness will allow us to make the connection. Or, there are other ways of bringing its operation to the fore. For example, hypnotists access it quite easily when they put their subjects into trance.

Clues about this can be found elsewhere in Gurdjieff's published teaching. He is emphatic about people being "dual beings" with two distinct kinds of consciousness. Now, this is where the real adventure begins. Commonly, it is just assumed by most that they are "one person", and so long as they persist in that belief then they won't progress from where they are. (Not that they ever really look at the belief, or have any sound or reasoned basis for persisting in it. It is just "assumed".) But as soon as they begin to feel two people inside themselves (ISOTM, p. 147), the game changes, and the real work of personal development is launched.

(Does the notion of "two people" seem odd? Well, take a look at pioneer psychologist Carl Jung's discovery of the subconscious in himself. It came with the realisation that he was "two persons" or "two personalities". He was quite capable of identifying the subconscious in himself, as we all are. It is a second, independent consciousness.)

Gurdjieff has given us an important key when he refers to feeling the two people. We "feel" the second person. It is by "feeling", rather than just thought, that we find the subconscious and confirm its presence. (After all, we can't literally 'see' it. We can retrospectively deduce and affirm its existence by thought. But actual contact can only be made by directly feeling it.

For those not yet confident with 'feeling', Gurdjieff had another exercise. He told them to "observe themselves", to see what was going on in the day-to-day functioning of their psyche. "Look inside and see what is there." When we can be aware of how we are thinking, we are observing our thought processes from another vantage point. Then we know we have a "watcher" as well as a "thinker" inside us. Or, we discover a second sense of self which is independent of the thinking self.

In Jung's "second person" experience, he became aware of a different person than the one he had always taken himself to be from his upbringing. Some people may find that they are already aware, however dimly, of such a "second influence" at work in themselves. There may even be a natural tendency to contact this dimension at times of quiet, solitude, or meditation. It is always there, and only requires a certain stilling or withdrawal from outward activity or the dominance of the thinking mind.

This second influence would clearly be one that departs from how we've come to think of ourselves due to our upbringing. It is almost always the case that, there is an abrasive difference between elements of the "outer self" (formed due to our birth circumstances, and our upbringing), and the character of our subconscious. They have been functioning independently of each other. And, how else would we ever recognise a second consciousness in ourselves, except by contrast with the established character of the everyday self? By contrast, the second self will be truer, kinder, and more at peace with itself. It will be a kind of "relief" to find it.

We move now then to a crucial feature of what we've always known as our everyday waking consciousness. It may be a shock for us now to be told that, what we've always taken to be our "awake" state is, actually, another form of sleep. I mean, we go to sleep at night (in bed), and "wake up" in the morning. But Gurdjieff says, when we've woken up (in the morning), then we've got to really wake up!

## "Mankind is Asleep"

One of Gurdjieff's most prominent claims, which almost everyone cites, is that "Mankind is asleep, and needs to wake up". It may be taken to mean that, the level of conscious awareness in most people is so low, they are virtually asleep. That's true enough. We are accustomed in our everyday waking state to simply not noticing most of what is going on around us in the world. Our conscious minds are so actively engaged in a narrow take on life, we are not observing and registering most of what is there to be seen. It also applies to what is going on in our own psyches.

This is apart from some scientific assessments that humans typically use only 10 percent or less of their brain capacities in everyday living. If a group of people were to independently experience exactly the same situation in an everyday context, they would afterwards typically remember and give differing accounts of what they noticed. Most of what is before our eyes is never seen. We are almost always taking in only part of what is there. Our focus is too narrow, and we are usually too absorbed or too comfortable in our own settled way of looking at things to stay alert to much more.

The person who takes themselves to be "one person" is definitely asleep. They're not seeing a crucial element of what is there – their own subconscious. But the person who is becoming aware of their subconscious, or its operation in themselves, is starting to awaken. Gurdjieff found in the students he attracted in the 1920s and 30s, that most of them needed a lot of work on themselves to assist their awakening. So he devised and gave them all manner of exercises to assist the process, some of them rather gruelling. He still thinks "work on oneself" is necessary in most people. Because, it is by the conscious intention and effort of each individual that awakening is spurred and advanced. Once found, the subconscious needs working with to bring its operations more decisively into our everyday life. It is similar to getting our conscious functions working after we've just woken-up in the morning.

All the great spiritual teachers of the past spoke of this sleep (of mankind) and the need to awaken. ("Sleepers awake!") We are fortunate in still being close enough to the living example of Gurdjieff, who awoke in our times. He can tell us how to do it, and in terms appropriate to our contemporary understanding.

Over time cultural understandings change, and these kinds of teachings are notoriously susceptible to being corrupted. New imaginings come to those no longer in touch with the source of their teachings. The sleep takes over again. And reasoning and thinking is modified by degrees to revert to its old default setting. The subconscious is then quietly but effectively dropped into oblivion again. (It is almost as if there is a quiet conspiracy to eliminate it from conscious attention.) The conscious mind, left to itself, has this constant tendency to dump the subconscious. Yet for Gurdjieff it was absolutely central, and the only way people could develop and become what they were capable of being.

So Gurdjieff presents us with this graphic picture of people in everyday life "who are asleep, but think they're awake". That might be amusing, apart from the gravity of its being literally true. When he refers to our "waking consciousness", he is simply contrasting it with our unconscious state of sleeping in bed at night. But it is also a kind of joke to him, or definitely ironic. Because, what most people who are awake in the everyday sense don't realise is, they are mired in another kind of sleep there.

He is talking about an hypnotic state. The sleep of everyday life is unlike sleep in bed, in that we appear to be awake, but it is nevertheless another form of sleep.

## Hypnotic Sleep

There are identifiable stages of hypnotic trance or sleep, from a general drowsiness or lethargy, to the deepest state, called "somnambulism". (That means literally "sleep walking".) People in this state can walk around, with eyes open or shut, and can be told to exhibit any feature typical of the normal everyday waking state. We might not recognise, from their external appearance, that they are hypnotised. Internally, they are not aware in and of themselves, or of the state they're in. We could not sensibly discuss their state with them. To an unhypnotised observer it would seem like a case of "The lights are on, but no-one's at home".

One or two things might be obvious to anyone who has watched demonstrations of stage hypnotism. People are so easily susceptible to being hypnotised, and the methods for inducing it are so simple. (Even members of the audience sometimes fall into trance while the target subjects are being hypnotised.) Yet it may not occur to those watching this, that they are seeing an accelerated or concentrated form of a phenomenon that already operates directly in the everyday world.

It is a person's susceptibility to "suggestion" that makes them vulnerable to controlling influences in the shared public world. There are plenty of those at work in contemporary society. From the youngest age, moves are made to induct new members "properly" into the prevailing everyday reality. (A certain religious figure once boasted: "Give me a child until they are seven, and I will have them for life.")

There are many forces in the world with a vested interest in controlling public behaviour. And, the knowledge of how to do it has been readily available for some time. Alternatively, or as well, there is a powerful inertia in the mass consciousness, and it operates to continually perpetuate the *status quo*. People want to feel safe as the member of the 'herd', rather than step out of that on their own. So they "copy" or "imitate" others, and generally curb any impulse to do anything which might show them to be 'different'.

We may presume that a small number of people knowingly act to keep the bulk of mankind in this compliant sleep. Because, their own power, influence or financial gain depends on that. A compliant population is an exploitable one. Unfortunately, the 'controllers' themselves are also the victims of another form of suggestibility. So you get layers of hypnotism behind hypnotism. (Just as, people already in the everyday hypnotic sleep can be further hypnotised by stage hypnotists.)

The great mass of people who participate in and perpetuate this somnambulant living, at whatever level, aren't aware of what they're doing. This is the great tragedy of the situation – those who are asleep don't see or realise what is really going on in life. Nor do they realise how different, and how much more fulfilling, their lives could be if they started to wake up.

The important issue here is whether a person who has become alerted to the situation, and "sees" what is happening, will take the steps for extricating themselves from it. Gurdjieff says there is no inherent reason for people to remain in sleep, and it is possible to wake up at any time.

"De-hypnosis" can begin by removing oneself from the constant reinforcement of everyday influences. Turn off the radio or television, and take some quiet time by yourself. Give yourself a break from the "internal chatter" as well. Feel the silence, while quietly refusing to be threatened by it. Think about things that are relaxing and personally pleasing. And this de-hypnosis process is assisted by contacting the subconscious. When one has connected with it again, one is no longer asleep.

## The Disharmonized Consciousness

Later in Beelzebub Gurdjieff explains why people are disposed and susceptible to hypnotic suggestion, and therefore the sleep in which they live their lives. What makes it possible at all is the disharmonised state of these two consciousnesses which we have been talking about. That is also why Gurdjieff wanted his teaching to begin with the state of our two minds.

He tells us that nowhere else in all of creation are (what he calls "three-brained") beings like humans susceptible to being hypnotised. There is not even the conception of such a state. It is only on the earth. And he says it was not always so here.

Many thousands of years ago, shortly after the continent of Atlantis ceased to exist, the way in which the human psyche functions was changed. It was split and divided into two parts. It then formed the two separate consciousnesses we have today. These two parts were 'disharmonised' thereby, because they cannot, and do not, work together properly in that formation. The conscious mind has a constant tendency to work by itself, and strives to be sufficient by itself, because it is 'independent'. And it also works in most people to ignore, nullify or discount the subconscious, which retreats into its own independent world. That is, until a certain robustness develops in an individual's conscious awareness, and they come across certain 'facts' about this subconscious which they can't ignore. Then the conviction starts to form: "Hang on! Something's not quite right here!"

Our conscious awareness had to align itself with the arising of the everyday self when it was born into a new life on earth. The greater mind of the subconscious was gradually forgotten then, due to the pressures of upbringing, and left to itself. Our awareness must also remain with the everyday mind. This is because it is needed there for the integrity and continuity of the life began on earth, no matter how hobbled it is in that role. And, the only possibility for reuniting the two minds depends upon it remaining there. People then persist in their state of "unresolved dualism", until the awareness in any individual grows sufficiently to recognise the true situation, if it ever does. (Most people live and die in sleep.)

Once the second mind is recognised within oneself, a person is faced with a choice. They can either drift back into hypnotic sleep, or take steps to continue their awakening.

This disharmonised state in people could be remedied much quicker and easier, if children were told from a young age about the subconscious and how to work with it. But there is a dominant regime which insists that the only 'real' objects of human perception are those experienced with our five senses in the everyday world. As a result of this, 'education' is biased, and the everyday consciousness of those being educated is one-sided. It is done by the inculcating and fixing of impressions which are hostile to the presence and influence of the subconscious. ("It's just your imagination!" and so forth.)

That is part of the hypnotising effect. The enforced suggestion, by the same people who tell children to "stop day-dreaming", is that one is only educated and trustworthy if one works solely from the evidence of their five outer senses. Although, mostly one is just told this in the case, and no experimentation is encouraged which could challenge it. Effectively, growth in, and proceeding from, the genuine inner mind is stopped.

## States or Levels of Consciousness

Gurdjieff gave a handy guide to different levels of consciousness in people, so we could understand and see where we were up to. He spoke of four levels.

Level One is ordinary sleep, which we do in bed at night. Level two is the typical hypnotic sleep of our 'waking state'. Everyday life is lived at that level. Real awakening starts with level three, which involves self-consciousness. Here we start to become aware of ourselves through the subconscious. With level four, finally, there is another possible state, which he calls "objective consciousness".

In this chapter one, and most of the book, we are essentially moving from level two to three.

## Further Comments by Gurdjieff

When he spoke with me in 1985, he added two

comments about this initial stage of development which are not explicitly stated in previously published material. He told me to

> *look at the aspect that in most people the subconscious mind is..asleep.*

And he added further that:

> *what's got to be done is that, the subconscious mind has to as aware..as the conscious mind is. Not for the entity living inside the body to be..as aware of it, but to stop the sleeping in the subconscious.* *(3/Jan/85)*

This is a step further than the initial wakening realisation that we have two consciousnesses. There must also then be an arousing of the subconscious from slumber. Awareness, along with the waking of the conscious mind, must be summoned in and extended to the subconscious.

If we go back to the hypnotic state, we might have presumed that it is the conscious mind which is hypnotised. Certainly it is put into abeyance by the work of the hypnotist, and that is the mind that is 'awoken' afterwards. In allowing oneself to be hypnotised, one has also allowed the hypnotist to assume a power of command over the subconscious. He can tell it what to do, and it does it. A compliant subconscious may not immediately seem to be asleep. After all, it is responding. But being a "dumb servant" is not exactly a sign of being awake, especially in a mind having the sort of capabilities we know the subconscious has. Its very passivity may be the defining characteristic of its sleeping.

In fact, in Beelzebub Gurdjieff identifies passivity with being asleep. The conscious mind becomes passive when we fall asleep. And the passive state of the subconscious, either under the command of the hypnotist, or when it has no active role in our everyday life, indicates it is sleeping also. It seems we've rarely, if ever, experienced in our conscious life, what it would be like for the subconscious to be awake.

Apart from Gurdjieff, I have never heard of anyone

claiming that the subconscious is asleep. It just does not seem to have been considered that it could be, or is, and therefore needs to be awakened. But this must essentially be the message of all the great spiritual teachers. Becoming spiritually aware means "waking-up" in BOTH consciousnesses.

**"Using" the Subconscious**

It does alert us, however, to the way in which we all just "use" the subconscious in either hypnotic state. We assume it is just there to do the bidding of whoever holds the power of command. And we don't even consider it might "have a mind of its own" or "be a mind of its own". It is just used for purposes formed by the everyday waking consciousness of people.

So, a stage hypnotist uses it to produce behaviours that entertain an audience. Hypnotic therapists use it to modify unwanted physical or mental characteristics we'd like to change. There is also a whole gamut of "new age" practices that involve contact with, or use of, the subconscious. Prominent among those is the huge "self-help" market. There, any number of teachers will tell you how to use self-suggestion on the subconscious to make yourself confident, charming, rich or successful. But they are all just "using" the subconscious to further our everyday mind's (or ego's) aims and purposes. One can't be sure how successful some of these practices are. But clearly they must all reinforce the sleep of those involved, at both the conscious and subconscious levels.

It is not surprising therefore, that Gurdjieff should find the subconscious asleep in most people. It is being "used" in a passive way, when used at all, for the purposes of the conscious mind and not its own. In general, we don't even understand what its own proper function might be.

**Reciprocal States of Waking and Sleeping**

An interesting clue as to what would happen if we recombined our conscious and subconscious minds is found in another passage of Beelzebub (p. 505). It occurs almost as an 'aside' while Gurdjieff is addressing something else. He notes how – as seems obvious once it is stated – the energy which enhances our everyday waking life depends upon a certain quality of sleep the night before. When we've had a 'good' sleep, we feel energised and ready for whatever the coming day holds.

He extends the idea to include the other way round – that our sleeping well as night will follow from our having had a good day, in a certain sense. Thus we have reciprocal states of the activities of day and night giving something to each other. He puts it down to the nature of the links that are made, presumably between our conscious and subconscious minds. This would assume a limited transfer from one to the other. Possibly the subconscious reviews our previous day's activities during sleep, and the conscious mind may benefit from dream activity during the night. (Our dreams are such a rich resource for subconscious analysis. And how often has a "good sleep" solved or clarified problems we've had the day before?)

Obviously a small amount of co-operation can go on here, between otherwise independent minds. While not yet in a combined state, each mind may take and use the results of certain activity within the other. And, when the quality of transfer is good, it is apparent we can experience two things – increased harmony and energy. We might deduce then that, if the conscious and subconscious minds could be recombined in our conscious state, there would be far more harmony and energy released into our lives.

## Not Aligned

Gurdjieff's second 1985 comment to me picks up the various problems outlined earlier above about the two consciousnesses. They are 'independent' of each other, and disharmonised in function, which leads to the 'sleeping' condition in each of them. They lack the meaningful connection to each other which they once had, and were meant to have. Gurdjieff refers to this as their being "not aligned". He then stated categorically to me that the rest of his teaching would be

> *of no use to anyone (until they had) aligned their consciousness and subconsciousness (with each other) (3/Jan/85)*

Again we see why the "conscious/subconscious" was of such concern to him, and had to precede all else in his teaching. It is an indispensable preliminary to the transmission of what he had to say. Any genuine personal development requires the conscious participation of our subconscious mind.

Alignment refers to the relative polarity of the two consciousnesses in people. Gurdjieff expresses the governing law in the commonplace, folksy observation that a stick has two points of termination, or 'ends' (Beelzebub, p. 11). What doesn't work one way, has to be turned around and tried the other way. For example, a battery won't drive the device it was designed for if it is inserted upside-down. The positive and negative polarity needs to be reversed. So we turn it right-side up to solve the problem. (The two forces which need to be combined, using direct current, to produce 'light' will only, in their wrong combination, by default, leave us with darkness.)

In the case of the two consciousnesses, they are disharmonised and won't work properly because their relationship is upside-down. (We might understand then why, elsewhere in Beelzebub, Gurdjieff refers to the perception of reality in people as upside-down or 'topsy-turvy'.) When the conscious mind is "active", and the subconscious "passive" - in our daily lives – little can operate as it should. What we need to do then is switch them the other around, or use the other end of the stick.

Gurdjieff actually foreshadowed the solution in the same passage where he told us about the two consciousnesses. He said most people mistakenly take their waking consciousness to be the "real" one. Whereas, he says it is full of falsity. He maintains our subconscious should be the active partner in the relationship, and the conscious mind should become passive to allow that to happen.

Only in that formation will the two consciousnesses start

to merge harmoniously, for the benefit of our life in the world. The 'split' can be healed, the dualism will dissolve, and the sleeping will disappear. (Remember, the possibility of hypnotic sleep didn't even arise before the split in the human psyche thousands of years ago.)

This wasn't just "theory" to Gurdjieff. What he affirms here is what he found in his own experience. That's the way it works. He had been through the process himself, and could demonstrate the results in his own psyche and life. That's what he did to get where he was. (He always tested things on himself first before attempting to recommend them to others.) And then he went through years of ongoing observation and research with the students who came to him to validate and confirm all the details of this process.

## Copernican Revolution of the Psyche

The solution to the problem of the two consciousnesses in people is simple enough to state, but its ramifications are enormous.

This is a "Copernican revolution" of the psyche. In the sixteenth century the Polish/Prussian astronomer Copernicus turned the prevailing view of the earth in the cosmos upside-down. He had studied the ancient writings, and carried out his own observations and experiments, and then declared the prevailing view to be wrong. (This was also how Gurdjieff proceeded.) Copernicus showed how the earth orbited the sun, and not *vice-versa*. It upset the powers-that-be, and outraged the general population, but he was correct. It was a crucial correction that allowed mankind to emerge from the Middle Ages into a new era of discovery and exploration of the cosmos. Today we wonder what all the fuss was about, because he was just telling it like it is.

Suddenly we see the point of everything in and surrounding Gurdjieff's production of his introductory chapter to Beelzebub. The REVERSING OF The POLARITY OF The TWO CONSCIOUSNESSES IS The PIVOT OF The ENTIRE MECHANISM. We would expect to find something integral to his message at the meticulously honed entrance to his "All and Everything". (He apparently revised and rewrote that introductory chapter dozens of times.) He would have wanted to have the major clues there, even when he couldn't spell the details out in simple terms to those not ready to hear it.

At the very beginning of all his writings, Gurdjieff states his aim in Beelzebub. It is to demolish without any mercy or concession, the wrong beliefs and feelings about the world inherited by his readers from past generations. It is to be an iconoclastic clearing. All the images from the existing external world must be swept away to make room for the new – the reality behind everyday reality.

Even given that all genuine spiritual teachings set out to dispel illusion, it is still a very big claim. But he is talking about turning the functioning of the human psyche upside-down. That is integral enough to change virtually everything.

## The Pivot Point

Once the pivot point is found and recognised for what it is, the overall plan and purpose for his teaching is revealed. Archimedes – the ancient Greek mathematician and inventor – once said, if he was given the right pivot point then he could move the entire earth. It is not by philosophies, or political doctrines or movements, or more religions, or the 'advance' of science or any existing human knowledge, that the world can be changed for the better. All of that has been tried many times, for countless ages. Our 'modern' civilisation is still based on a small number of people exploiting the rest, and no real progress is possible by any of the prevailing means. Gurdjieff didn't see a great difference between so-called 'civilised' society and savages in primitive communities. The finery and sophistication of some contemporary cultures and countries is still belied by the warfare, killing and slavery which continues around the earth.

Something more fundamental to the human condition needs to be addressed and corrected. It lies within the psyche of people. The transformation must proceed in individuals, by correction of their upside-down and disharmonised state, in order to impact and change the world.

**The Work of Ashiata Shiemash**

In Beelzebub Gurdjieff describes how the work of one enlightened individual transformed a whole area of Central Asia in ancient times. He calls him Ashiata Shiemash. (There is no historical record of a person by that name. It always seemed to me - the present writer - that he was talking about an incarnation of Hermes. But Gurdjieff clarified the matter in his messages for this book, and that can be found in chapter 11.)

Anyway, Ashiata Shiemash found the psyches of the people at that time (around 1200 B.C.?) were as disharmonised and dualistic as they are today. He then set out to bring certain functions of the subconscious mind into the everyday waking presence of a small group of people. (This was effectively recombining the conscious and subconscious minds of these people.) Once successful, the members of this group spread the work to other groups. Within 10 years, very definite changes were manifesting in a wide social area. Various forms of enforced social control disappeared, along with divisions of social classes. Slaves were given their freedom, and exploitation stopped. The desire for warfare evaporated and war stopped entirely. Leadership was given entirely to those recognised and acclaimed for their merit and worth.

This extraordinary social transformation was finally decimated by factors beyond the inhabitants' control. It concluded with the military invasion of Alexander the Great, which swept right through the region. Even the records and traces of what had been achieved were largely lost to posterity. But the knowledge of it was preserved in secret circles and passed on for future reference. Gurdjieff had found the clues and fragments about what was possible from that time. He put it together early in the twentieth century. The pivot point for individual and social transformation was known. Certain facts, truths and understandings resident in the passive subconscious have to be brought into active awareness at the everyday level.

Once Gurdjieff had found the pivot point for reorganising the human psyche and restoring it to its proper function, he then devoted himself to finding the means to bring it about in practice.

**The Path of Awakening**

The quickest way to wake a sleeping person is with a jolt. You shake them, or set off a loud noise near them, and they wake instantly. This applies to physical sleep, and by extension to hypnotic sleep.

This is the method of what is generally called "shocks". (In computer terms, it is the equivalent of rebooting your system. If the computer freezes or malfunctions, booting or rebooting will restore it to proper functioning.) The effect of a shock on people, in their everyday 'sleeping' consciousness, is instant. It solves at once both of the problems which Gurdjieff explained to me. He said shocks have the double function of

> *ceasing the somnambulance of the subconscious, and aligning the consciousness with the subconscious... (3/Jan/85)*

These natural consequences of the shock also demonstrate the accuracy of his account of our psychic functions.

In his published teaching Gurdjieff variously describes shocks as necessary for moving a person from one point to the next, of effecting crucial stages of development. A shock at the right time makes the transition successful.

Of course, there are "shocks and shocks". There are "life shocks" which happen in the course of a person's everyday life. For example, they might lose a friend, a partner, a job, or their home, and so forth. These are disruptions or rearrangements of the settled and valued circumstances of one's life, sometimes intensified by their suddenness or manner of occurring. Psychologists have listed and graded these kinds of shocks for the typical intensity of their effects on people. We might also call them "traumas".

Gurdjieff's own spiritual development proceeded via a series of such shocks from his earliest years. They started the processes in him which resulted in him becoming the person he was, and achieving the things he did. I will review those stages of development for him in chapter three.

These kinds of shocks are life-rearranging. But not all are positive in their outcome, depending chiefly on the person and how they react. They work far better for some people than others. Over time, Gurdjieff was able to determine which 'types' (of people) respond better to shocks. Often a trauma is the beginning of awakening and spiritual growth, and many psychics too trace the onset of their abilities to just such an event. But only in certain types of people.

**Managed Shocks**

Gurdjieff knew that shocks were the best tool in his arsenal for awakening people and aligning their two consciousnesses. But of course, he couldn't summon up "life shocks" to use on people for this purpose. So he did the next best thing. He employed a range of kinds of "social insults" on those who came to him to learn, to "kick start" the process of their awakening. It was akin to stamping on peoples' corns. Some he just turned away, because he could see no immediate possibility of their making any worthwhile advance. (Not everyone has the ability to make important advances in any lifetime.) All the time he was being informed by his subconscious of the inner state of every person he encountered. He could walk into a room and instantly feel where every person there was within themselves. And he strove constantly to put out the teaching, and prepare those who came to him to understand and use it.

As you might imagine, the greater formality in social interaction in the 1920s and 30s in a 'civilised' country like France made his unexpected social insults rather effective. He could also do something like this and 'get away with it'. People might put up with a lot if they thought he knew what he was doing, and it was leading somewhere. And, dealing abruptly and autocratically with his pupils was also put down to his strange Eastern manner. He could also use it to dispense with much of the rubbish that some tried to engage him with.

Some people who saw him fly into a rage, and then return to total calm and composure almost instantly, knew it was a kind of performance that he could turn on and off at will. He was "acting". He did it for the effect on those he was verbally assaulting, and had no personal investment in it. It was part of what he called his "artificial life", where he devoted himself to doing whatever was necessary to awaken others. But personally, he would much rather have retired to a quiet place where he could just spend his days in peace.

**How Shocks Function**

I pressed him for more information on how shocks worked. He told me then that five of the "28 types" (which I will explain later in the book) were better placed to benefit from shocks. They will react positively rather than negatively to them, picking themselves up and moving on. The effects of a shock are slower in others, and in some seemed to have no discernible benefit at all.

In the five types who benefit most, it is because of a "fine balance between the intellect and the soul". So trauma acts more like a "kick in the pants" for them, to get some changes moving in their psyches and lives.

Pressing him further, he told me I was "not a bio-physicist", but nevertheless gave me the following account. Especially in the five "poised" types, the shock has an immediate electrical effect on the nervous system, altering the pattern of impulses. This impacts the pituitary gland, which swells and then implodes, releasing porous secretions into the bloodstream. That in turn stimulates "part of the right-brain". (This is a physical sequence, but it has its corresponding effect in the consciousness. Later, more of the relationship between the major bodily glands, the chakras, and the essences/types will be spelt out.)

(His reference to the "right-brain" was also interesting. "Right-brain" and "left-brain" are terms used especially since the 1950s, after research into different functions of the two virtually separate hemispheres of the human brain. Left-brain functions resemble those Gurdjieff attributes to the everyday consciousness, and right-brain to the subconscious. This research began properly in the decade after his death. But since he knew what was happening with me, and the Gurdjieff groups, in 1985, I'm not surprised he was also fully acquainted with the right-brain research.)

**Other Shocks**

There are further types of shocks, which a person can actually administer to themselves. They are every bit as effective as 'life' or 'social insult' jolts, but without the drama or negative trauma. If you want to advance in this teaching, by all means use them. However, most people aren't likely to see their point and start using them until their awakening has begun. But, if you want to "get going", then use them.

Later in this book I will detail two important exercises that Gurdjieff acquired and used on himself for his personal development. They are known as "the Bow" (chapter 6) and "the Dance" (chapter 9). The first one involves breathing, and the second one spinning around. They are necessary when one embarks on the group work associated with the essences, to be explained later (chapter 10). But both of those exercises can be done apart from that. Both administer beneficial shocks and assist the flow of development.

However, the shock *par excellence* in the Gurdjieff work is to "remember oneself". That will get everything moving, and can be used straight away and in all situations. It is not an external blow or impact, but an inner direction of the awareness using something absolutely integral to the work on oneself. This really speaks to the subconscious, in a way it understands. The inner self one is remembering here <u>is</u> the subconscious. It would be the equivalent of the subconscious suddenly saying "Hello!" to the conscious mind. (You'd get a jolt it that happened.) So, give a jolt to your subconscious by talking to it!

More and more, I found, as I got into this teaching – if

you directly address your subconscious, then it will respond to you.

**Remembering Oneself**

One might immediately see the resemblance between Gurdjieff's telling people to "remember themselves" and the ancient Greek injunction to "know thyself". But it is a very clever adaptation. (Gurdjieff didn't originate this practice, but it became integral to and distinctive of his teaching.)

"Knowing" has become so externalised in our modern culture, under the dominant regime of trusting nothing but the five senses, that the idea of "knowing oneself" is often misunderstood. A person, for example, might take it as a cataloguing of their external life features, or as seen by a more impartial observer. (Like, place and circumstances of birth, social background of parents, schools and formative influences, and so forth.) This misses the point, or the real point of those who tell us to "know ourselves". Though, a person might even catalogue their external life features, and realise it's not who they thought they were!

The self we need to know is the inner self. How we might "know" it is not immediately obvious to the modern mind. But to "remember" it is a more appealing proposition. In fact, the subconscious mind was born with us, and was the sense of self we had as a very young child, before the outer self was formed. It could be remembered, even by the reckoning the conscious mind would employ in these matters. One might usefully try to recall one's earliest childhood memory, and go from there.

In order to "remember", we search our inner sense of things to reconnect with something once experienced. Remembering is not exclusively a left-brain function, as knowing has tended to become. There is apparently no single repository of memory in the human brain, but all sorts of cues serve to draw back conscious recollections from various areas. These are often 'feeling' cues, like emotional tones associated with past experiences, or synchronistic connections.

It may not be necessary to delve back into childhood.

People with a rich "inner life" have a readier sense of when they are "touching base" with themselves. It can often be something we retreat to when the outer circumstances of life become harrying, confusing, annoying, distasteful, or so forth. It's our "place of peace". Or, it might be identified as our "secret place", away from the world.

People have their hobbies in everyday life. It will be something they enjoy which takes them right away from the tensions and pressures of doing what needs to be done in life. With jobs, earning a living, the family we have, or just getting on with other people, there is often little choice in what we need to do while there. But if one has a chosen hobby that one can "lose oneself in", then it will probably be noticed that one's perception of time and space alters when engaged in it. That is a sure sign that one is working with the subconscious. We find that we feel better about ourselves in such a space, and when that is seen, then one is remembering oneself.

There is no 'judgement' about oneself in the quiet inner place where one remembers oneself. One is never judged as being too much, or too little, of this, that or the other. One just "is". That's pretty close to what Gurdjieff calls "being". And "being" is "just being". It is like its own reward. People also contact this state through meditation.

## Reflections of the Inner Self

Generally it is "older souls" who have more of a sense of a "self" to remember. They tend to be those more accustomed to "enjoying their own company", or even "communing with themselves". This doesn't exclude younger souls though, who sometimes make great strides in spiritual matters.

Gurdjieff thought it was important to find some aspect of the world where one can just feel at peace. He found solace and great peace in nature. His early years were spent in a quiet rural setting, and he always longed for the peace of nature in the countryside he knew as a child.

This is reflected in his writings, where "nature" and "Great Nature" are presented as bountiful and healing. In his

1985 comments to me, however, he wished to modify one aspect of his published teaching about this. He had realised since passing over that the love of nature was his personal "foible". He said that other people could have the same experience in different ways to him, in a variety of contexts. For some it might even be by staring as a brick wall, or at the texture of a brick. He said:

> *You don't have to be in touch with nature to do it. All you've got to do..is be in touch with yourself. (3/Jan/85)*

What is important here is finding some context that will reflect back to you the peace of your inner self. It might be the sea, or gardens, or mountains, or walking, or chocolate, a log fire, or a hearth, or any number of things. Find the one, or ones, that work for you.

Finding such contexts, or even just imagining them (imagining one is there), will serve to reflect the inner self. Repeating the experience periodically will reinforce this sense of self. Then it can be summoned up easier at will, while you are doing anything at all. One can then move to remembering oneself at all times and in all situations. (Not that one will always be mindful to do so. But it can always be picked up again, quietly and with no sense of judgement, whenever one notices one is not doing it.)

**Breaking Patterns**

While working to contact the subconscious with the direct practice and the attendant shock of "remembering oneself", the grip of the everyday conscious mind can also be loosened.

Gurdjieff says everyday outward living is "mechanical". We have learned and then use certain moves, which are kinds of "going through the motions" routines. Most of it we could "do in our sleep", which we literally do. There is little conscious effort involved for the awareness in us. From the time our feet hit the floor in the morning as we get out of bed, there are routines of bathroom and dressing and eating. Then we take the same route by the same means to get to work or wherever. Much of the rest of the day can be spent in the same way. The monotony of routines reinforces the sleep in the conscious mind.

In respect of this "mechanicalness" Gurdjieff says:

*The patterns have to be broken.* *(3/Jan/85)*

One exercise Ouspensky recounts from Gurdjieff is helpful in this regard. Every day one should deliberately do something differently to how one normally does it. Say, get out of bed on the other side, or change the sequence of one's morning routines. Prepare food differently, or prepare different food. Find a different route to work. Do 'morning' things in the afternoon, or *vice-versa*. And so forth.

He says that all consciousness will revert to mechanical patterns if you let it, or haven't trained it to do otherwise. So the aim is to be as aware and alert as possible in whatever one is doing, and take steps to avoid the mechanicalness. Do it in stages to avoid any sense of onerousness, and you will soon discover a freedom here.

## Grandma and the Chief Lever

"Doing things differently" to avoid mechanicalness was part of Gurdjieff's secret to success from his earliest teenage years. He cites it as crucial to all his subsequent development. In Beelzebub he calls it the principal lever for effecting what he had altogether become (p. 27). That is a massive claim, which underlines its importance for our spiritual development.

It is encapsulated in a piece of advice which he says his dying grandmother passed on to him from her death-bed. Actually, it wasn't quite as dramatic as that. He dramatised it for effect in Beelzebub. But, it was given to him by his grandmother, and he did always remember it and use it.

His grandmother told him that always he should not do things as other people did them. In further explanation of that she said, in effect, to avoid just 'going along' in life as others do. He should, instead, look to doing things that no-one else does.

He claims then, in Beelzebub, written much later in his life, to have always followed that advice – doing absolutely everything in a way not done by others.

This is a very individual, unique, even eccentric way to live one's life. It always hit a chord with me, from the time I first read it in the mid 1970s. It seemed to licence, without restriction, a freedom to just be myself. But it was also reinforcing a similar impulse I'd felt from my earliest years. Sometimes I just wanted the freedom to do something a bit odd or outrageous, just because it was what I wanted to do.

Of course, living in the 1970s was a great relief, after growing up in the more restrictive 1950s. There were all those parental cautions about what one should and shouldn't do, especially in public. But the 1970s introduced us to a new social philosophy or dictum, expressed very well as "doing one's own thing". The rebellion of the young of that era introduced a new freedom that quickly permeated many levels of society. And you could say it was very close in essence to Gurdjieff's prime directive.

In 1985 Gurdjieff restated his "grandma's advice" to me in a slightly different way – not to amend it as much as to more fully express what there was in it. He said:

> *Trust the judgement of no man! Or Never trust the judgement of others!*

And further:

> *Don't consider what other people have got to say as being real, as..being true. You've got to always find out for yourself and do it your..way. Always look behind (others') words. Always look behind (their).. actions. Go by what you feel in your solar plexus, and go by your..instincts.* (10/Jan/85)

It was part of Gurdjieff's genius to be able to express what could be difficult and complicated instructions for spiritual growth in a condensed and pithy way. It came from his peasant background, and his penchant for using few words to express the essence of something. He was very intelligent, but, by choice, always reverted to simplicity in communication.

"Grandma's advice" is a gem of compact and accurate instruction – not simply rustic folklore. It expresses exactly what is needed to find and use the influence of one's subconscious in everyday life. The younger one starts with it, the better. But it can be followed by anyone as given – never too late - and be perfectly sufficient by itself. It is worth unpacking a little though, to exhibit what is in it.

## What is in Grandma's Advice

The chief means for inducting children into the hypnotic sleep of everyday life is through their trust in, and subservience to, those who explain the world to them. They are taught, and learn to defer to, 'authorities', who tell them 'what's what'. Once they simply accept this, they can be led up the garden path all their lives.

But 'authorities' are notoriously unreliable. Their claims need to be tested. We know, for example, that there are vested interests involved in the appointment and payment of many authorities. Many can also be self-appointed. A lot of these people are dysfunctional, who find a social role for themselves in telling others what they should believe or do. Often they don't believe or do it themselves. Then there are the imitators, who just pass on what was passed on to them, without validating it. In fact, it doesn't take a lot of attention or effort to find inconsistencies and fallacies in the claims of various authorities. (They won't thank you for pointing that out, but the real point of the exercise is to find the truth for oneself.)

One of the by-products of gathering groups of children in schools can be the way they learn to conform and become part of a "herd". Young people need to avoid the default path here of merely copying or imitating those in their group. Conforming can become a habit reinforced by earning praise or avoiding censure. The ability to "think for oneself" is fostered by thinking beyond the confines of a group, to determine what is or isn't appropriate to oneself.

To "not do as others do" throws a person very much on their own resources. Practising this is the only way that genuine individuality can be reliably fostered. That part that is uniquely "me" has to come from something intrinsic to me, not the second-hand beliefs and impressions of others passed on during upbringing and education. Only then can I genuinely "think for myself". One can, of course, review ranges of possibilities offered by others in the world. But something inside oneself should always be decisive in choosing what is right for oneself.

Over time one will develop a sense, that can be relied upon, about when the claims and advice of others 'gel' or 'make sense', or don't. We could call this an independent "truth-sense". Learn to be guided by that. Also, the "doing not as others do" will lead slowly but inevitably to a sense of one's own unique path in life. The subconscious that was born with us obviously had a purpose in choosing the life circumstances that it did for us. By reconnecting with it and bringing its operations into our everyday life, we are surely on track to discover, or re-discover, "that for which I was born".

CHAPTER TWO

# Working With The Subconscious

So far we have reviewed the fact and presence of the subconscious, and the need to 'wake it' and bring it into active prominence in our everyday life. General means of contacting it have been outlined, which anyone can use in their daily activities. General effects of that have also been noted. It is time now to look at what Gurdjieff says is "in" the subconscious, and more particular ways of working with it.

Once we have "discovered" the subconscious, then the adventure has well and truly begun. The overall process involves moving from an "outer-directed" to an "inner-directed" life. What Gurdjieff calls "work" - as in work on oneself – is learning to recognise and use what is there

He talked of two functions or properties which reside in the subconscious or arise from it. They are "conscience" and "essence". Now we are ready to respect and employ its legitimate functions, rather than just "use" it as a passive slave for our everyday purposes or fancies.

## Conscience

Conscience is universally misunderstood today. In all the dictionaries it is invariably described as an inner moral faculty or sense. But according to Gurdjieff, the morality people talk of has nothing to do with conscience.

He says the two things should not be confused. This is confirmed by the etymology or original meaning of the word. Conscience is literally, and only (through the Old French *conscience*, from the Latin *conscientia*) "inner knowing", or "knowledge within oneself". Even according to the Oxford Dictionary of the Christian Church, its original meaning was inward knowledge only in a generalised sense.

The subconscious "knows things" - in fact, an extraordinary number of things. This is apparent even from the work of hypnotic regression. During hypnosis, meticulous details can be recalled from specified periods of a person's past. The subconscious even records things our eyes saw which never registered in our conscious awareness.

When we have a conscious connection with it, and therefore a 'flow' from the subconscious to our ordinary waking consciousness, then we can know what the subconscious knows. Not all at once, of course. It won't swamp us with information. It does literally know "everything at once". But it also knows that our conscious minds are designed for dealing with a limited amount of data in relation to living a life in the world. It has to protect that, because its own future prospects for expression and growth through our life in the world depend on it. So it typically delivers only bits and compact summaries on what is of particular relevance to us at any time.

Perhaps the subconscious can be seen as containing a vast reference library. It is at least that. And, conscience is its super-efficient recall service, available when we need it or call on it. Obviously those who coined the word "conscience" in ancient times must have known about this reference library of inner knowing within ourselves. Gurdjieff told me it was regarded then as

> *a medium to great understanding..(or) as the decision or higher centre.* *(9/Feb/2012)*

**The Invented Moral Conscience**

Owing to the basic degeneration of the human psyche even in centuries just past, the 'independent' conscious minds of people over time invented an alternative use for conscience. When people are no longer in touch with their subconscious, then they don't get any 'knowing' from there.

So they began to refer to this function as an internalised sense of what is morally right or wrong. All those things which parents, teachers and others involved in our upbringing told us we should or shouldn't do, are instilled in the memory. Recalling them is supposed to be a guide for making choices and living our lives. This is only a recycling of what a person has consciously experienced and learnt from 'outer reality' earlier in their everyday lives. So the subconscious is effectively by-passed and dispensed with.

Gurdjieff contrasts what he identifies as the genuine, objective conscience with the modern, shallow, mistaken moral-sense one. He says that the knowing of the true conscience in one person could never contradict that true knowing in another person. It is universal in that way.

Morality, on the other hand, is always an artificial and relative thing, and there will always be conflict between what different people see and claim is morally right or wrong. Morality differs from place to place, from culture to culture, and according to the differing beliefs of its various advocates. You can even make-up your own moral beliefs. Many do. And you don't need to go to another country to have a moral dispute. You have probably already had dozens of them with family members or neighbours.

You will no doubt find that the true conscience, when awakened and connected with, will not sanction the harming and misuse of other people. This will not be because it is "morally wrong". But, understanding people <u>as</u> people will bring an automatic recognition of how they should be treated as such.

You use yourself as the example when working this out. Obviously this is why Jesus said: "Do to others as you would want them do to you." With morality though, it is quickly used as a justification or excuse for the most atrocious inhuman behaviour towards others. A study of the most hardened criminals will quickly show you that they all have their own 'moral sense'. And, no-one <u>consciously</u> acts to do wrong or evil (in their own terms, however self-delusional). Even Aristotle noted that.

Even those who mercilessly kill and slaughter others, represent it to themselves as necessary for some imagined 'good', as they understand it. So much for conscience as a moral sense! It seems to operate more as an aid to self-delusion. Or, moral beliefs are a "buffer" to mask the true nature and gravity of some of our actions from us.

In Gurdjieff's terms, self-delusion would be a prime example of the inability to be sincere. This is one manifestation of the disordered psyche of split and disharmonised humans. The "duality" in the consciousness of everyday people naturally translates into double-dealing, duplicity, two-facedness, or any of the other 'dual' attributes. It is healed by bringing the two consciousnesses into alignment. Then a person can be sincere, and sincere people never carry out or attempt to justify outrageous acts of abuse towards others.

We might even see the 'moral conscience' as a kind of silly game that many people play. It is often used by the more dysfunctional 'types' of people as a justification for trying to interfere with and control the behaviour of others. Or, it is good for creating conflict and emotional agony for those who like to generate and feed off such energies. You will also find that the most vehement advocates of moral rectitude are the very people with most to hide about their own moral failings.

### The True Conscience

The true conscience can tell you how to act always and in everything, in relation to the real world rather than any relative version of morality. It is an informed counsel that a person can have. We don't have to work from moral precepts, rules or principles. Instead, there will be an instant feeling-knowing. We will know this because the subconscious knows "how things really are" - in the real world, not the illusory one. (On one occasion Gurdjieff said to me, "The subconscious never lies". It knows "what's what", and it is totally trustworthy.)

One merely needs to ensure then that one can access the true conscience. Problems can only arise if that access is blocked, and one is not sure of what it is saying. There are two conditions Gurdjieff spoke of which could block or obscure the deliverances of conscience. (These are particular factors which perpetuate the "unresolved duality" of the two consciousnesses in people.) We will review them briefly. They are "buffers" and "negative emotions".

**Buffers**

The true conscience is obscured by psychological "buffers" in a person. It cannot be accessed by anyone with strong buffers. These buffers have their primary function in hiding contradictions within a person from themselves. They are partitions which have been put up in the psyche, to stop people seeing themselves as they are.

Buffers in general are used to cushion from shocks, and whatever lessens shocks makes it harder to 'waken' a person from their 'sleep'. But they make life more tolerable for people who still have much to work through before they can awaken. Buffers perpetuate self-delusion. They consist in false opinions, prejudices and beliefs which have become fixed in the mental functioning of a person.

We might also recognise such buffers as "mental blocks". Their presence can be painfully obvious to those around a person when they aren't to the person themselves. The removal of buffers depends crucially first of all on the person who is carrying them coming to see them. Nothing can be done without that. In fact, the criticisms and comments of others will only increase the need of the buffered person to justify themselves (with more self-delusional strategies or fiction), so long as they're not ready to dismantle them. Perhaps all we can tell such a person is to "observe themselves", until they start to confront their state and move to change it.

**Negative Emotions**

Since the conscience resides in the subconscious, it too can only be directly accessed by 'feeling'. Now, there are "feelings and feelings". Gurdjieff distinguished between what he called the "lower" and "higher" feeling, or emotional, centres in us. They may merge or overlap a bit, but the lower one carries the everyday emotions.

Perhaps if I point out that "all emotions are feelings, but not all feelings are emotions", you will see where this is going. An insightful person once said that "e-motions" are "earth-motions". All emotions arise in relation to earthly experience, although we've usually learnt to have and express them by the example and teaching of adults during our childhood.

In line with the dual psyche, emotions are strongly polarised. They will always be either negative or positive, or, pleasant or unpleasant. You might immediately recognise that many 'feelings' can be neither, or neutral. (We can know many things by 'feeling' that we have no personal investment in.) The problem with emotions arises solely from the negative ones. Although, if you examine the whole catalogue of them, you will see that the overwhelming majority of them are negative.

These negative emotions are a problem for the person experiencing or expressing them in two ways. Firstly, if you entertain them and allow them to "get a grip" on you, they will suck your energy mercilessly, and leave you feeling depleted for hours or days. Secondly, the very strength of such emotions will swamp and block out the perception of finer feelings.

Negative emotions are held to serve no useful purpose for the person on the path to development. If you got rid of them entirely, then you would only benefit and not miss anything worthwhile. In everyday life a person may not be aware that they can dispense with them. (The old patterns just keep replicating themselves, with inertia and no realised reason to change.) Gurdjieff once said the last thing a person is inclined to give up is their suffering. Look at what negative emotions do to you! (Do you like suffering, or would you rather be without it?) They may not be dispensed with overnight, but they can be phased out over time, given the willingness to do so.

He said to just drop them down the drainpipe. They

must be caught in their onset stages, because once they get a hold it seems one just has to wait them out. We do it by the choice to "not identify" with them, or to "not express", when they start to arise. Sidestep them. They are <u>never</u> justified. (As if it could be an entitled indulgence for us to emote and suffer for a while!) They are often a concession of powerlessness in the face of others' behaviour. But it is always better to remain 'cool' and consider useful ways of acting in those situations. Or, it is even better to do nothing, rather than react emotionally. Once the bulk of negative emotions can be cleared, then the feeling-atmosphere within oneself will be far more conducive to the inner knowing of conscience. The harsher screaming of negative emotion will no longer block out the finer feeling of inner knowing.

## **<u>Messages from Conscience</u>**

The knowing that comes from the subconscious mind then is basically "felt". (It could be experienced as a "sensing", an "intuition' or as an "impression", depending on the essence of a person. Different essences can have different modes of picking up what is perceived through feeling. More of that later.) But in all cases the knowing is instant. Feeling operates much faster than thinking, and the subconscious instantly knows things it would take the conscious mind a great deal longer to work out, if it could at all.

So the deliverances from our conscience come very quickly. They're typically 'there' before the conscious mind would even think of asking for them. In most people these instant messages are <u>already</u> coming to them, but they're either not seeing them, or they're discounting or ignoring them. It depends where our conscious attention is, or how far we've come to recognise what is happening in this area.

A way to experience this is, <u>notice</u> next time you meet someone new, or visit a house or place where you haven't been before. The conscience will typically, first thing off, shoot you a message about that person or place. Look for the "first impression" you get, along the lines of "I am comfortable with" or, "not at ease with", and so forth. The stronger warnings or endorsements are easier to pick up initially. But there can be a whole gamut of first impressions given to us. Even in common folklore we are counselled to listen to, and trust, our first impressions. We may need that information as to whether to avoid, or have more to do with, a particular person or place in future.

Or, next time you hear the telephone ring, see if you get a sense of who it is before you answer it. (Like, "Oh. That'll be so-and-so".) If someone is late for a meeting with you, see if you can pick up a feeling of why. When hearing news through the media, where not everything is said or explained, see if you can fill in the missing pieces. (This is the ability to "read between the lines".) Then there may arise feelings while someone is explaining something to you. Could it be that they are hiding something, or not telling the whole story? You might get a kind of "clunk" or feeling in the solar plexus. Has something of concern to you happened, or be about to happen? The "inner knowing" will come to you if you practice with it, which Gurdjieff always maintained was necessary. Tell your subconscious you want it to happen.

The true conscience can also be felt when one is faced with a decision to act against what one firmly feels to be correct. That is a Gurdjieff example. It is an instant road right into it.

## Another Gurdjieff Example

Gurdjieff gave me a particular example we might use in looking for the activity of the subconscious. It involves situations that the young, or not so young, might find themselves in – when experiencing sexual attraction to another person. He said there is a powerful upswelling of the subconscious in such situations.

This immediately reminded me of an incident recounted in Pauwel's book Gurdjieff (pp. 39, 40). He tells how an

American writer friend of his was lunching at one table with a female novelist colleague. Gurdjieff was sitting at another table nearby. The writer asked his female friend if she knew Gurdjieff, and when she looked across at him, their eyes met. Gurdjieff was seen to consciously breathe in a particular way, and the woman became pale and faint. She later said the encounter was weird, and she'd felt sexually transfixed.

There was speculation, of course, that Gurdjieff had used some magical trick picked up in the East to enhance his sexual attraction. People were always imagining exotic explanations for the way he behaved. There were occasional episodes of apparent 'magic'. But Gurdjieff went along with many of these things, real or imagined, to increase the interest and curiosity of people, which promoted his teaching. In my experience, some interesting phenomena may be sparked between two people with high energy signatures. Possibly the breathing that Gurdjieff did was just his use of the breathing exercise detailed later in chapter 6. It summons up the activity of the subconscious. But you may also find an explanation in the following exercise he gave me to pass on during 2012.

The activity that Gurdjieff was recommending was as follows. In any situation where elements of sexual attraction with another person arise, ask yourself: "Is it me, or is it the other person who is initiating this?" Then "remember yourself" and look to the subconscious to give you the answer.

He also made the point that, "The subconscious is not a flock of angels". That is, it is not some distant angelic-type force, but a very present and accessible aid within oneself for handling everyday situations. Look for its input in precisely those circumstances where one needs to make decisions about what to do, or not do.

## More Dimensions to Conscience

Everyone acquainted with hypnotic research knows the subconscious has a vast encyclopaedic capacity. Some of the more adventurous hypnotic therapists have found they can elicit information from there about a person's "past lives". There is a good deal of published material which talks about this. When looking for the basis of a particular life problem, a therapeutic hypnotist will typically tell their subject to "Go to the cause of your present problem, and explain it". In a fair number of cases this entails the detailing of a past life experience.

If the subconscious also knows the details of lives we've lived prior to this one, then its encyclopaedic knowledge is vast indeed. (Remember we were 'born with' the subconscious. It came with us from wherever we were 'before'.) The understanding of karma and life lessons would typically be involved here. (One should not seek to resolve those kinds of issues <u>just</u> through hypnosis though. We don't <u>learn</u> if things of this nature are summarily altered by hypnotic suggestion. But there are some techniques of past life regression which provide clues which can then be consciously worked through by us now.)

The more we look at the functions of the subconscious, the greater its capacity seems to be. While it has a phenomenal memory, its abilities must extend far beyond that. For example, the "self" we are remembering when we "remember ourselves" either <u>is</u> the subconscious, or resides "in" the subconscious. It must include a sense of 'self' at least substantially equivalent to our everyday self. (This is the "second self" referred to in the previous chapter.) Maybe this is all part of what Gurdjieff meant when he said the subconscious is an "independent" consciousness. It is not merely an encyclopaedic appendage to our conscious selves, but has its own operating system and ability.

Looking for more information in Gurdjieff's writings about conscience, we find something a bit unexpected. Suddenly he starts to talk about it as "divine"!

### <u>The Conscience as "Divine"</u>

In <u>Beelzebub</u> Gurdjieff moves at one point from talking about the real or authentic conscience to another characterisation. Suddenly it is said to be "sacred" or "divine". The change takes place as he begins his explanation of the work of Ashiata Shiemash. (Remember, in our previous chapter, this individual was identified as transforming a large area of Central Asia in ancient times.)

Gurdjieff never calls the subconscious itself divine. But he accords the highest, most exalted praise to the mission and work of Ashiata Shiemash, who he said had been sent from "Above". By extension, it is Shiemash's restoration of the activity of the conscience in the waking consciousness of people which earns the "divine" and "sacred" labels. There is more to the reinstatement of the human psyche and proper social relations between people than Gurdjieff cares to spell out in the first book of Beelzebub. But at the very end of his first series of writings he says that heaven and hell exist right here, amongst us on this planet, and not elsewhere. It is the goal of all religions to guide us from one to the other. And the restoration of the conscience plays a pivotal role in bringing divine order into being.

If we look at all the "saints" that Gurdjieff talks of in Beelzebub - including Buddha, Jesus, Mohammed, Moses, and so forth – then no greater veneration and praise is accorded to any of them than Ashiata Shiemash. It is apparently because he didn't provide more "teachings" like the others, which could be subsequently corrupted and misused. But he actively demonstrated how an important change to the human psyche could restore "the kingdom of heaven" on earth.

Giving more "teachings" to mankind, of the kind where we are told to "believe this rather than that", doesn't seem to alter the fundamental problem that exists in humanity. Just working with the everyday conscious minds of people doesn't address the duality and 'sleep' which keeps them locked in the *status quo*. As long as there is duality, then people will continue to misconstrue any teachings to perpetuate conflict amongst themselves. And as long as there is 'sleep', then people will be led to align themselves with causes that effectively only promote conflict, warfare and the interests of the few over the many. Only when the true conscience is restored in peoples' everyday consciousnesses will the divine vision of "peace on earth" and "good-will" come into being.

**The Sleep of Conscience**

Since the subconscious is asleep in most people, then so is the conscience which resides in it. It also is assisted by shocking and stirring people. Gurdjieff says that periodically, usually after times and great warfare and human slaughter, some groups of people start to recover their sanity for a short time. They are shocked to the point of revulsion, and start to say things like, "Never again", or "That has to be seen as the war that ended all wars." But, without the reorganisation of the psyche for a proper awakening, the 'sleep' takes over again, and people start to find new reasons to start killing each other as before.

There is an old reassurance given to people who are about to be hypnotised. It is said that the hypnotist can't make them do anything which is against their conscience or moral principles. Ha! But we know the conscience is asleep in most people, and moral principles are pretty relative and flexible. In terms of stage hypnotism, it is probably only true in the sense of people being more resolutely reluctant to do anything that could be seen as morally wrong in front of others. Stage hypnotists who want to remain popular won't outrage their subjects' sensibilities in that regard by testing the resolve.

Apart from that, when the conscience is asleep, or put to sleep, people can be coaxed into doing all sorts of things. After all, that's how soldiers are trained to kill the 'enemy'. It all depends how the commands of hypnotists, or 'suggestions', are framed. People can be coaxed into all sorts of evils if you can get them to believe they're acting to avoid still greater evils.

**The Essence**

The second property or function that Gurdjieff identifies in the subconscious is the "essence". We are moving now to the most central concern of this book. An essence, as any dictionary tells us, is the inner, distinct nature of something. It inheres in that thing in a fixed way, and makes it fundamentally what it is. Our essence is our inner nature.

'Essence' is almost always coupled and contrasted with 'personality' in Gurdjieff's teaching. We can also link this with the "conscious and subconscious" of chapter one. The essence is to the subconscious mind what the personality is to the conscious everyday mind. They are the "selves" of each consciousness, or vehicles of conscious and subconscious expression.

Since essence resides in the subconscious, we are born with it. A new baby or infant is all, and only, essence. The personality doesn't start to form until the 'outer' learning of upbringing and education starts. At birth, there is only pure essence, while the conscious mind is a blank sheet of paper waiting to be written on.

The personality is our way of relating to, and coping with, the particular circumstances in which we are born into the world. Interestingly, 'personality' comes from the Latin word *persona*, meaning "a mask". It suggests it is the mask we put on to establish an identity in the everyday world. Personality is very necessary though, both to give us a "self" in everyday life (which also helps install 'life lesson' and 'karmic' tasks), and to set things up for bringing the essence into prominence later.

Unfortunately, in the way things presently are, most people never come to realise their essential selves. There could be some partial knowing and transfer, but it rarely comes in fully.

From a review of published and unpublished sources, I can put together a list of claims of the way Gurdjieff contrasted essence with personality. This helps to inform us how both function.

**<u>Essence as Opposed to Personality</u>**

We can note the contrasts under the following headings:

| <u>ESSENCE</u> | <u>PERSONALITY</u> |
|---|---|
| Arises from the subconscious. | A 'construct' of the conscious mind. |
| What belongs to us or is "our own". | Doesn't really belong to us. It is contrived, and used. |
| Innate. (We're born with it.) Our <u>inner</u> being. | Acquired after birth. <u>Outward</u> learnt behaviour and understanding, even though internalised. |
| It cannot be separated from us. | Can be altered or removed, quickly and completely. |
| The genuine basis of our individuality. | Derived entirely from other peoples' influence. |
| Our one central stable "I'. The gifts and traits peculiar to a person. | Many inconsistent and changing "I's". Derived from external influences (place, time, environment), and dependent almost exclusively on them. |
| Although we always retain the <u>same</u> essence, it is given to us to grow it in expression. | Personality is 'accidental', according to circumstances. |
| Not able to react <u>as</u> <u>such</u>, but it 'understands' and assimilates experience, growing thereby. | Reacts immediately and superficially, to extend the range of its 'roles'. |
| We know essence when we <u>feel</u> it. | Personality is a <u>mental</u> construct. |
| When we know something in our essence, we <u>really</u> know it. | Mental knowing is always susceptible to challenge and modification. |
| We're "in our element" when we feel it. | We're alienated from our true self when submerged in it. |
| What is true in a person. | The lie or falsehood in a person. |
| Subject to planetary influences. | Not open to those influences. |
| The key to one's "fate". | Life events are just 'accidents'. |
| Enables one to "be oneself". | Generates any number of superficial 'roles' or 'selves'. |
| Central to life. | Marginal to life. |

Many of these characterisations could be further explained. They are given in summary form here to enable an overall picture or grasp.

**When the Consciousnesses are Aligned**

It is through the functions of the personality and essence that the principal changes take place to restore unity and harmony to consciousness.

When our two consciousnesses are being aligned, it is chiefly through the relationship of the essence to the personality that the change is effected in our psyches. This is where the swivel turns most decisively on the pivot point to restore upside-down to right-side-up, by switching 'active' and 'passive' to their proper positions. This is how to do it for oneself.

The process is as follows. The personality which has been contrasted with the essence – in the long list of differences listed above – is by itself a kind of empty shell. It has a currency, and a necessary place in the everyday world, but left to itself leads nowhere. We have learnt to grow up and live in the everyday world through internalising the various influences surrounding us since birth. But none of that is "us", or "the real me". At this stage in our explanation, it is what Gurdjieff calls the "false personality". But it has its most important use in allowing the next stage to unfold. Indeed, it was necessary for that.

Real change in an individual, here, begins by conscious realisation and choice. It won't "just happen" by itself. Nature prepares us only to the point of having a functioning personality. But there must be realisations then within each individual, with corresponding choices and actions to take it further. That is the process being explained in this book.

Briefly, when someone begins to feel and see the reality of their essence, and starts expressing it in everyday life, the swivel starts to move. They are thereby remembering part of their inner self. Then by degrees, by bringing more of their essence into expression, the personality starts to transform. The inner elements constituent of the real "I" will slowly eclipse the outer elements of the false personality.

What is 'false' in the personality will metamorphise into becoming the "true personality" - one that reflects the essence. And through the true personality the subconscious at last becomes the active force in a person's life.

**The Seven Essences**

So, what of this "essence" in each of us, whose finding and expression transforms us and takes us beyond duality? Gurdjieff only gave general characterisations of it in his available teaching, such as in the list provided immediately above.

In some traditions, a person is urged to find that part of themselves that "never changes" (its being a "fixed nature"). That can take a while to work out. But now that teaching can be supplemented, and the process streamlined. Gurdjieff previously alluded to there being a particular number of essences, but he even fudged that a bit. And he talked of 'types' along with 'essences', without properly explaining the relationship.

In fact, there are seven distinct essences, or fixed natures, and we are all born with one of them. There are no exceptions. Each essence has its own cluster of interests and abilities, and they can be readily characterised. (The list is provided in chapter 6 below.) Knowing our essence entails feeling what is integral to the expression of the one we have.

All people with the same essence have, at the deepest level, the same impulse within them. But the expressions of it will vary, according to the trajectory of previous and past life experiences each one has come through. That individualises each person's use even of the same essence, but not so as to change the central impulse and features.

The seven essences are characterised in chapter 6 in a way that Gurdjieff never expressed them in his previous public teaching. He did give people all sorts of partial clues about their essences, without spelling them out explicitly. He wanted them to take the steps themselves to realise their own inner natures, by feeling the impulse within. But frankly, almost no-one was ready for that.

There has to be a sufficiently stirred inner-feeling for

the process to develop in earnest. And people needed to demonstrate their willingness to identify and work with the subconscious. He wouldn't have told anyone things they weren't ready for. In that situation, they would have been apt to misunderstand and misuse such information. He was always anxious to avoid that. The biggest problem he faced in his public teaching was people misquoting and misconstruing what he told them, because they weren't really ready to hear it. That's why so much was left obscure.

This transaction of finding and expressing the essence is so important - along with the group experience it leads on to – that Gurdjieff wouldn't just give it away. He needed to supervise how it was used. People tend to adapt what they're told to fit their current understandings of things, when they're not ready to use the information properly. And he certainly didn't want the operation of the crucial pivot point for human transformation confined to oblivion by half-baked misunderstandings.

## A Word of Caution

A word of caution should be added before we proceed further. As Gurdjieff said to me more than once, "This book (you're to write) will not be for everyone." It will have a magnetic appeal to those ready and able to use the information.

There are conditions in some people which would make it impossible for them to participate in this work. The ideal state would be having an already equal development between personality and essence in a person. (Or, where feeling-awareness is recognised alongside of intellectual-awareness.) Most people like that are what we would call "old souls". Where either the thinking or feeling abilities in a person have been seriously stunted, no meaningful work can proceed.

Gurdjieff says in some people the essence has been permanently disconnected, or has 'died'. Nothing can be done there. But it is highly unlikely that such people would be interested enough to pick up this book, far less read as far as this.

Then, as for 'conscience', there may be some barriers to cross for even those who could proceed. The first one is the same as for conscience, reviewed earlier - "buffers". No one with strong buffers can advance meaningfully with essence. The person themselves must recognise and remove them first.

Two further obstacles are the chief feature or fault, and then the chief fear. Both can be cleared. But they need to be seen, understood, and worked on. Both of these factors hold the *status quo* for the false personality. They keep people where they are. They are like the last gates that need to be opened before anyone can proceed in earnest. Beyond our giving of a few examples of each here, and explaining in general how they function, each person themselves must work to identify and remove any final obstacles.

**The Chief Feature or Fault**

The chief feature is a central characteristic of any false personality, around which it rotates. Because it is so central, so intrinsic to it, the person who has it can hardly ever see it unaided by themselves. In ISOTM Ouspensky records Gurdjieff saying that a teacher is needed to name it and show it to a person. But later in that book, he also says those around them can see this feature and often draw attention to it in a 'nickname'.

In 1985, Gurdjieff told me it is "usually the way" that someone will find their chief feature through interaction with others. But it doesn't always need to be overtly pointed out. It speeds up the process if it can be. But then

> *one can be shown one's fault (or feature) many times over without being able to accept it. (9/Apr/85)*

The sorts of examples of chief faults or features we find in published sources are:

a) someone "talks all the time"; or
b) you can hardly get them to talk at all; or

c) a person won't "project a self" in their everyday relations; or
d) they show no 'shame' over anything; or
e) they're always arguing with people;
f) or they wait, or bait others, then snap at them.

The person in a) might attract the nickname "motor-mouth", or the person in f), "crocodile". As for e), one example I know was called "the great contradictor" - to which they immediately retorted, "No, I'm not!" And so forth.

These are all recurrent personality features. The solution in each case, once the characteristic is seen and appreciated by the perpetrator, is to work on behaving in the opposite way. Deliberately setting out to undo the construct unlocks the existing false personality.

**The Chief Fear**

Gurdjieff was very emphatic about the "chief fear" in our trance sessions, although I cannot find it in the published teaching. He said that when we are on the earth-plane, there are always fears. Everyone has them. A person will find themselves struggling with a particular fear as a major life task. One can certainly work on identifying this in oneself. Ask yourself, what is that thing you fear most of all? (Like, "What is the worst possible thing I can imagine cropping up in my life?") Any fear will tend to attract the circumstances in life which correspond to it, especially when you won't look at it. So it tends to "dog" you periodically in everyday living until you can come to terms with it. But, a fear is just a fear. If one can identify it, face it calmly, and see through its fearfulness, it can be dissolved.

Examples of some fears are:

A) fear of failure; or
B) fear of success; or
C) fear of not being "good enough"; or
D) fear of "lacking support", or
E) fear of being vulnerable.

People can see these applied in various ways in their individual circumstances. Failure for some may be in relationships, or in a job, career, or even just their ability to cope with life. And so forth, with each of the categories.

This fear holds the false personality where it is, because as soon as the prospect of it arises, we back off from going further. So we need to be able to walk through it or past it. Remember, a fear is just a fear. So, stop entertaining it. It won't grow into anything more if you can look at it calmly and just say. "No, thank you."

All these obstacles have their uses in keeping us where we need to be at certain stages in development. But as awareness increases, and the timing becomes right or appropriate, or, we gain the understanding of what really needs to be done to go further in our lives, they become redundant. Then, by seeing through the fear, and dissolving it, we can step past it.

It also needs to be said that, some people will be more advanced in this work than others. The older the soul, the greater the sensing of one's essence and the 'knowing' coming from it. Some are "ripe" for aligning themselves with their inner self and getting on with this work. These people will step past the obstacles more easily. Others just need to spend the time to look their fear in the face, and slowly do what it takes to dissolve it.

## Gurdjieff's Experiment with Essence and Personality

Gurdjieff once demonstrated the reality of the personality and essence in each person when he hypnotised two subjects during a group meeting. It was in St. Petersburg in 1916, and Ouspensky gives an account of it in ISOTM (p. 251-3). When I asked Gurdjieff about this, he gave a slightly differing account of the occasion than Ouspensky.

Essentially, two subjects were hypnotised and instructions given to remove their (false) personality constructs. Each behaved in rather different ways to their 'normal' everyday selves. (Gurdjieff was quick to tell me that, "Those personalities were back intact after the hypnosis". 26/Feb/85)

The first subject had a position of social prominence. They used to speak often and at length, with very definite opinions about themselves and everything in their personal and social life. When this personality, with its outer ego, was stripped away, they fell silent. They couldn't be engaged on any of the matters they'd previously talked so earnestly about. In fact, they then claimed they had no interest in such matters, and even denied they had previously talked about them! When pressed at length to mention anything that interested them, they eventually just said they fancied some raspberry jam!

The second subject was not thought to be a serious person by those in the group. They often engaged in foolish antics and put themselves down. They also used to engage in the most abstruse arguments, about little or nothing, where everything was mixed up and confused. But when that personality was stripped back, they became extraordinarily serious and eagle-eyed, and astonished everyone with the intelligence, accuracy and relevance of their comments.

Gurdjieff told me the second case had become

> *very calm and very much at ease with himself. Very peaceful. Almost enlightened.*

But,

> *The other personality was a screaming wreck when it got down to the ego-less self. It had been the (everyday) ego that had kept that person not in a screaming heap.* (26/Feb/85)

Gurdjieff had shown the huge contrast between the personality and the essence in these two people. He obviously chose the subjects to display that maximum contrast. It need not be so great in most people. Also, the essences of the two subjects were also very different to each other. The second person was the most able of the seven essences, but hobbled in everyday life by a crippling false personality. They were playing a sharply contrasting role in everyday life – a parody of their true selves – due to their upbringing and socialisation.

The first subject had the one essence which in its "central core isn't always at peace with itself". In that case, it was the outwardly constructed personality which kept that person 'together' in life. Without it, they would have been a "mess".

It should be noted in the light of that, <u>one</u> of the seven essences will not benefit that much from the development being outlined in this book. (Even though, their presence is required for the group work to be detailed later.) Their real growth and development often comes in other ways. When I expressed my misgivings to Gurdjieff about this, he said <u>no-one</u> gets it easy. And everyone must work with what they've got.

Even though older souls – who are more in touch with their essence – do have it easier with this form of development, they've had it harder in life than others. They have been the proverbial "ugly ducklings" who've never quite 'fitted' in everyday life. They are often made to feel like ugly misfits. Life in the everyday world as most people live it, doesn't make much sense to them.

The path of the older soul is to experience the greatest conflict between the outer conditions of everyday life and their inner sense of themselves. But this conflict is ultimately productive in what it leads to. It brings the equal growth and balance between the personality and the essence. And that makes them ripe for the development outlined in this book.

**<u>Distinguishing Essence from Personality</u>**

Gurdjieff's hypnotic experiment was an excellent demonstration of the "two people" composing each person, which we looked at in chapter 1. It was a practical vindication of the truth of that teaching.

We have come across the one essence of the seven where the relevant advice given to other six doesn't always apply. Even meditation is not recommended for these people. Since their inner self is unstable or "not at peace with itself", and they need the outer ego to keep them "together". Even "remembering themselves" and "not identifying (with outer reality)" are mixed blessings.

But for the other six – which are the "essences in general" - the plan is to weaken the activity of the personality, or outer self, in order to bring the essence into more active prominence.

Look at the second case above. So long as that person continued to identify strongly with their outer selves, then the different character of their essence was concealed from them. The personality was indeed operating as a "mask". It was masking their true self not only from the world, but also themselves. You can see the relevance then of telling such a person to "not identify". That means to stop taking the everyday self, as we know it, to be who we really are. We just start standing back from it, inwardly, in the way we think of ourselves. We let it continue to operate outwardly, as it always has (at least for the time being), but increasingly we are no longer so personally invested in it. Our real self lies elsewhere, and we begin to know that.

As we no longer identify with the outer personality, we start to notice things about it. We can watch "it", as it goes about its normal routines. How adaptable it is, as it employs a selection of roles in different life circumstances! We adopt one stance for dealing with parents, another for friends, and another even for different friends, for employers, strangers, and so forth. Our personality is the original "man for all seasons". We easily slip into each successive role as the demand of the moment calls for it.

But while there is this adaptability, we also start to realise there is no <u>one</u> stable "I" or self amongst the numerous roles we play. If we used to think we were a stable, whole person, there is no basis for that there. We see the personality is an adaptation mechanism. It is to the essence we must look to find a stable, non-changing sense of ourselves. As a "fixed nature", it is the reliable self that doesn't change.

**A Further Range of Differences**

Between the essence and personality there are many differences. Working with the subconscious begins to effectively change the character of our lives as we live them.

In 'normal' everyday life we are accustomed to seeing and dealing with "accidents". So many things seem to "just happen". You cut your finger with a knife, you walk into a lamp-post, or someone is injured or killed in a car crash. We see them and deal with them as "accidents". Gurdjieff says that people living in their false personalities are subject to a kind of "law" of accidents. And that applies to the whole life. There is no apparent reason why these things happen. Perhaps they're linked with astrological events, or maybe they're just chance occurrences.

But to be in your essence takes you under a different law – the law of "fate". Important changes become, and are seen to be, more inevitable or necessary. But they're more explicable, and as we become active players in life through the essence, we understand how certain choices lead to certain outcomes. Therefore, we're more actively in control of what may or may not happen.

Being now more connected with this chain of cause and effect, we see how the major events of our life all relate to a <u>chosen</u> course of manifestation. Through this, we're not just seeing things differently, but life itself starts to function differently.

Another distinct difference is in the quality of our 'knowing'. It comes to us in a different way – inwardly, through feeling. In our false personality we sought to make sense of the world through the claims of various 'authorities'. We also weren't consciously seeing the manipulation of outer life by those with vested interests in certain agendas. Through gaining independence of that by 'feeling', we start to "see through" so much of what is happening around us. We see more of the "why" of things happening as they do. And the clarity of our feeling-perception brings its own certainty, which we can depend and act on.

It is through knowing our essence that the ability arises to "grasp the essence" of things around us in the everyday world. (Gurdjieff often talked about his grasping the essence of things.) The inner self grasps things intrinsically, or implicitly. Feeling-perception is far more insightful and holistic than sense-perception. It goes to the meaning of things.

With the essence, both we ourselves and the world start to make better sense to us. We are working from something "real" within us. We can go beyond the second- or third-hand (and often mixed-up) views of the world of our false personality. We start to "think for ourselves", because we're in touch with the basis of our individuality.

Once the essence is brought into play, and operates to start superseding the false personality, then we get growth in essence expression. This is a link with all our past lives, and has within it the knowing of why we were born into our present life. (We have the same essence in all lifetimes, and its growth proceeds through each successive lifetime.) Then we can start to make our present life count, instead of wasting it as so many do on lessons that aren't being seen and learnt from. Then our real reason for "being here" can be confronted and worked with. We have a history, of which our present life is the latest chapter. We just stand on firmer ground, and life itself makes a great deal more sense.

## CHAPTER THREE

# **Gurdjieff's Early Development**

A crucial component of Gurdjieff's teaching – as reviewed in chapter one above – is that 'shocks' are catalysts for awakening, or moving between stages in development. The impact of the shock changes things in a person's body and psyche, and reorients them to become more of who they truly are.

This must also be understood with the cautions given in chapter one, that (external) shocks – the traumatic kind - work efficiently in this way for 5 of the 28 types (or 3 of the 7 essences). They work slower for most of the rest of the types, and possibly barely at all for others.

These kind of shocks were indispensable for Gurdjieff himself. He was one of the 5 types, or 3 essences, where they work most efficiently. His whole early development, if not his entire development, proceeded from a series of such shocks. In fact, there was no other way for him to "crash through", to get to the level he needed to attain.

As he explained his early life to me, the facilitating shocks began from the age of three. He gave me details of some events not mentioned or recorded elsewhere, and expanded accounts of other things previously published. He even revised more than one claim he'd made in the two main sources of his early autobiographical details. (See chapters 2 and 3 of Meetings with Remarkable Men, and the introduction to Beelzebub.)

What Gurdieff went on to become in his life was effectively instigated and set in motion during his 'formative' years. He continually contrasts both "formative years" and "preparatory age" with a person's "responsible being", when the crystallisation into settled adult life has occurred. I take it, from another reference of his, that is around 25.

So the earlier phases must embrace both childhood and adolescence, extending into young adulthood.

**The Birth Date**

I took the opportunity while in direct communication with him to try to dispel the confusion over his birth date. It seemed like a fitting way to check the authenticity of his claims, both for myself and others. Serious biographers have long been exasperated by the lack of reliable detail on this matter. Indeed, they often complain that his whole chronology is dubious prior to 1913. After that, Gurdjieff's public movements could be mapped and cross-referenced from others.

There are differing and conflicting claims about Gurdjieff's year of birth in the existing literature, with estimates ranging from 1866 to 1877. He had apparently told J.G.Bennett he thought he was born in 1866. While, one of Gurdjieff's sisters also told Bennett she thought it was in 1877. A surviving passport gives the birthdate as 28th December 1877. Bennett eventually found both of these dates hard to reconcile with Gurdjieff's claim of new vistas opening for him in 1888. Also, his birth region of Alexandropol had been ravaged by the Russo-Turkish war around 1877.

So, Bennett chose 1872 as the most likely date. Most writers think 1872-4 is most probable. James Moore, who constructed a chronology, stuck out for 1866. While, James Webb (The Harmonious Circle) nominated 1874, on the basis of identifying Gurdjieff with someone called Narzunoff, who claimed to be born on 26th July of that year!

Gurdjieff told me he was born in 1867. He admitted he liked to play games with some people over this (and other things). He had later purposely revised the date to 1877, "for reasons of vanity". (To make it appear he was younger than he was.) I have to add that, a month after his 1867 claim to me, he said it was possible the date could have been 1869. It was certainly either 1867 or 1869, but he believed 1867 was the true date.

The difficulty here arises from the kind of circumstances

Colin Wilson refers to, where reliable records were rarely kept in those regions. Relevant records no longer exist, if they ever did. There is nothing to refer back to. And in Gurdjieff's own recollections, the upheavals surrounding the family's move to, and settling in at, Kars (around 1877/8) were rather disorienting and distracting. He was unsure later about the passage of time at that point.

## The Initial Shocks

He affirmed to me that major 'shocks' occurred for him from the age of three. He was born in a calm rural setting in Alexandropol – in the region close to the Caucasus and Kurdistan, between the Black and Caspian seas. His father managed a large herd of cattle there. Gurdjieff was the first-born of five children. (He had a brother and three sisters. He said:"There were 5 of us.") We would call them a peasant family, which they were in lifestyle. Although, the large cattle holding and the land gave a certain richness and comfort to their lives.

As the first-born, Gurdjieff was feted, over-indulged and 'spoiled'. He was given everything he wanted and allowed to run free, chiefly under the supervision of his paternal grandmother. The setting was idyllic and carefree for him. Then suddenly in his safe little three year-old world two large thunderclaps crashed around him, and changed everything. They were the arrival of military fighting forces and the death of his brother.

He tells of the inner terror which he came to identify with the sound of massed troops marching through their safe rural haven. And he links it, time-wise, with the death of his brother.

A revision of the record would be called for here. In Meetings with Remarkable Men it says the brother was present when Gurdjieff was seven. "That's wrong." he told me. "That information is not correct. My son will tell you" (26/Feb/85). If Gurdjieff was three at the time, and the first-born, then the brother could hardly have been older than two at the time of his death. James Moore identifies the brother as Dmitri, and suggests a birthdate around 1870-72.

But it would have had to be 1868-70. In later life there was a Dmitri who was referred to as Gurdjieff's brother. But he must have been another close relative, not his brother.

What the real brother's name was, I have no information.

As to the circumstances of the brother's death, much was left unsaid. Checking and re-checking this during the trance sessions, Gurdjieff merely insisted that he did have a brother, and that he "was killed" or "died". He showed the medium a well. (The kind of well that water is drawn from.) That was all. However it happened, it had a huge impact on the three year-old Gurdjieff. (Apparently three year-olds are very aware, especially of such things as grief.) That triggered everything off for him. From then on, it was said, he "turned into a little old man – even as a child" (20/Dec/84).

## The Move to Kars

In the 1870s there was a reversal of the Gurdjieff family fortunes. Disease ("foot and mouth") devastated the cattle herds, and most of the family possessions were sold to cover liabilities. The father opened a lumber yard, which failed. Only his business as a carpenter's shop remained. After the Russians took over the fortified city of Kars from the Turks in 1877, the uncle persuaded Gurdjieff's father to move there. They left their rural home in Alexandropol for a very different urban existence.

Gurdjieff intensely disliked the move. Urbanisation replaced rural peace and freedom. They had been led to Kars with the promise that life would be better. But they only found that it got harder. There was no 'spirit' or 'reality' there. Gurdjieff had to work with tallow to make soap and candles. This is when the longing for nature took root in him, and urbanisation was seen as what alienated a person from themselves.

At the same time his paternal grandmother went into serious decline. She had moved with them to be with her son. But she was also very attached to her husband, who had died some years previously. And his grave and their life together had been in the rural home. So when they moved to Kars, she sort of died with what they had left behind. She used to just sit by the hearth, near the fire in the stone fireplace. The mantle was barely five foot high, but she was shorter in stature than that. She just sat there in the wooden chair her son made for her. It was less than two years then before she died, under a patchwork quilt in bed.

**Grandma's Advice**

This was the grandma who gave him the advice he recounts in the introduction to Beelzebub as the principal lever of his wholeness. Gurdjieff includes it as the first of the three specific and special "data" which he says became solidified through his whole being during his younger years.

In Beelzebub the giving of this advice is presented in a dramatised form, with him being called to the bedside of his dying grandmother for its bestowal. But the advice was in fact his last recall of what the grandmother had told him. It was substantially what she had always told him. There was no actual death-bed scene. As a matter of fact, she was in a coma for about 3 days before her death. But her spirit had left some time before her body succumbed.

The grandmother and father were very significant for Gurdjieff. The three of them shared a special affinity and implicit understanding. They all had the same essence, and were older souls. He always missed them more than anyone else during his later life, and longed for the 'reality' of their company.

Since Gurdjieff was born in 1867, then he would have been about 11 years old when they moved to Kars, and 13 when the grandmother died. She was his link to his carefree rural childhood, and that died with her.

**The Grandmother and Childhood**

I was given further pictures of the childhood atmosphere. At age 3, Gurdjieff was under the supervision of the grandmother. He was decidedly unruly, running around with a stick in his hand, not paying credence to anyone. He was a really happy child, and lost within his own world. He was pretty headstrong, very spoilt, very indulged, and very adored.

The grandmother, rather short, had big hips and a gathered skirt coming out from the waist. They wore dark-coloured clothes, and all had 'funny' wooden shoes. The smell around their dwelling was a sort of mixture of both animals and cooking.

Gurdjieff was a chubby child. All the family members were stocky. Even at age 7, he was resistant to learning to read, and a bad student. He didn't want to do what they asked him to. The books with wooden covers were there. But basically he wanted to do it for himself, and he was reading before anyone else realised he was doing it. Towards age 11, he slimmed down and had a large shock of thick, dark, wavy hair.

The grandmother was a profoundly religious woman. They had icons sitting around in the house. But she had her own firm beliefs about how to live one's life. One had to always work things out for oneself, by learning to trust one's own instincts. She had a very enquiring mind, quite unusual for women of her times. Gurdjieff inherited this kind of mind from her. She also understood and pursued various methods of folk medicine, herbal remedies, the body-mind connection, and things like that.

We also find, especially in Gurdjieff's father, some political-mindedness and political activity. There was his Greek ancestry, but also a strong feeling of being Ukranians. They had moved to Kars after the Russians had overturned the Turkish occupation there. But with the "clear-thinking" characteristic of grandmother, son and grandson, and concern for fairness and justice, they were rather critical of the Russian government of the city.

A curious sidelight is that the young Joseph Stalin stayed with the Gurdjieff family while he was studying as a student in Kars. Gurdjieff's father didn't like to see anyone "going without their bread". So they took him in. When Stalin left, he did so without paying what he owed them.

## Gurdjieff's "Ashokh" Father

Gurdjieff's father was an amateur "ashokh". These were sorts of local 'bards' in the area who put together, or recited or sang poetical, musical or traditional legends and tales. Many were illiterate people, but with well developed memories. Even vast amounts of material were mastered by some of them, and performed over hours or days. This was an astonishing oral tradition, stretching back into the remote past.

Gurdjieff tells of one evening when he was present in his father's workshop, along with his uncle and a Dean Borsh (from the Kars military academy). His father began performing a legend of 'Gilgamesh' – a hero from Babylonian times. Part of it was recited so many times that Gurdjieff still remembered it years later. In subsequent years he was astonished to find that, new archaeological discoveries had recovered this same "Epic of Gilgamesh" on clay tablets. When freshly discovered, the text was four thousand years old, and virtually identical to the oral tradition passed on by his father!

He told me he was about 23 years old when he came across the new archaeological evidence. It significantly rearranged him at the time. In his terms, it was a "spiritualising factor", and a "shock" for his mental and feeling associations. I will explain more about that presently, because something else happened for him that night when his father recited Gilgamesh.

This is not recorded in the account of the evening given in Meetings with Remarkable Men. He was lying in the wood shavings in his father's workshop, and had not been sent to bed as usual. Then he had a kind of vision. His father was reciting the sequence about the "flood before the flood", when something extraordinary happened. In a kind of red mist, he saw chariots entering a city.

## Clairvoyant Episode

It was, in fact, the first real clairvoyant episode he had, of which there were many during his life. (I could relate to this. I had one myself with a person appearing in a red back-light not six months before our Gurdjieff trance sessions began.) For Gurdjieff it reinforced what his grandmother had said about not trusting others, but doing it himself. Such a thing had never been spoken of to him by any other person. But he knew what he had seen, and it had been very real. This episode helped to compound the idea for him that there was an "otherness" - another way of thinking and experiencing.

After I was told of Gurdjieff's vision, I checked the "Epic of Gilgamesh", looking for the mention of chariots in the "story of the flood". But there was no reference to chariots there. What Gurdjieff saw then, was not a depiction of something from the Gilgamesh story. I sought clarification from another channelled source, through the same medium, and was told the vision had a specific meaning for Gurdjieff. The chariot is the vehicle of the messenger on an information-carrying mission. Like the prophets of old, some people have a life-mission to pass on messages from elsewhere. It would therefore have been a graphic preview and confirmation of Gurdjieff's coming life-mission.

## Dean Borsh

Another significant figure in the young Gurdjieff's life was Dean Borsh, from the Kars Military Cathedral and Academy, who was his first tutor. He describes the Dean as the third component of his 'inner god', and the one who played a crucial role in establishing his individuality (p. 34, Meetings with Remarkable Men, hereafter MRM.) By this he must have meant the Dean was the third person, after his grandmother and father, to influence him greatly. The learning he brought was integral to Gurdjieff's realisation of his individuality.

Being of the same essence, and of similar soul development, we find there was an immediate and deep connection between Dean Borsh and his father. The two men met often. Gurdjieff talks of the strange way they proceeded with each other. He would see them asking and answering questions nonchalantly of each other, in an incomplete way, in a serious and quiet tone. Only later did he come to understand what they had been doing.

Dean Borsh and his father had telepathic communication with each other. They had previously been reincarnated souls together, and there was a certain level of non-verbal affinity between them. They had already had half of the conversation directly in their own minds with each other, before parts of it surfaced. So, when they resorted to verbal communication, it seemed strange and incomplete to a third party. With few verbal clues, they already understood intrinsically what the other was talking about. Later in life, Gurdjieff found he had this telepathic communication with a particular woman, apparently one of his sisters.

**The "Wisdom" Tooth**

The next important experience in sequence is a curious story told in the Beelzebub introduction (pp. 30-5). It is the second of the three important personal experiences he recounts there, after 'grandma's advice'. (I have given the background to grandma and her advice above, with the grandma connection earlier in this chapter, and the advice itself explained in chapter one.)

Gurdjieff tells of a rascally scuffle between himself and a couple of other young boys. It resulted in his wisdom tooth being knocked out! The events as described there never actually happened. It seems he was a bit young to have a wisdom tooth. The story is simply symbolic, as can be appreciated from what he explains about it. It was of vital significance however, for Gurdjieff's seeing of the seven essences, and for his coming to identify and express the qualities of his own essence.

We get the timing from his saying it was in his youth. So we're probably looking at mid teenage years. In saying that it was purposely instigated by some external forces, he is highlighting the extraordinary coincidence of the event for his personal development. At the same time its fortuitousness could hardly have been just "chance".

Dean Borsh was involved in it. Gurdjieff says elsewhere how Dean Borsh persuaded his parents that he should leave the local municipal school and be tutored at home by him. The Dean was very knowledgeable about ancient and esoteric things, which he often discussed with the father.

The "wisdom tooth" is the basis of the story. Gurdjieff said his displaced wisdom tooth had seven prongs. The number "7" is integral to the "ancient wisdom" and a general collection of ancient references and writings. We know, too, that "wisdom" is the knowing of the heart, or intrinsic knowing. That transcends mere knowledge in the common outward sense. The "wise person" knows more, and is more adept than the merely knowledgeable person. They are working from their essence, and have that connection to their subconscious minds.

After telling how his wisdom tooth had seven prongs, Gurdjieff adds that each of them had a drop of blood, and shining in each drop was a succession of colours. They were the seven colours of the rainbow, which are the seven colours which fragment through a prism from white light. For him to explain this much, shows he had a reasonable grasp of the significance of 7 in the ancient writings. They represent the seven essences. And to locate and understand the character of one's own essence in that cluster or sequence, gives a personal understanding of the basis of one's individuality.

## The "7" in Ancient Writings

It is worth reviewing "7" in some ancient writings. We can start with the recovered text of "The Epic of Gilgamesh", which Dean Borsh and Gurdjieff's father had talked long and often about. In the prologue of that epic (Penguin edition, p. 61), it tells how Gilgamesh built the city of Uruk, and its foundation was put down by the 'seven sages'. This text was recovered on clay tablets from an Assyrian library, and the Assyrians collected their texts from older libraries in Babylon, Uruk and Nippur.

Chapter 9 of the biblical book of Proverbs begins with a personification of 'Wisdom', and her constructed dwelling had seven supporting pillars.

A rich source of information is H.P. Blavatsky's article "The Number Seven" (The Theosophist, June 1880). She refers to a competent and dependable treatment of the topic in the German journal Die Gegenwart. That, in turn, attests to 'seven' being a sacred number in virtually all Eastern countries in ancient times. And later it was also considered significant in Western nations.

Closer to our own times, the writing of Hermes called the Pymander identifies a mystery associated with "seven". It is claimed to be concealed, which would make it part of the secret learning that initiates were inducted into. It is also linked with "harmony", and seven men and seven women, and the "natures" of what are apparently the seven planets of antiquity.

These Hermetic writings may be a link with the Ashiata Shiemash which Gurdjieff talked of. But even closer to our own times is the historical account of the tradition of the "seven wise men" in ancient Greece. They are credited with having dedicated a temple of Apollo at Delphi, where the injunction "know thyself" was inscribed.

Over hundreds of years a group of seven very enlightened men was maintained in ancient Greece. When someone died, they were replaced to keep the group intact. They came from all over the country, but met periodically at Delphi and other places. The group consisted of one of each of the seven essences. We know the names of many of them – people like Solon, Thales, Pittacus, Bias, Periander, Pythagoras, Epimenides, and so forth. The pretext for their meeting together was for political administration, but there was an implicit spiritual purpose behind it. (The ancient Greeks were following the example of the Babylonian city of Uruk, where the "seven sages" became the foundation of their governance.)

It seems that Dean Borsh introduced Gurdjieff to this ancient wisdom tradition. While he was still a "rascally young lad" in his teens, he got the impact of the ancient wisdom.

**The Oozing from the Cavity**

In this story, Gurdjieff says there was a kind of discharge and flow from the cavity of his displaced wisdom tooth. It is said to have caused a change in his consciousness, so he intrinsically grasped the meaning of his grandmother's previously given advice. And, connected with that, it developed into certain characteristic behaviours in him thereafter. It formed into an intense interest in getting to the bottom of every strange phenomenon and fact he came across. Anything out of the ordinary caught his attention. He was starting to "play Sherlock Holmes" with the mystery of life in general. Through an understanding of what was his essence, or the impulse central to it, he found himself projected into a tremendously absorbing, fruitful and satisfying life-quest.

He had what we call the "essence of Mercury", which Buddha was also said to have had. It causes one to seek out and confront mysteries, and strive to understand and resolve them. He had a passion to understand the real purpose of life. Once the quest was recognised, every strange fact about the human condition became a clue to follow. The "game was on", and he pursued it from that point for the rest of his life. The subconscious was now coming to prominence through his essence.

His grandmother's advice had been the original activator, and then he "found the essence" in himself. It was like, "This is what I really want to do!" But it didn't stop there. There was one further aspect which was shortly to combine with what he had achieved to that point, and it would drive his quest much faster and more effectively.

**Priest or Physician?**

He might have been expected under the tutelage of Dean Borsh to prepare for the occupations of either priest or physician.

Ouspensky obviously believed Gurdjieff had once qualified for and taken up the occupation of priest. In a visit to Gurdjieff's original family home with him in 1916, he says an interesting portrait caught his attention. He was sure it was Gurdjieff in a black frock coat. He said it immediately convinced him, without a doubt, what Gurdjieff's profession had been. But he then says, rather strangely (in ISOTM, p. 341), that he wouldn't tell anyone! (As if we didn't know what wearing a black frock coat in an important family portrait would mean!)

When I put this to Gurdjieff, he said simply that Ouspensky was mistaken. The portrait had been of his uncle, not himself.

Gurdjieff told me he wouldn't consider becoming a priest. Look at the sayings of his father about priests listed in chapter 2 of MRM! He endorsed those sayings. He saw foolishness, wrong advice, and assaults on peoples' faith as endemic to the profession. (Dean Borsh, of course, was a striking exception to that.)

He did look seriously for a while at the possibility of becoming a physician. This was mainly for his family, and how it could provide a means for looking after them. He was interested in it, and learned a lot about the body and physiology. But when it came down to having to make a choice, he didn't want to practise it.

## The Final Compounding Shock

In Beelzebub Gurdjieff goes on to describe the third experience in sequence which was crucial for his development. He omits from that account the final shock that brought it about. (There must also have been a shock connected with his wisdom tooth episode, but we don't have enough information to say exactly what it was.) The shock for the third episode is clearly referred to in Herald of Coming Good. (See page 14. To be called just HCG in future.)

It was a hefty spiritual blow, brought on by the death of a very close friend. As he explained it to me (2/Apr/85), it was "the final compounding shock". There had been a number of reverberations throughout his life, from very early childhood. Those shock effects had continued over time, like expanding circular ripples from a rock thrown into a pond.

By about age 17 the effects of the earlier traumas had dissipated into a period of quiet and smoothness. Then there was the next decisive step. As the final compounding shock, it unhinged something, or loosened a constraining mechanism, to set something new in motion.

In Beelzebub it is the 'datum' which followed or accompanied the shock which was of most concern to him. In HCG he talks of the shock having triggered in him a striving that couldn't be repressed. That is further explained in Beelzebub as issuing in a comprehensive principle – like, "If you're going to go for it, then really go for it!" It was akin to "letting go" as if you were on a 'spree', and not concerning yourself about any distracting blocks or limitations.

Earlier in that book he claimed to have engaged since childhood in the practice of doing a great deal of anything which he did. It reminds one of the old biblical advice, that when your hands find something to do, you should do it with all your strength.

Whatever constraining mechanism was released by Gurdjieff's final shock, it brought a rush of bodily and inner enthusiasm or striving. It was an enlivening factor. He tells us in HCG that it did not overwhelm his general functioning. He found it could be tapped or put into abeyance, according to what he chose to do. But it slowly penetrated his entire being, and was constantly "there" for him after that.

**The New "Vivifying" Factor**

In the light of his later teaching, we can see how the three important stages or episodes he recounted in his Beelzebub introduction correspond with the three parts of the psyche of "modern man". (It is in modern man, but basically has been there since the end of Atlantis.) In the main body of his teaching, modern man has a problem with these three parts. They are 'split' and work independently of each other. They are "disharmonised". He claims that, even in the time of Babylon (second to first century B.C.), there was a period when proper integrated functioning had been restored for some, for a time. This happens when the three independent parts work together again as one.

This book began with the problem of the "two consciousnesses" in people. Those needed to be brought into alignment with each other. Now we see a third factor in the situation. Something else must then be brought into play, <u>after</u> the conscious and subconscious (or personality and essence) have been integrated. It isn't a consciousness <u>as such</u>, but a functioning of our organism nonetheless. The terminology Gurdjieff uses here isn't precise. It is variously called a bodily functioning, or an 'organic instinct', or the 'moving-instinctive' centre in us. He says in <u>HCG</u> that this third part is an automatic or self-moving thing, according to the way these bodily systems have become accustomed to functioning.

It was the automated mechanism which had previously locked him into functioning as most people do in the everyday world. But when the expression of the essence was advanced enough in his consciousness, the final compounding shock "switched" this organic mechanism for him. It then began to support his new 'unified' self with gusto. This irrepressible striving served to greatly advance his essence aims, to find and disseminate the teaching it was his mission to bring to the world.

So, what started with grandma's advice had roused the subconscious. In the second place, what happened with the 'wisdom tooth' episode brought his conscious mind into tandem with subconscious/essence knowing. And the third episode switched his automatic functioning to support this new direction in life. He had then, what he referred to later in <u>Beelzebub</u> (p. 38) as the combined outcome of consciousness, subconsciousness, and organic automatism.

There is more to be said yet about this "3-in-1" functioning, which we will return to in chapter 5. It is the restoration of harmony to the human condition. Gurdjieff had identified the elements in himself in his early experience, and later found some references about it in ancient Hindu writings. He then put together his distinctive teaching as a means of assisting the development of others. More of that later.

## <u>**And the Kundalini Rose**</u>

Gurdjieff's achievement of the "3-in-1" state by age

17 was a major accomplishment. He must have been ripe and ready for it. (He was an "old soul", with past life development.) We know it was triggered in practice by external shocks and 'coincidences'. He himself refers to extraneous forces (beyond himself) having a hand in it. The development was clearly integral to his pre-chosen life-purpose or mission. It would need to have been allowed also by his willingness to proceed (his free will). All the elements were in place for forward movement.

Perhaps this "3-in-1" state could have been sufficient in itself. But I don't know enough to be sure of that. What is clear is that, in Gurdjieff's case it triggered a further accompanying experience. He was moving quickly to a more advanced level. As he describes it, and also fuelled by the same impetus which switched over the vivifying automatism, he experienced the classic symptoms of "the rising of the kundalini".

A "racing" and intensity enveloped his internal processes, and continued for some time. Simultaneously, an almost unendurable itchiness proceeded along the back around his spine. There was severe pain in the solar plexus. After these symptoms had continued for a while, they were mercifully replaced by an unparalleled inner peacefulness.

In Eastern – especially Indian or yogic – teachings, the kundalini is the "coiled serpent" which sits at the base of the spine. It is an energy that sits there in a primed state, ready to rise up when summoned or released. When one has reached the required state of personal development, the kundalini can rise up through the "chakras" in the body – along the spine – to bring enlightenment. It must travel up through all the 7 chakras to the top one, the "crown", to bring total enlightenment. The crown is then said to open up like a lotus flower, when one's understanding and life is transformed.

It must be noted that in Gurdjieff's case, he did <u>not</u> have the full kundalini experience. He had part of it. It was the major part, but not all of it. He did not even know when he had the experience what the kundalini was. Only later did he read and learn about it, and gain more understanding.

During his later life, he believed or assumed that he'd had the full experience, when he hadn't. It was not until he passed over that he saw or realised that, the kundalini had only risen to the neck, or the fifth chakra. That was astonishing enough, but it wasn't complete.

He told me, if the kundalini had risen completely for him, then he would have simply retired from all activity in the world. All his earthly experience would have been complete. But there was still much for him to do during his lifetime. He still had his mission to collect and disseminate teaching. So it was by choice at an unconscious level within him, as well as by the wise over-seeing of his soul, that the kundalini rose only to the fifth (throat) level. That gave him sufficient enlightenment and ability to do what he needed to do in his life.

**Pointers About the Kundalini**

Gurdjieff gave me some advice about the kundalini. He said it very rarely rises completely at one time in people. Hardly anyone is prepared within themselves for that. It would simply blow all one's circuits, or one would be unable to cope. So what you get, virtually all of the time, is partial arisings, when it begins its ascent. It is an important accomplishment if it only rises through even one or two chakras. These partial arisings are progressive. It may go further later in the same lifetime, or carry over into later lifetimes.

This is a very dangerous energy if not approached correctly. One should <u>never</u> set out to trigger its rise by specific practices. (There are plenty of warnings in Gurdjieff's writings about wrong crystallisation and damage to peoples' psyches.) What one can and should do, is "prepare" the path for it. Then it can arise easily and safely when the time, chosen by the soul, arrives for its advance. 'We' don't choose the timing, the soul does. Achieving the "3-in-1" state prepares the way for it. So also does the spinning exercise detailed later in chapter 9.

(I was curious when Gurdjieff was giving me this advice. I had previously tried to make sense of the warnings about the kundalini that Ouspensky recorded from Gurdjieff. [ISOTM, p. 220] They seemed to warn one off entirely about having anything to do with it. When I asked Gurdjieff about this, he said Ouspensky didn't always have the empathy, intuition and psychic insight to correctly understand what he was told. Though, if you read the ISOTM passages closely, you'll see that they merely warn about misunderstanding of what the kundalini was.)

**The Publication of Gilgamesh**

I do not have any specific information about Gurdjieff between 17 and 23. His early investigations are discussed in chapter 3 and onwards of MRM. The "out of the ordinary" events which attracted his attention there were apparently 'supernatural' things which arose around him. He continued with his formal studies. And he earned money by his resourcefulness and practical ingenuity in making and repairing small household items for people.

Despite his "3-in-1" and kundalini accomplishments, he was not immediately elevated to a place of implicit or universal knowing. He still had to search and find things, and start to put them together for himself. Though, doors and understandings opened for him when he chose to progress. The next important breakthrough was finding the newly published text of Gilgamesh.

According to archaeological literature, Gilgamesh and his epic had been "wholly forgotten" before the old clay tablets were unearthed and translated in the late nineteenth century. Gurdjieff read the magazine article about them in 1890. It was a great shock for him to realise the text was virtually word-for-word the very story passed down by *ashokhs* for thousands of years. He had heard it from his father when he was a child. What an amazing coincidence!

At this stage in his development it produced a shock for his mental and feeling associations. Just prior to his discovering the Gilgamesh text, he'd had a kind of religious crisis. He was breaking away from formal religious belief, rejecting the bible, and even doubting there had ever been a place like Babylon. He'd started to develop his own philosophies, and dealt with anything religious by assuming that none of it existed.

There was a certain pattern to his thinking. He'd start to put together a new way of looking at things. But when he came across inconsistencies or new refuting evidence, he'd ditch the lot and just start again. Things were constantly reassessed. So, after he'd just dispensed with anything religious or ancient from his early upbringing, suddenly the reality of Babylon hit him full on. Everything had to be reassessed again. Before long it was taking him off on long journeys to discover the truth.

## The Gunshot Wounds

There are references in his writings to gunshot wounds he had received. I wondered if they were further shocks in his development, or even warnings to him during his later wayward phase. But he told me the two occasions that he was wounded were both accidental, and of no real consequence. One was a hunting accident, and the other an accidental discharge of a gun while it was being cleaned. One impacted his knee, and the other his left shoulder. They were just minor flesh wounds.

Whenever he made anything of the gunshot wounds in his writings, it was only as a teaching point. He could turn anything ordinary into something exceptional or dramatic if he saw the chance to make an instructional point out of it. That's how he taught.

## The Headaches

He said "the headaches" gave him far more trouble than the bullet wounds. These headaches made him look at himself far more effectively than anything else. They started from age 17, and were prominent during his formative years. When he started going off on long journeys, the headaches went away. And every time he stopped 'looking', the headaches came back. So, as long as he was wandering, he was alright. He travelled mainly on foot, and went through many countries in Europe and Asia, and even northern Africa.

The headaches were created by his spiritual guide, or guardian. It was a way of pulling him up and saying, "Look at yourself!" They had a really profound effect on him. And he found that people, crowds, and cities brought the headaches on. They stopped after he was 40, returning only briefly between 56 and 58 (1923-5). That's when he had to make more journeys, to resolve some more questions. He was allowed to settle after that.

## End of the Formative Years

I was told that by age 26 the formative phase was ending. By then he was ready for a lot of profound thinking. But he spent another 14 years before he gave himself fully to the work. He still did a lot of travelling during that time. But it was a phase of coming to terms with his outer ego, the world, worldly ways, and women. By then he had learned how the world worked, and he used it to indulge his ego.

Evidently he could have gone further in his final development if that period hadn't lasted as long. It was necessary learning for him though. It wasn't karma, but just "life lessons". He said of it in retrospect: "The (outer) ego is such a waste of time!" Without it, he could have been doing at 26 what he went on to do at 40. About 1907/8 is when his real life work began.

CHAPTER FOUR

# The Teaching Phase

Gurdjieff began his real life work from age 40, around 1907. That is when he started teaching.

The information given to me in trance sessions corresponded with available records. James Moore, in his chronology of Gurdjieff's life, has him situated in Tashkent from 1908-10. There he taught as a kind of instructor in supernatural studies - the first mention of his public teaching. Tashkent was annexed to Russia in 1865, and was the largest city in the Central Asian Russian-dominated area at the time. It acquired its own university in 1919. It was therefore a large enough city, located not too far from Gurdjieff's homeland.

## Beyond the Personal Ego

It had been necessary for Gurdjieff to transcend the dominance of his outer ego in order to teach effectively. The ego is an essential part of our psychological make-up, which we all need to function in the everyday world. It is our "sentry", and will come out strongly when we are under threat. Alternatively, when we are trodden on or walked over by others, or life circumstances, our self-esteem suffers, and the ego is diminished. It causes problems for our spiritual advance when it is out of balance in either way. It shouldn't remain under- or over-inflated when it doesn't need to be. Some people continue to use it when it is over-inflated to intimidate or manipulate others. Other people may become too comfortable with being a "martyr" and continue in low self-esteem.

When its balance is lost through over-inflation, it can't work for other people. We lose our "feel" in spiritual work. The essence then becomes non-usable. We are no longer effectively in touch with it. When the ego is under-inflated, it won't work for others. And it under-estimates the essence.

Gurdjieff had spent a long time in that over-inflated ego condition, from ages 26 to 40. He still did a lot of travelling, driven by the headaches. He still collected much information and teaching. But he wasn't putting it together properly, and he wasn't using it. He was still working in a sense, but nowhere near as well as he could have. In our trance sessions he said he "talked in another way than he felt".

This was a "very internal, private thing" for him, and he never spoke of this phase in his later communications with people. The period is glossed-over with references instead solely to his travels and meetings with remarkable people. There had been "women", and marriages, and alcohol, and self-aggrandisement". He had learnt how to see through people and manipulate them, and he just used it.

His transcending of his own outer ego consisted essentially in his giving up or curtailing the power he knew he had for manipulating others. He would no longer use it to exploit the weakness and suggestibility of people. But he would commit himself instead to assisting others in coming to know themselves.

He previously smoked hashish, but continued that later as an occasional recreation. (It was a social custom in Turkey and other countries.) Also of course, he was still fond of good food and alcohol later. He continued to indulge those "vices" - as he called them – sporadically, or periodically, as an occasional "rest" from his gruelling work. That was along with a number of liaisons as well. (He said he was "fond" of women, and had a weakness for being flattered by them.) In fact, it wasn't until his 50s (after 1917) that he went beyond seeing women merely as pretty "dolls", and developed an interest in the female mind. But his 'chauvinism' was basically a reflection of social attitudes at that time.

It took him until 40 to transcend his own world. Then, he said, he "dropped the self", and started to "live the way he thought and felt". He also talked of his ego being "imploded", or "taken within". It can never be dispensed with while living in the everyday world. But it can be brought into balance.

**Under Guidance**

When Gurdjieff dropped his controlling ego, his attendant spiritual guardian moved in closer to him. (I discussed the guardian in the preface, and explained how his advice was passed off in Beelzebub as that of the Mullah Nassr Eddin.) Note how Gurdjieff says there that he'd always used the Mullah as a "guide" (p. 57).

(I refer to the guardian as "he", to reflect the Mullah identity. But our guardians are typically of a level of development where they incorporate both maleness and femaleness within themselves. They may project as being either male or female.)

He told me he was "working hand-in-glove with (his) guardian from 40 onward" (3/Jan/85). The advice of the guardian was usually brief, pithy and couched in the kind of folksy language Gurdjieff loved and appreciated. The guardian's advice is almost always of the direct off-the-cuff sort, like someone commenting over his shoulder, rather than a teacher sending him advice and directions from another country!

There was a very affectionate bond between the two. Strangely, Gurdjieff never asked, and was never given, a name for his guardian. He just used a "pet name", like "Joe" or "Fred" in personal communication, or "the Mullah" in Beelzebub. The only other information I have about his guardian is that in appearance he was very tall. (This would have a meaning for those familiar with such things. It probably meant his guidance came from a rather exalted level, as we might expect.)

We might even say the guardian "used" Gurdjieff to get out as much teaching as they could into the world. (I was told: "The guardian attached itself to the entity – not the entity to the guardian".) Gurdjieff had a mind to teach as often as he could, and he had the necessary back-up and support with him. The guardian often influenced his thought patterns, and then he ran with it.

In his after-life reflections from the other side, Gurdjieff said he realised later how the guardian enabled or assisted him in grasping "the incomprehensible". They had also assisted him with the finer details of understanding the "28 types", after Gurdjieff had done the initial work by intuition and hypnotic experiments. The guardian was very close indeed with him after his motor car crash in 1924.

## The Charisma

Gurdjieff certainly had a "presence" to him. But the "charisma" came both from his mastery of himself and the close bonding with his guardian. Others could sense and feel it. Unfortunately, people turned the charisma into a "mystique". This elevated him and what he had far too highly, and separated him off from his students.

Gurdjieff didn't like it, and didn't want it. He took steps most of the time to try to puncture those assessments of himself. He did outrageous and contradictory things, and even his closest followers despaired at times of his antics. Adulation worked against what he was trying to achieve with people. He needed them to show personal initiative to get somewhere in their work on themselves. Over-deference to him only led to enslavement of feeling. It also obscured the fact that, underneath he was just a normal man. People weren't seeing that. He felt things as deeply and sincerely as anyone else. He was a feeling, sensitive person – behind the roles he had to play for his 'work' – and almost no-one saw that.

The fact that he could talk about and do things which many of his followers considered amazing, became a demarcation. The more they separated him from themselves in their minds, the less they could imagine doing what was required to be like him. Yet, if they could have seen the "ordinary man", they would have better grasped the possibility of attaining the same level of development themselves.

## Beginnings of the Wider Teaching

After the initial teaching at Tashkent, around 1911,

Gurdjieff planned a new way of working with people. The idea was first floated of setting up an "institute" where he could work more intensely with a chosen group of students. His 'circles' needed to be organised on different lines to the occult ones in Tashkent, with a different 'method' of transmitting the teaching. He also needed to find a locality where a far wider range of human 'types' were available to him.

He was expanding his horizons. He said the people of what he called the "U-Krine" had the "spiritual accent" for participating in his work, and he could have achieved much with them. But there were very limited ethnic pockets of people there, and they were barely one generation out of their peasant origins. His work would have become lost there.

Initially he decided to move his efforts into the heart of Russia, which was quite prosperous and peaceful in 1912. He also specifically moved to Moscow to meet Ouspensky. This was something organised on the "other side", and known to Gurdjieff through his guide. Ouspensky could present the ideas in a form more appealing to the educated Western mind. His background of searching for the unusual and miraculous in the East, and writing about cutting-edge scientific and metaphysical ideas, was an appropriate preparation for that.

As Ouspensky tells the story, Gurdjieff first came to his attention through advertised public performances of "The Struggle of the Magicians" - Gurdjieff's dances, in 1914. That was fortuitous, but strange. As Gurdjieff said to me in 1985, he never wanted his dance exercises to be performed in public. That is, he probably wouldn't have minded some limited public exposure, for attracting students. But they were never intended as "public, public" performances.

He wanted the dances in a written form "for people to do in private". They had their essential point in a sequence of steps for individual dancers to do, but not outside that. But his followers took them into the public arena, and he just allowed it to happen. In fact, the dance exercises were only for the benefit of those doing them, not anyone watching. As a public performance, even though of dubious entertainment value, they became general publicity for him, and an introduction to a wider range of people.

Anyway, Gurdjieff ran groups in Moscow from 1912 while he worked on his teaching method. He was getting the feel of the 'scientific' and how to present things to those embracing this rising current in Western thought. In Moscow and St Petersburg he was attracting a number of intellectuals and scientific people. Land was acquired near Moscow for setting-up his Institute. But then war broke out – the start of the First World War. His plans were put on hold.

## Complications and Progress

One complication that arose for him was being pressed into service for the Russian spy network. There are references in some books alleging he was a Russian spy. The truth is not quite as glamorous. At about age 43, in 1910, he was faced with the demand to undertake military service. He was able to avoid this, which would have disrupted his teaching plans, by volunteering to become a courier in the spy service. He said about that, he "didn't mind playing the game".

(Along with the 'spy' rumours, there is speculation in some books that Gurdjieff was the person Dorjieff who spent some time as a Russian ambassador in Tibet. It is simply false. He had indeed travelled in India, and even got as far as the border with Tibet, but never entered that country. But he says he knew Dorjieff and corresponded with him, and Dorjieff used to expound many of his ideas at times. That may account for the confusion. Also, the two men looked similar, and had the same build and height. Further, he said, as a final means of distinguishing the two of them: "Dorjieff had hair!")

For the first 2 years of Gurdjieff's courier duties (1910-12), the demands on him were spasmodic. But from 1912-16 they became more intense. His job was to carry "crudely coded messages contained in books". He had to take them to and from other countries. He mentions Spain in particular.

His last mission was when he left central Russia with a group of people in 1917. First they stopped in Essentuki, but started to find themselves trapped there. Then Gurdjieff led a band of his followers on foot, by a dangerous and circuitous mountain route to the Black Sea. They crossed the lines of the warring factions a number of times, but got safely through due to some ingenious planning and cunning. (He told me recently, he could do this because he had no attachment to either side in the conflict. He just told those who confronted him what they wanted to hear.)

That momentous retreat from the civil war in Russia also coincided with the Bolshevik revolution and the collapse of the Old Order. He had carried messages under the Tsarist regime, and it probably wasn't safe for him to return after that. Those involved in the old order were often summarily executed. It shut the door on further teaching plans in Russia.

There have been some criticisms that Gurdjieff didn't see the war coming when he set-up operations in central Russia. When I put this to him, he said he knew it was brewing, but neither he nor others expected the scale of devastation and changes the First World War would bring. He'd seen smaller wars in many countries most of his life, and used to just carry on by working around them.

He had, however, met Ouspensky in Moscow in 1915. He included him in the intensive teaching of the 1915-7 groups in Moscow and St Petersburg. It was the richest, most extensive phase of his formal teaching. This set Ouspensky up with most of the material he needed to lecture for many years in London, and for the publication especially of ISOTM. That was the single most important book for spreading Gurdjieff's teaching to the world.

## The 'Method'

The 'scientific' emphasis in his teaching after 1912 was part of a general change of method. At Tashkent he had used the role of a "Master and His Students". But that was changed experimentally, and by degrees, to the "Scientist and His Assistants".

What he was doing here, as he explained it to me, was "trying different paths to the same end". He was trying to adapt the teaching to "different personalities, different cultural and social groups and outlooks". The 'scientific' manner of proceeding had a much wider application for all the 'types'.

He complained to me that Marshall McLuhan's 1960s claim, "the medium is the message" had been <u>his</u> idea first! According to McLuhan, the form of a message embeds itself in the message, influencing how the message is perceived. Gurdjieff was certainly alert to this fifty years prior to McLuhan, and actively using it in his own work then. Form and content, for him, were part of the same message. We respond to the "role" a teacher is playing as much as to what they are saying.

Not only in his general teaching, but also in his one-to-one dealings with people, Gurdjieff adapted his manner to suit the particular occasion and audience. His role-playing repertoire was so adaptable and diverse, that many people could hardly credit they were dealing with the same person. He dealt with different people so differently. He did this, of course, to attend specifically to the development needs of each person. It was not merely an exhibition of his role-playing skill. He said it was a mark of the perfected person that they could play any role outwardly while remaining inwardly detached and free.

## **<u>Towards the Institute in Paris</u>**

For about two years he moved from place to place in the southern Russian-annexed territories, until he was forced to retreat to Constantinople in Turkey. It was a year there, and then 1921 in Berlin, before the final move was made to Paris in mid 1922.

The years after 1912 saw at least three unsuccessful attempts to set-up his 'institute'. A lot of his time and energy also had to be spent on business and money-making ventures, to support himself and those with him. In 1918 he evacuated most of his original and extended family from the Alexandropol region, because of the renewed Turkish invasion action. He also had to find means to support them. His father and oldest sister remained behind, and his father was killed during subsequent fighting.

He told me of the frustration of these years, of always "living in a bag". (We would say, "living out of a suitcase".) He wanted "somewhere to roost". People were like "shackles on him", always needing something from him. Two important relationships arose for him during this time, but he just turned his back on them. More than ever he was longing for a way to set-up a stable 'institute' somewhere, chiefly now so that he could deposit all these people there. He wanted to be able to get away by himself and reassess everything.

The prospect was raised of acquiring a property at Hellerau, near Dresden, in Germany. Most of his party of people moved to Berlin in anticipation of this. At the same time, his English supporters were also trying to arrange residential status for him there, and a property. Both possibilities fell through in quick succession. The Hellerau property was legally barred, and the application for residency in Britain was rejected. His past spy associations were known to the English, and they were unsure if he might then be working for the Bolsheviks.

The large party of people moved from Berlin to Paris in 1922. Shortly after, a sizeable house and property were taken over at Fontainebleau-Avon, near Paris. (The "Prieure des Basses Loges", or the "Prieure" for short.) At last the stable 'institute' was established. A large group of his followers and extended family moved in. Gurdjieff had shifted his operations decisively to Europe, and he now had the widest cross-section of 'types' available to him. Even though, at this point he could speak neither French nor English. There could have been no more suitable location than cosmopolitan Paris in the 1920s though. He also rented an apartment in Paris for his teaching activities.

## Restlessness and Reassessment

All through the enormous difficulties surrounding the five years of the retreat from central Russia to the arrival in Paris, Gurdjieff had been teaching both widely and intensively. He told his chosen followers of the "super-human efforts" they needed to make in work on themselves. His own efforts were clearly super-human, and a brilliant example. But he did not need to work on himself like that to dissolve suggestibility, or transfer the existing automatism, as they did. He was driven by his sense of mission.

He also had said he swore an oath in 1911 to devote himself for twenty-one years to do whatever was necessary to advance his teaching activities. (That claim needs to be reviewed in the light of the Moroccan episode to be dealt with in chapter nine. The important oath behind his work is explained there.) He needed to be pretty tough to carry out what was demanded of him. We know from a published source that during adolescence his father had made him rise early, be splashed with cold water, and then have to run around naked outside. That would have hardened him up for much that he had to go through later.

With all the effort and dedication he was putting in from 1917, the results he was expecting weren't materialising. The people he was teaching weren't finding and using their own initiative, but continued just looking to him. He said they were weighting on him. (That's "weighting", like being a heavy weight.) He told me he took off for a while in 1919, with just 6 people with him, to Trieste and Bonn. He was weary, he was restless. The headaches had come back, and he had trouble with his feet. He just needed to get out for a while.

By the time his 'institute' was set-up in Paris, he was still decidedly restless. Even before he got there, he knew this structure wasn't going to work as he'd originally thought it would. It offered the possibility of more stream-lined group work for advanced stages of development, such as he outlined briefly in HCG. But the people he had with him weren't ready for that. At least this property was somewhere he could deposit all those people while he got away by himself to rethink everything.

## "I Want to Get Out!"

His sense of being trapped persisted for some time at

the Paris institute. He felt he was being "choked" for about 6 months. He left two men in charge of the set-up (de Hartmann and Orage), and took off on travels. He went out, and back, a number of times. He had a bag of papers on his back, and was constantly going out to "cogitate, to ruminate, to go over the words (he was writing), to work on them". But the predicament persisted. All the time he was thinking, "I want to get out, I want to get out, I want to get out!"

He was tired of the simplistic explaining he had to do with his students all the time. For him it was like a person of Ph.D. standard having to coach kindergarten kids in finger-painting. He did his 'seeing' psychically, and then he had to analyse it and put it into words. He would rack his brains constantly to think up more and more "little exercises" and techniques to get them to make the simplest advances. He was quite ingenious at this, but it gave him little satisfaction. He was constantly asking himself, "When are they going to get real?" Those who did the cooking in the kitchen seemed more real to him than his students.

Time and again over weeks, he told me of his frustration with this situation at the Institute. He used to sit at the big oak/walnut desk in the study provided for him, with books and papers spread before him, just staring at the wall. He didn't like the interruptions, or the feeling of being couped-up, or the regimentation involved in running the place. He'd given his students "practices" to do, but they were adhering to them in a "mind way, not a soul way". No one was "thinking for themselves". They weren't finding their 'individuality'. If only they would embrace "grandma's advice", which was so simple and straight-forward. That was the key to it all. Then they could have seen past all the seriousness and the rubbish they didn't have to own. They would have seen the 'ridiculousness' of all that.

He knew the teaching, but couldn't get it to work with the students he had. So he felt trapped, unable to advance. He longed to have some people around him like his father and Dean Borsh, who were "real". The only person he mentioned to me that he had some soul contact with was de Hartmann.

He says he talked "with" him, not just "at" him, unlike the others. Also, to a lesser extent, there was Orage.

**An Early Glimpse of the Institute**

We get an early glimpse of the Institute from the correspondence of the writer, Katherine Mansfield, to her husband John Middleton Murry, the well-known literary critic, in late 1922. (A book was published of her letters to him from 1913-22. Gurdjieff told me to look for it.) She was a celebrated short story writer, and in her mid 30s was seeking a cure for tuberculosis in southern France. She heard of Gurdjieff through Orage and Ouspensky. When she visited the Institute to meet him, she was invited to stay, barely a fortnight after it had opened. We have her correspondence from October to December, 1922, and she died there on January 9, 1923.

She described the daily activities of the 40 or so people at the Institute. It was a 'grounding' experience for her, as she struggled with what she called her artificiality and pretence. She said she was looking for something 'real'. She related warmly to the people in the Russian contingent there, and even claimed they were her 'own people'. On the other hand, she found the other group, the mainly English students, to be very tedious. They just weren't seeing the spiritual qualities the Russians were displaying in the course of basic common work. She complains about the foolish Londoners who come to the Institute, just don't see what's there and go away with that mind-set.

Over some weeks, she began to see some interesting possibilities for herself, and talked of wanting to continue in it. But despite some advances, she succumbed to her illness.

When I asked Gurdjieff about her, he said she'd had some veils lifted from the front of her eyes, and could see more clearly. She had apparently accepted some of what he told her, but not all of it. She was too heavily imbalanced in the intellect, and a bit too physically lazy. She played along with Gurdjieff's suggestions, giving lip-service to them, but "underneath it was a big ego".

Gurdjieff had a couch installed for her on a high shelf

above the cows in the stable, and she was asked to watch the cows. If she had made the mental or spiritual changes possible through this, it would have cured her. Apparently her tuberculosis didn't arise from any hereditary or physical causes, but was chosen by her in her teenage years. However, she wasn't willing to make the step to recovery. She was moved back into the main house, and died three weeks later.

(Since I had read criticism of Gurdjieff for putting a tuberculosis case in the cow shed, I asked him about that. He said she was placed up high, and the rising warmth had carried her exhalations upwards. He had acted on guidance in putting her there, for her own best chance of recovery, and that there was no risk for the cows, or other people, involved. There were no adverse effects.)

**Lack of Cohesion**

Differences between the two "groups" at the Institute were quite clear to Katherine Mansfield. Gurdjieff knew he had a problem with these major factions, but also saw important conflicts right through the assembled company. There was nationality against nationality, male against female, 'interest' against 'cause', and various moving factions. He wanted them to co-exist in an harmonious way, but didn't know how to achieve that.

Some of the contemporary accounts of Gurdjieff present him as a kind of white Russian autocrat, who one might think ruled with a rod of iron! He could give that impression at times, but it was just another of his many contrived roles. He never forced anyone to do anything. He was very conscious, always, that you can't force or intimidate anyone into personal development or enlightenment. That was the very suggestion or hypnotism by 'authority' that he was trying to overcome in people. Genuine development can only proceed by conscious personal choice. He also knew that forcing any sort of development could damage the psyche, which was also directly opposed to what he was trying to achieve.

Of course, he did engage in various kinds of "staging",

as shocks to get things moving. And he tried another ploy at the Institute. He thought that it might be possible to create a tension between himself and everyone else staying there, where they might all unite against him. Thus his autocratic stance. At least that might bring them all into a common cause with each other. But it didn't work either. Their differences with each other were always greater than he could overcome with his contrived alienating efforts.

**Research Amongst the Basques**

One of his trips away from the Institute in 1923 was to research how group harmony was achieved amongst the Basques. When he ran into a problem, he often sought secret teachings that would help him overcome it. He had some earlier theoretical understanding of group dynamics from Morocco, and some previous acquaintance with the Basques in northern Spain. But at this point he needed more.

The Basque people had a very, very old oral tradition, going back many thousands of years. Cave systems and records had been left in areas of Spain and the Pyrenees mountains from Lemurian times onwards. Even Seth mentions them, in Seth Speaks. There was a tradition of group adhesion in the face of harsh conditions and physical threats. Apparently the physical records in the caves are now too damaged to be of much use. But in 1923 Gurdjieff knew of the Basques and their way of life. He went there to observe how they functioned.

The austerity of the Basques was surprising even to Gurdjieff. Amidst great deprivation and threat, they had learnt to survive through their group organisation. By intuition and the wisdom of their oral tradition, they were using and promoting their inner essences in this way. He said this was where he "first perceived the idea of group interactions". So much of the advice he gave us for our group of 7 in 1984/5 actually "came from the mountains of Spain".

It is as well that Gurdjieff collected what he could of the Basque oral tradition in the early 1920s, because it didn't last long after that. The civil war with Franco in the 1930s disrupted and put an end to the tradition.

What Gurdjieff saw amongst the Basques was very interesting to him. It was a practical demonstration of principles of group work he had learnt in Morocco and amongst the Dervishes. Unfortunately, he couldn't use it at the Institute. There was no "cause" he could invoke to galvanise the people there into a cohesive group, such as the threats to their survival faced by the Basques. Moreover, he knew that the "finding of oneself" was more efficient and effective in conditions of peacefulness rather than threat. If there were to be conditions of social and economic breakdown in the West, such as some were predicting for the "end of the Age", then the Basque example would have had an application. Essence work could be quite effective where people were banding together for survival. But, barring that, the Basque insights had limited application.

The dynamics of group interaction worked sufficiently for our group in 1984/5. There was sufficient commonality of purpose amongst us. But it wouldn't work at the Paris Institute. The spiritual paths and soul ages of those gathered there were too diverse, and they kept bickering against each other. They just weren't ready for that kind of experience. Gurdjieff eventually realised he couldn't get a cohesive group going. He then turned his back on group work. He was left with "writing and travelling", but was too drawn into ego interactions with the people around him, which were going nowhere.

## Frustration and Going Nowhere

Of course, the writing and travelling just faced him with more frustrations. It impacted greatly on his sense of mission, boxing him up and driving him to desperation at times. He told me he had been waiting for a long time for the "right person" to come along, who could understand the writings he'd put together. Then he could pass on what he had, and that person could take it from there. But he waited, and waited, and the right person never came.

It was becoming clear to him that no-one in the West

was ready to hear what he knew! He could put out a lot of general teaching, but there were things those around him simply weren't ready to hear, or which he couldn't say to them. When he tried to involve them in "soul work", they misconstrued or ignored it. Presumably that is the extra material he gave me for this book – or some of it. Over 60 years later he could say certain things to me, and it would be over 90 years before it could be published. In that respect he was a man generations before his time. But yet, he had to collect his material when he did, and somehow it had to be passed over time to those who could use it later.

At the Institute for the rest of 1923 he was entertaining more of the Paris *avant-garde*. I asked him why he couldn't make more progress with the bright thinkers of the day. He said there wasn't much to them. While it was a rising intellectual class, they were still very limited. He said the big names of that era were hardly more cosmopolitan than the average Melbourne University student of the 1980s. At his Saturday feasts, when everyone was treated to a good meal with wines and spirits, he played the role of "Master of the Feast". He introduced the ritual of the "Science of Idiotism", said to be a custom in Turkestan. There were toasts to all manner of "idiots".

There was a kind of double reference for "idiot". The person who steps out of the everyday illusion is taken to be some kind of idiot by those still focused in everyday living. But he was also highlighting the dysfunctional aspects of the majority of humanity so painfully obvious to him. When he talked of the "twenty-one gradations", it was also a reference to the twenty-one "types" of persons who aren't true to their essences.

The toasts at these gatherings were all to generalised forms of idiots. The "ordinary idiot" was the most common form, and celebrated first. Then we find numerous variations of that, with words like "hopeless", "squirming", "square" or "round", and so forth added. The lists are numerous in a number of accounts. A large part of this celebration must have been Gurdjieff venting his own frustrations with those he couldn't otherwise get through to. He didn't aim his remarks at anyone in particular, but included them all in it. He added enough instructional pointers to make the content worth pondering for everyone. The highest category of idiot was reserved for 'God", because he "didn't know himself". That is worth thinking about. (Hmm. "God just doesn't know himself!")

The first half of 1924 was spent on his first trip to America. He visited major cities, attracted some new pupils, and founded the New York branch of his Institute. He was in dire need of funds at the time, and the American trip netted adequate donations to pay off all his debts in Paris.

He wasn't travelling well in himself in 1924. He told me that any teaching he put out at that time should probably be disregarded. He was playing with the notion of 'evolution', and it wasn't coming out right. In fact, something was seriously wrong. Then, in July 1924, he was involved in a serious motor car crash. He hovered between life and death for days or weeks. And as he slowly came together weeks later, the whole game-plan changed.

## The Car Crash

The information I was given about the car crash was, he needed to be pulled up decisively. He was seriously out of touch with himself at that time, and very stressed. If that phase had continued, he would have undermined his whole work and credibility. So the crash was something that "had to happen". He was taking too long also to confront the writing he needed to do, to record what he knew. He was still bogged down in things that were going nowhere. For the person who has found their inner self, there are no 'accidents'. Everything happens with purpose, "for a reason".

Meanwhile, J.G.Bennett tells us (Gurdjieff: Making a New World, p. 163) that in London Ouspensky was hinting that Gurdjieff had gone mad. One is not told if this was a reflection on him before or after the car crash. But it probably relates to his frustration and desperation as it built up to that event. Ouspensky loved his teaching, but found aspects of Gurdjieff's behaviour very hard to take. The car crash threw everyone connected with him into shock and confusion.

Weeks before the crash Gurdjieff knew "something was coming", but didn't consciously know what. He had acquired a motor car a while beforehand, and used to drive like a maniac. On the evening in question, two people who were due to have driven back to the Institute from Paris with him, were delayed or otherwise occupied. It was at the time when dusk was turning into night. He'd been drinking, and fell asleep at the wheel. The car veered off the road and crashed headlong into the trunk of a sizeable tree.

He was half thrown out of the car by the impact, and managed to drag himself onto the ground outside with a small red cushion under his head. Published accounts talk of lacerations and bruising to his head, arms and legs. I was told that the main problem was impact to the abdomen from the large steering wheel. The abdominal problems weren't picked up, but the impact went through to his lower back, pinching a nerve going around his hips which affected the legs. He'd also had a minor stroke, which wasn't picked up. The doctors didn't know if he'd live or die. He was quickly taken from the hospital back to the Institute, to be nursed by his family.

Apparently he dragged himself out of bed in five days. But it was really six weeks before he started to feel anything again. He was very grouchy during the convalescence – not as an 'act', but because that's how he felt. He was very, very tired. At last he started to face the fact that there wasn't much he could do for those at the Institute, and they would have to find their own way. He was "sick of everybody, sick of everything", and he realised there was no point in trying to go on as he had been.

As soon as he could, he took himself off by himself, north to the Swiss mountains. He got into opium and "pipe-dreams" for a while. His guide moved in very close after the car crash, and that's when the plan was hatched for his enigmatic writing which we see in Beelzebub. Many of the things that couldn't be said, or accepted, in a straightforward way, could be hidden or hinted at in a larger work. Only people with a keen inner sense of things could pick them up, while others would flounder around without comprehension, or get hung up on the superfluous. It was akin to the old Hermetic practice of hiding secrets from the unworthy in what was otherwise plain sight.

**Writing for Publication**

After the car crash, many people left or drifted away from the Institute. It was clear it couldn't operate as it had previously. Gurdjieff devoted himself to his writing as he recovered his strength and functions, and no general teaching was given.

The first draft of Beelzebub – the first, longest and most important of his writings – was written substantially in the three years to 1927. But revisions and amendments went on for many years after that. Gurdjieff began by dictating it. But when he was able, he started typing up drafts himself on an Armenian typewriter. It was then translated into Russian, and then into English and German, and later French. This was long and tedious. The successive translations also increased the likelihood of his original meaning being distorted. This could be one reason why he spent such a long time on translations and drafts, and had them read constantly to groups of people. He was continually checking people's responses. It was a slow, torturous process.

When the first draft of Beelzebub was finished, he moved to the second book, MRM. That was finished more easily. But the current of the times was starting to intervene and impact on him towards the end of the 1920s.

**Disillusionment with the World**

Beginning around 1927, Gurdjieff saw the direction in which Western society was heading, and was appalled by it. The material opulence and decadence affronted him, and he saw it going against everything he was trying to achieve. Then, increasingly, he turned his back on society and became more reclusive.

As part of his reclusive retreat, he started to send

many of his closest followers away. He told them they were making his life too comfortable! These were the people most devoted to him, and they were hurt and bewildered by being dismissed and sent off. His prime concern was advancing his work and teaching however, and he was pushing them away to force them to stand on their own feet. He knew he might not be with them a lot longer. So they needed to find their own way.

He was always kind to the Americans. In his greatly reduced circumstances he needed to foster the American links, where he could gain the donations to keep him going financially. So he welcomed them at the Institute, and made a number of visits to America. This wasn't necessarily because they were making important advances in his teaching. If anything, they understood less. But there was a fascination and a following there. He saw them as wanting a religion-substitute. So he said to me:

> *They wanted a religion. So I gave them a religion. (19/Feb/85)*

He gave them what he felt they would be happy supporting. Perhaps this was also part of his disillusionment.

### New Efforts in Himself

During a February 1985 trance session the medium said she was surprised Gurdjieff had lived as long as he had. Because, she saw that by 1929, at age 61 or 62, he was "ready to go". (This could be linked with why he sent his closest followers away during the previous two years, in anticipation of that.) His great despondency and frustration with the world and people, coupled with having no meaningful company, impacted greatly on his will to continue. It would seem that virtually anyone else would have decided to pass over at that point.

Yet, Gurdjieff went on for another 20 years. By 1930 he was finding more energy within himself. Then I was told that, he did his most brilliant work during the revisions of

Beelzebub in 1931. What had given him this new lease on life?

The prolonging of life is something he directly addressed both in his earlier teaching, as recorded in Views from the Real World, and in the final chapter of his last book, Life is real only then, when "I am" (hereafter LIROT). He both believed a person could extend their span of life, and had suggestions as to how it could be achieved.

**A New Teaching Initiative**

By 1933 he had launched a new teaching initiative. It came in the form of a small book (87 pages), which he produced and rushed into print that year. It was his HCG. It was not part of his planned series of enigmatic writings, but a "one-off". It gave a condensed version of his teaching, and outlined plans for a reinvigorated institute. But it provoked a howl of protest from his old students, who saw it as too brash and out of character with the previous material he'd given them. They prevailed on him to withdraw it from sale and destroy copies of it! Fortunately, a surviving copy came to light later, and it was published again some years after his death.

HCG had been a direct appeal to people at large, outside of his established students and groups. They didn't like that. The existing students and followers thought they knew better than he did how his teaching should be presented. Gurdjieff was still gripped by the vision of his mission, and wanted to get his basic message out to anyone who could use it and benefit from it. But he was then locked back into the structure of the students who still couldn't grasp and use the essential parts of his message. He could only continue with his enigmatic form of writing. (Bennett says that by the mid 1930s, he was finally giving up the hope of organising a general awakening amongst people by his direct efforts.)

**His Final Book**

In 1934/5 he wrote the final, and smallest, text of his major trilogy - LIROT. It had been intended to demonstrate, to those ready for it, the world as it actually existed in reality. But he had lost most of his enthusiasm for trying to explain things which were far beyond the comprehension of the students he had. He told me he'd written it "with a different kind of heart", and it was actually "far more literal" in its contents. He wrote comparatively little in this final book, and didn't spend much time on it.

His gave this book to the 'groups' he organised before his death, and told them to publish it only when they were sure the time was right. It eventually appeared in print in 1975. When I asked him about that book in 1984, he said:

> *Don't worry about it. No one understands it. (19/Nov/84)*

He then said he would work with me later to understand it. That only started to come to the fore this year (2012), because the original trance sessions terminated in May 1985 without work on it.

The most important key to <u>LIROT</u> is the "I am", which appears in the title. It is linked with, and arises from, what is identified as the "eighth nature" in chapter 10 below. It is the natural culmination of working with one's essence, and carrying out combining work with all 7 essences. But you will need to make your way through the following chapters to get a grip on that.

The "I am" is the further stage of development which Gurdjieff was still working on in himself through his final years.

**<u>Final Years</u>**

For his final years up until his death in 1949, Gurdjieff worked on constant revisions of <u>Beelzebub</u> in particular. Then there were the other trips to America. And lastly, from the mid 1940s, he was preparing nominated students to carry on "groups" after his death. The things he couldn't explain simply, and get people to use during his lifetime, had to be protected in the enigmatic writings for future generations.

One intriguing aspect of his preparation for the future was his naming of Fritz Peters as his successor. We would have to say it was never understood by the rest of his students and followers. It puzzled, and maybe even incensed, the rest of those who considered themselves far more able and worthy to fulfil that role. More will be said about this later.

CHAPTER FIVE

# The Fourth Way

Any commentator on Gurdjieff will tell you that the "fourth way" is central to, and distinctive of, his overall teaching. Mention the "fourth way", and one immediately thinks of Gurdjieff. His is credited with having introduced this way of development to the Western world. Just what it consists in, however, is not so clear. This matter is so important it deserves a separate chapter.

## It's Brief Disclosure

What is generally known about the "fourth way" comes almost solely from a brief characterisation of it in a talk Gurdjieff gave in 1916. It was recorded and recounted by Ouspensky over about 7 or 8 pages in his ISOTM. After Ouspensky's death (in 1947) his lectures from 1921 to 1946 were collected and published under the title The Fourth Way (TFW). It is a thick volume, containing over 400 pages. Yet, references to the fourth way only appear in about 10 of them.

But the title "fourth way" developed a life of its own, apparently from the way Ouspensky treated it and talked of it. It came to be used as an identifying title for Gurdjieff's teaching in general. Fourth Way schools and teachers appeared in some places after his death, and the transmission of teaching under that title has gone on until the present day.

I point this out because Gurdjieff told me he had never explained the fourth way! (Take that as, "never explained it properly".)

## What Gurdjieff Had Said

This idea of a "fourth way" was introduced by Gurdjieff in distinction from what he called the other three ways of development of the 'fakir', the 'monk' and the 'yogi'. These were categories representing all the available and widely known ways in which a person could seek personal immortality. He pointed out that the 'fakir' sought <u>physical</u> mastery of himself to that end. The 'monk' sought <u>emotional</u> mastery, and the 'yogi' <u>mental</u> mastery. We then recognise what they were working on, individually, were the three disharmonised aspects Gurdjieff pointed out in the human condition. But they were only working on them one-by-one.

These three parts were disharmonised because they weren't working in unison with each other. But there was also disharmony <u>within</u> each part, or their functioning was not what it could or should be in the unified state. So the 'ways' of the fakir, monk and yogi were addressing just the problem presented in each separate part.

Gurdjieff pointed out what a long and exacting task it was in each case to pursue such mastery. There had to be serious renunciation of ordinary living, and then faith and commitment, to get anywhere at all. If a person could achieve physical mastery – which was the hardest of all – they then had to move on to the emotional part, and then the mental. In practical terms, it was all far more than any person could hope to achieve in a lifetime. So he concluded the situation was hopeless, unless a fourth and better way could be found to streamline the process.

But, he said, there <u>was</u> such a fourth way, where people could work simultaneously on all three areas at once. It wasn't always available. But where it was, <u>and</u> a person could find it, they could make rapid progress with minimal dislocation to their everyday life. There were no special preparations, and neither renunciation nor faith were required. Further, a person could achieve the desired mastery in all three areas in one lifetime. This was how a 'sly' man proceeded. (<u>ISOTM</u>, p. 50).

("Sly", of course, may mean "cunning" or "wily" or "secretive", or such things. But Ouspensky took it to mean "indirect" [p. 99, <u>TFW</u>]. Perhaps he got this from Gurdjieff, though it isn't explicitly stated in <u>ISOTM</u>. But it <u>is</u> a fair assessment of what is implied there about the fourth way.

Because, somehow the work proceeds in that 'way' on the physical, mental and emotional areas without working directly on each of those functions. It <u>is</u> an <u>indirect</u> <u>method</u>. Perhaps the sly man is cunning or wily because he uses an indirect method.)

Gurdjieff also said the person using the fourth way could achieve so much because they knew a "secret" which the fakir, monk and yogi didn't. There is even the claim that the sly man prepares and swallows a tiny tablet, and in very little time obtains what he is seeking. (This is the generally understood teaching about the fourth way.)

## Never Transmitted

Essentially, Gurdjieff hints at what constitutes the fourth way in what Ouspensky recorded, rather than spelling it out. Since it is a way that causes minimal disruption to our everyday lives, we might presume that inner practices like "remembering oneself" and "not identifying (with the everyday self)" play a part in it. We can do them while carrying on our ordinary everyday lives. But clearly a substantial part of the explanation is still missing.

In another one of his early comments to me, Gurdjieff said point blank that he'd never taught the fourth way! He said: "The fourth way was never transmitted" (3/Dec/84). He'd certainly mentioned it by name, compared it generally with the other three 'ways', and made some broad comments about it. But as to exactly what it was, he never explicitly said. Quite a few people presumed they knew it, and still do. But it remains to be seen how those presumptions stack up against what he went on to tell me.

We need to ask ourselves here, what is it that could indirectly but effectively bring mastery over, and harmony and unity to, the three wayward aspects of our everyday functioning? What could have that potential?

## The "Soul Way"

He told me: "The fourth way is actually the 'soul way'." So the 'sly man' is really, or also, the "wise" or "spiritual man". Perhaps this is not such a surprise. It is entailed in his explanations about the "four bodies", which immediately precede his fourth way comments in the 1916 lecture. (ISOTM, pp. 40-4) The first three bodies there are the physical, the emotional (or astral), and the mental (or etheric). The fourth is described as the divine or "causal body". It is the Master. With it come unity, will, and immortality. (Most commentators I've read don't seem to include that explanation.)

The implication is clearly there. But Gurdjieff told me he "negated" this aspect of things, or didn't explicitly express it, in relation to the fourth way. He didn't spell out the involved spiritual element. Because, he'd chosen to follow a 'scientific' mode of teaching, and the "soul way" couldn't be easily explained in those terms. The method of transmission he'd chosen had enabled him to impact the rising tide of scientific thought and the Western mind with his general teaching. But it limited what could be said spiritually.

In a sense – as he himself continued to explain – he had been trying to get to a spiritual end via a scientific means. This fitted well enough with his personal understanding of what "material" was. Since, for him, the physical world and the spiritual world were merely two ends of the one continuum. "Spiritual" didn't mean "airy-fairy", but was just as substantial, and even more so, than the world of physical objects.

But, to explicitly declare the "soul" aspect of the fourth way would have been seen as a reality of a different order by many, if not most, of his early twentieth century students. Possibly it would have been seen as beyond what they could understand or embrace. He was very conscious of the threshold of credibility with those who sought his teaching. It was always a great restriction on him. He couldn't get them to move within themselves to where he could speak freely and frankly of the things of the soul.

In another sense, he told me, he had constructed the lead-up to the soul element in such a way, that it could be deduced by its absence. If one followed the sequence and logic of the lead-up explanation, it would be seen or felt to be what was then "missing". But, of course, even that assumed its absence could be felt. Sufficient "feeling" had to be operating in those following his fourth way comments. Otherwise, you just had a group of 'everyday' people waiting to hear more 'everyday' comments.

(Possibly this is why he added the teasing reference to the 'tiny tablet' that could be swallowed. People strongly focused in everyday reality are apt to look for such tiny pills to cure them or provide solutions. The recovery and reinstatement of the soul might seem like a tiny pill to those open to it. But to others it could have been a "big pill" - too big to swallow.)

Time and again throughout his teachings, he had pointed out the lack of unity and mastery in a person's everyday functions. He had asked his students to "observe themselves", precisely to see what was there, and also what wasn't. When they started to 'feel' there must be "something else" which should have been there, but wasn't, they would have at last started to reach for it.

**The "Missing" Element**

What was "missing" was the fourth part or element which could effectively tie the other three together. In our trance sessions, Gurdjieff showed the medium three asparagus spears, and then tied a ribbon around them to bind them together. (A rather folksy example.) But he pointed to the finding and following of our essence as what effects that binding, which leads to the "crystallisation". As he put it:

> *The fourth function is the first, before your one, two, three. The fourth one is also the first (as well as) the fourth. And once the essence is tapped, the intrinsic self is tapped. You've got control of the externals. It crystallises the other three into one mass.*
> *(26/Feb/85)*

He also said:

> *The crystallisation only occurs once you're aware of the self. Everything crystallises once the self is tapped, once the centre is tapped.*

He also explained the difference between the first three, and the fourth elements in the following way. The understanding of our emotional, mental and physical aspects is "fairly intellectual", because they're

> *see-able, knowable, dissectible, understandable – by words.*

But that fourth element is a

> *feel-able, knowable, understandable, (yet) unspeakable thing.*

**The "Unspeakable" Thing**

By "unspeakable", he means that there are no ready words for it – not in the straightforward way everyone understands they have a body, mind and emotions. We might be able to "talk around it" a bit, but not everyone recognises what is being referred to.

The "knowing and understanding" of the soul proceeds from the feeling ability. This used to be the way knowing and understanding functioned in (learned) people even in ancient Greece. They called it "noos" or "nous". But the notion has barely survived in English as a sort of synonym for "savvy" or "common sense". Perhaps you've heard it said of someone that they should, "Show a bit of nous [nowse]!" As if, "Why aren't you using the common sense or knowing that God gave you?"

When whole cultures model themselves on something like a 'modern' scientific way of proceeding, they revert to a low common denominator. 'Modern science' imagines the prime reality to be three-dimensional physical objects existing in a three-dimensional physical space. (Like, "something you can get a grip on".) To a spiritual person this is "outer reality", maybe, but takes no account of "inner reality".

It is very much "young soul" stuff. We've all been there. The price for being born into the everyday world is, you have to totally lose yourself in that kind of reality before you can begin to find it again. Everyone has to progress on that path of self-discovery at their own pace. Some are ready to feel or 'see' the reality of their soul and such things again, and some aren't.

This is why Gurdjieff told people they had to work to attain the possibility of a soul. It respects the right of those totally absorbed in the everyday reality not to know about any soul. It serves no identifiable function for them. But when inner awareness begins, they can start to feel there is something to be attained.

Gurdjieff also sought to make the unspeakable speakable by dissecting our three everyday functions, and trying to highlight what was missing from them. If anyone examines closely how they function in everyday reality, they can see there is no stable or unified self there. Strangely, almost everyone just seems to assume it is there. They "think" they are a single unified consciousness. So getting people to see through that illusion was something he could work with.

In fact, the fourth part (in the fourth way teaching) is also the first part we originally started with. We used to have it from birth, before we started living in the disharmonised way called for in everyday life. So, finding it is really a "finding of it again". It is recovered, or remembered. (Thus the emphasis on "remembering oneself".) And to remember, is to "re-member" our selves – adding the fourth missing part to become a unified whole again.

With the fourth way, Gurdjieff was also seeking to teach by example, or by demonstration. It was "by the way he was", or the command and control that he had – not over other people, but over life, as such. He himself was a present, living embodiment of what his students could come to see was missing in themselves. His "charisma" was an effect of that cause. He said:

> *when you're in control of that (inward) self, you're in control of your externals.* *(26/Feb/85)*

When he couldn't explain it to them in words, his presence was meant to be an instruction by example. If they could have seen that he, too, was just an "ordinary man", like they were, it would have been so much easier for them. (I think there is evidence that Fritz Peters, at least, could see that. See what he says in Balanced Man.) Then, the "something extra" he had would have been more obvious and potentially obtainable by them.

**Teaching Not Formulated**

He told me that, even though the fourth way was "understandable and knowable", he had never attempted to find what words could be found for expressing it. He said he "knew it", and that the explanation was implicitly obvious to him. But his students had never reached the stage where he was called upon to try to make it clearer for them. The demand never arose.

That is the way that things work with "subconscious thinking". We grasp them inwardly first, in outline, in overall conception. The 'feeling' is there, and we 'see' it through that. (The seeing of it at that level is the implicit knowing of it.) But then it is a further step to find the words to express it outwardly. So he had never reached the stage of trying to articulate it during his lifetime – as far as it could have been.

In 1984/5 he told me he had to "find the words" to explain the fourth way to me. Thus the "knowable but unspeakable" characterisation given above, and his other comments. Amongst his "words" then, was an insistence on the word "melding" to explain the unifying process with the fourth element. My suggestion of "integration" wouldn't do. He definitely wanted "melding". And melding, of course, is a kind of fusion of the two notions of "melting" and "welding" something together – a very substantial blending and unifying. Something 'melded' is well and truly locked into place.

It invokes the illustration Ouspensky records from Gurdjieff in ISOTM (p. 43). There are various metallic-type powders contained in a vessel. As powders, they may float around in an accidental way if their container is tapped or tilted. They remain in this free-flowing state until a special kind of fire is lit under the container. By thus heating and melting them, they are then fused together. They have been "melded". They are then unified into one mass and inseparable. That is the kind of explanation he wanted.

We may notice that, the four parts involved in our human melding correspond with the traditional "four elements". 'Earth' is the physical body. 'Air' is the thinking mind. 'Water' is the emotions. And the fourth one – 'fire' – is what melds them all together.

## The "Complete" Person

The end result of this melding is now an indivisible whole, which he calls the "whole" or "complete person". He had often said that modern "man" is only a pseudo-person, and could only be called a "man" in quotation marks. It is only when the melding had re-created the unity of all our everyday functions that we could be called a genuine complete person.

## And Enlightenment?

Becoming a "complete person" is not yet enlightenment, which is another important stage further on. But it is a necessary and crucial step on the way to that. At times Gurdjieff said there was a marked resemblance between the complete person and the enlightened one. As if, "You'd almost think they were enlightened!". On another occasion he said the 'complete person' could be seen as "enlightened into person-hood", but not "godhood". There has to be the final eruption of the kundalini for full enlightenment. Remember too, the kundalini only rose to the throat level for Gurdjieff, and he says it tends to only rise in stages for us. That could be a quick, or a slower thing, depending upon our preparedness – what tasks we still need to perform on earth, and the readiness of the soul to "sign off" on one's earthly journey.

Being a complete person enables us to become the genuinely "normal" person in the everyday world. That's not just what passes for normal in the current state of things.

Genuine 'normality' opens up possibilities and dimensions which couldn't even be imagined in one's previous fragmented and disharmonised state.

You will, of course, come to clearly see from this 'complete person' perspective the kind of dysfunctionality that operates in the everyday world. If it wasn't obvious to you before, it will be after this melding. As older souls, we may have become used to "doubting ourselves" during everyday living, and giving everyone else the benefit of the doubt. (It is the most dysfunctional, unfortunately, who are the most self-assured in everyday life.) But from the viewpoint of the unified self, we start to confidently see both ourselves, and others, as we/they are. Any incompleteness and dysfunctionality becomes obvious in the people around us.

If you wondered why Gurdjieff used to talk about enduring the unpleasant behaviours, or manifestations, of others, this is it. Once you can see it, what do you do with it? To a large extent, it just has to be "endured". You may attempt to point it out to the dysfunctional person, but until they're ready to own and drop their 'buffers' or mental blocks, they won't see it. They may resent it, think you're "attacking" them, or otherwise engage in strange or irrational defensive reactions. The idiot doesn't know they're an idiot.

(Think for example, of the second of the two subjects hypnotised by Gurdjieff in the experiment detailed near the end of chapter 2 above. If you tried to tell them their reasoning abilities were being misused in the way they operated in everyday life, they would resent and reject your comments. They wouldn't "see" it until they were ready to abandon their mental buffers.)

**How This Teaching Got Lost**

The explanation of Gurdjieff's teaching phase from the previous chapter can now be extended. His great frustration was that his students were adhering to what he told them in just a 'mind' or 'head' way, rather than a 'feeling' way. So they weren't going anywhere, except in circles. He told me that, since he'd missed it had just been picked up by the 'head' people. When, really, it needed to be embraced and used by the 'feeling' people.

He said: "That's why it's gotten so very lost". It is why groups established to transmit his teaching have turned into kinds of exclusive secret societies, or intellectual clubs. They've got all the words he left, but there isn't any real foundation they can give you. He said that Ouspensky got the fourth way, but turned it into a trip for analysing four different kinds of 'ways'. When, the fourth way is really the soul way, which he failed to spell out.

(This explanation followed my telling him about a friend who visited the U.S. in 1982. He had contacted a Gurdjieff group, but was told he'd have to sell up all his possessions and join the group before any teaching could be shared. Gurdjieff was contemptuous of this, and just said drily: "The truth's not that exclusive!" These groups have the trappings as if they are harbouring a great secret, but they can't give you the basis of the real work. They want people to become intellectuals like they are, and then just "sit around and armchair it".)

## The "Coach" Illustration

Gurdjieff gives us the overall picture of the fourth way of development with his "coach illustration". It was introduced briefly in ISOTM (p. 41), as derived from some teachings from the East. However, in the final chapter of Beelzebub he elaborates it over several pages. There we find a coach, a horse, and a driver. The coach is our physical body, the horse our emotions, and the driver is our mental faculty. These three parts are the only components needed for a coach trip, and yet something is still "missing". Not until the owner, or passenger, enters the compartment, and gives the order to proceed somewhere, are the three component parts brought together with purpose. The whole combination then works "as one", with a single goal.

The owner or passenger is the "Master", and their word and purpose sets the three parts in unified and co-ordinated motion. There is no need for any further work on the separate parts. They are indirectly brought together by the fourth element in the situation.

What we then lack before we've found the fourth way is the Master in ourselves. Is it any wonder then that, after he elaborated the illustration of the coach earlier in the final chapter of Beelzebub, he should virtually finish the whole book by saying everyone should make it their principal aim to become a master (p. 1236).

A "master" in this sense is not a commander or controller of others, but someone in control of themselves. It is a spiritual master, not a worldly one. Or, to the point with this fourth way teaching, they are master of all the parts of themselves. That's exactly what a spiritual master has always been. They have "found themselves", and they are "in charge of themselves". They have always been the true owner of the coach, and the one waiting to resume control of it.

With the "master", you get "mastery" of the disharmonious separated mental, emotional and physical parts. That's what the fakir, monk and yogi were trying to achieve in their separate ways. And this "master" is the fully-realised "intrinsic self". It is the soul restored to its true role. Everything is then "one".

And, how do we get there? Well, Gurdjieff spelt it out in his 1985 quote recorded above:

> *Once the essence is tapped, the intrinsic self is tapped. You've got control of the externals.*

Finding one's essence is integral to the process. We'll go on to that in the following chapters. We'll also see that the "melding" has a second aspect, beyond the "3-in-1", to do with restoring full functionality to the essence area. In the meantime, it remains to unpack the rest of the mystery surrounding the fourth way.

**An Ancient Esoteric Teaching?**

Westerners in the 1920s loved the idea of uncovering mysteries or ancient secrets, which almost always had been hidden somewhere in the East. Archaeologists were still digging up significant artefacts from past civilisations, which had previously only been hinted at or known through references in old histories or documents. It also excited the imagination that there could be unbroken traditions from that time passed down in remote communities, untouched by the ravages of time. Ouspensky had travelled through the East, looking for "schools", "groups", "esoteric orders" and "ancient secrets". So had Gurdjieff.

Psychologically, this may also have been fuelled by limitations on human experience imposed by the growing fascination with 'science' in the West. The commitment to new scientific ways played a crucial role in breaking the authoritarian rule of the church over society. But it brought its own problems, as the suggestible masses changed their allegiance to a new hypnotising influence. The robust new sense of the everyday and obvious may have given Westerners automobiles, telephones and electricity. But it also brought a keen sense of an inner vacuum and disconnectedness from the point and meaning of life.

Gurdjieff's "arrival" in the West excited an interest in what he had discovered, and knew, from ancient sources in the East and elsewhere. His teaching and methods had a "difference" about them, which Ouspensky characterised as fragmented parts of an apparently unknown teaching. To some extent Gurdjieff fostered this or allowed the fascination to grow. Curiosity can be a healthy motivation. And what people pursue outwardly is often just a reflection of what they are looking for inwardly.

When it came to the "fourth way", which certainly caught the interest of many, there was a desire to know where Gurdjieff had found such teaching. Indeed, there seemed to be more interest in identifying its source, or valuing it because of that, than assessing it for what it was. So he was pressed to reveal the source. He played along with some of this, mentioning the Sarmoun Brotherhood, which apparently both pre-dated and was contemporary with the old Babylonian civilisation. There was also a tradition that they held the key to great secrets, or even received them from Atlantean times. Alternative access to the same information was available through Egypt, especially in the monument of the sphinx.

**The Sphinx**

As related in Beelzebub, the sphinx was supposed to resemble the emblem of the learned society of Akhaldan in Atlantis. (This kind of information came to Gurdjieff through his guardian.) Curiously, he also said its name was "conscience". It is in the sphinx that we find the best clue about the blended parts of the melded or complete person. It has four parts to it. There is the trunk of the bull (for the physical body), the feet of the lion (representing the astral or emotional), and the wings of the eagle (for the etheric or mental). But it also has a human head. It is "one body", but with four parts. Here are all the elements of the fourth way teaching.

One can find other channelled teaching which links the sphinx to Atlantis. For example, both Edgar Cayce and Rudolph Steiner spoke of these things. We get the picture there of the Atlantean population being divided into four castes or groups, based on the four parts we find in the sphinx. (This was supposed to be the basis of the caste system still surviving in India, but whose real point has long ago been lost.)

Apparently, the youngest souls were focused in physical reality. Their abilities, hopes and goals in life were linked with physical achievements. Examples would be physical work, or sporting prowess. More developed souls had emotional hopes and goals. They would have aims like love, commitment, devotion, and so forth. Even more mature souls had mental goals. Finally, the older soul had put all these functions together, and had emerged with a human face and blended capacities.

These were the antecedents of Gurdjieff's fakir, monk and yogi. People of each caste looked for mastery in life in accordance with their level of awareness. This three- or four-fold division was apparently very, very ancient.

**Esoteric Christianity**

When asked on another occasion about the origin of the fourth way, Gurdjieff referred in a roundabout way to "esoteric Christianity". Some then linked that with "true Christianity", which he claimed had existed in pre-historic or pre-sand Egypt, thousands of years before Christ.

"Esoteric Christianity" was mentioned by Blavatsky, and then Annie Besant wrote a book about it in 1901. You will find occasional references in what Gurdjieff taught to the real meaning of some Christian teaching and practices. But he had something very specific in mind when he drew the link with the fourth way.

It is hidden in plain sight at the very beginning of Beelzebub. In the first paragraph we find the Christian prayer or benediction, naming the Father, Son and Holy Ghost. So, why did he, surprisingly, employ this Christian prayer?

It is about the "trinity", which as you know, is a "3-in-1" formulation. This is also "esoteric-speak" for the three blended or melded parts of a complete person. In Beelzebub the law of three, called "Triamazikamno", refers both to the theory of the three parts, and to the completed process of the blended, harmonious person. To confirm his identification of this law and process with the Christian trinity, Gurdjieff refers later in the book to the three forces integral to it as, again, the Father, Son and Holy Ghost.

God – in virtually all religions – is affirmed to be "One". But in his manifested form, he appears as "three".

In her explanation of the trinity in Esoteric Christianity, Annie Besant says that the idea is found no less in the extinct religions of ancient Egypt and elsewhere. She refers us to archaeological and recovered textual evidence for this.

The difference between the exoteric (open) and esoteric (hidden) forms in religion is, those "with eyes to see" find another significance in what is presented. Gurdjieff also talked of a "legominism" in Beelzebub. When initiates in the past wanted to transmit important truths to future generations, they wouldn't just state them in written texts. Those were always being altered or destroyed by the ignorant, or the power-grabbing people. Also, languages and the meanings of words change over time. Messages in symbolic form are more precise, and speak to the important right-hand side of the brain. So they incorporated their truths into certain more symbolic forms that would endure over time, and even be protected by the non-comprehending.

So we have this 'trinity' of the manifested godhead as an article of faith in major religions. The non-comprehending hand such things down with reverence. "Those who know" get their message through. And so, 'esoteric Christianity' gives us the "3-in-1" formula. The symbol of the sphinx illustrated it in more detail. It remained for someone to see the relevance of the clues, and put together the method for achieving it.

**Gurdjieff's Contribution**

It is one thing to see that the three basic everyday functions of a person need to be blended and unified to constitute the 'complete person'. But it is another to know how to do it. The "method" for this obviously hadn't been transmitted in the traditions which depicted the complete person.

This is where Gurdjieff's genius came to the fore. He found a method, and a very good one, for how to do it. In one way it had been implicit in the stages of his own personal development, where he had achieved the basic "3 in 1" state by the age of 17. (See explanation in chapter 3 above.) But the communicable understanding of exactly what had happened, and why, came to him over time and through his extensive searches.

As I mentioned in chapter 3, he had found clues in some old Indian or Hindu writings. I was given no particular information beyond that. But it set him looking at the process in certain ways. He was then able to put it together and work it out.

I asked him at one stage in our trance sessions, what was the most important component he himself had contributed to his teaching. (I was looking for his "master's-piece" - from which we get the notion of a "masterpiece".

It is the unique contribution each master makes and leaves to the world.) He nominated his method for the harmonious development of people, after which his Institute was named. Confirmation of this came to me from another channelled source later. It was affirmed that this had indeed been Gurdjieff's own unique method of development.

It wasn't just for him though. It was a way we could all use and benefit from. When the fragmentation of the parts of our human functioning had occurred, shortly after the Atlantean period, it was not known how they would be recombined again. There was just the faith that "the soul would find a way".

Strangely, for all the effort that Gurdjieff's students put into trying to track down and find his 'sources', he himself was the most important source for the method of the fourth way. There was no further secret about it waiting to be discovered in a remote 'school' or monastery somewhere. He was holding it, right in front of them. He was also intent on passing it on to anyone that was ready to receive it. But there was no one ready for it. So he hid it in obscure writing.

As recorded in the same chapter of ISOTM as the fourth way, someone once asked Gurdjieff why important knowledge was carefully concealed, instead of being made freely available. He must have just about choked on that question. He explained that no-one was hiding anything, and those who had such knowledge where doing everything they could to pass it on. But you cannot force this on people, and immense effort was required from both givers and receivers to successfully pass it on. But, until someone is ready to receive this, it simply cannot proceed. Gurdjieff's father had often said to him, "Don't give away your treasure". It can't be given away until the receiver is in a position to understand what they're being given. Otherwise, it would not be seen for what it is, or valued, or used as such. It would be rejected, ignored, devalued or debunked.

**Gurdjieff's Method**

The 'indirect' method of working with the three disharmonised parts of a person must in the end be the only effective way of restoring overall unity. Working on the individual parts doesn't tie the three of them together. This was emphasised by Gurdjieff in the 1922 prospectus he put out for his planned Institute, repeated in HCG (p. 28). He said the proper outcome for each person could only possibly be ensured by what co-ordinated the functions of the three disharmonised parts.

The method for doing this has been reviewed slowly, both by explicit teaching and the account of Gurdjieff's own development, since the start of this book. It involves:

*The subconscious needs to be brought to the attention of our waking conscious mind.*

*We must find and separate "oneself from oneself", or realise we are "two persons".*

*Or, beneath the 'thinking' mind, we need to identify the 'feeling' mind.*

*The inner self needs to be "remembered", and the sense of it recovered.*

*"In" the subconscious are the conscience and the essence.*

*We there have a "knowing" and a "nature" to work with.*

*The essence must be distinguished from the personality, and what locks the personality in place must be loosened.*

*We are then ready to start "tapping the essence". (More particular details of doing that are explained in the next chapter.)*

*We recover more of the sense of our inner self, which expands and grows through that recognition as 'personality' is weakened.*

*It then moves from being the 'passive' self to the 'active' one.*

*The 'false' personality yields to the 'true' one coming into being, as feeling informs more of our thinking.*

*As we continue working in that way, at a certain point the automatism of our physical system will switch itself over to support the new consciousness arrangement.*

*That gives us the "3-in-1", where the three parts are thereby co-ordinated.*
*Mastery of the three parts makes us master of the externals, which is the principal element of our becoming Masters in fact.*

**The Characteristics of the Fourth Way**

Gurdjieff says of 'modern man' in his disharmonised state, that he does not even understand which one of his three parts has the potential to control and co-ordinate them all.

It is not the physical centre, which would be the logical place to start for either the young soul or someone attempting the 'ways' of the fakir, monk and yogi. It is not the thinking centre, which is normally the ruling centre for the person who has looked at their life and decided that something needs to be done about it. The intellect by itself can't get you there. But it is the refined emotional centre, where "the subtle has been separated from the gross". (Beyond everyday emotion is inner feeling.) Then we can see beyond outer experience and reaction to find the inner knowing. It alone has the ability to harmonise our three parts and restore them to their proper functioning.

The fourth way requires no renunciation, faith, or special life conditions for someone to start the process. You just start where you are. Nothing needs changing outwardly to embark on this journey. To attempt to change anything there would only complicate and confuse things. So Gurdjieff told his students to do nothing at that level. They were to continue to do nothing (outwardly) until they had acquired sufficient understanding, and were personally satisfied they understood what they were doing.

Each person's way is "individual", and their path of development must be strictly so. It can only be informed by the understanding that comes from their own essence.

A person could be "helped" in this quest by someone as advanced as Gurdjieff was, who could reliably assess the state of peoples' psyches and what they needed to do. He attempted to do this for those who came to him. But none of his students was ready to benefit much from this at the time.

We find some claims in ISOTM that people needed to be supervised by someone who knew what they were doing. Or, they were told they should become part of a school or group to pursue this 'way' under a teacher. Gurdjieff was referring to himself, and the 'help' that the students who came to him obviously needed. But he told me in 1984/5 the need for such a special group was "over-stated". A person can pursue this development on their own, and indeed must in the absence of an available special group or teacher.

**The Times Have Changed**

Times change, and conditions are much more conducive now than they were in the 1920s. Many more people are much further along in the West now for productively pursuing their own development. Gurdjieff couldn't explain many of these things simply during his teaching phase. As he said to me, while relaying basic elements of his teaching in 1985:

> *Had I written in this way back in the 1920s, no-one would have listened to me!*

There was a much stronger division in those days between the "peasants" and the "intelligentsia".

> *If you wrote it for the peasants, the intelligentsia wouldn't accept it. And if you wrote it for the intelligentsia, the peasants couldn't understand it. ..but now, with the much more universal education..this can now be written quite simply, and both will accept it.* (5/Feb/85)

So both the vehicle for transmission, and the readiness of people to listen, have now come together. The message can now be given as it couldn't before.

CHAPTER SIX

# Tapping The Essence

The "tapping of the essence" is the most crucial move for bringing the three disharmonised parts of a person together, and melding them into a unified whole. All the teaching reviewed above has been a necessary preparation for that. The subconscious must be distinguished from the everyday conscious mind, and we need to find and get a working relationship going with the essence.

Gurdjieff's teaching can be compared with that of the entity Seth, who said that what we call the subconscious is where our inner and outer selves come together and meet (Seth Speaks, p. 10). That is our entrance into the great "otherwhere" beyond limited everyday reality.

## Another Self

We go 'inside' to find it. Its prompting of us may come via urges, impulses, intuitions, specific feelings, implicit seeing or grasping of things, or convictions not mediated by anything else. Trying to understand and assimilate it with the 'outer' capabilities of the (false) personality will not work. It needs to be seen or felt in distinction from the false personality, which is only possible when the personality is weakened sufficiently. In chapter 2 we reviewed the mechanisms which hold the false personality in place, and how to move past them. Then we are ready to discover that "something else" which has always been inside us. It will be recognised as a "truer me" than anything experienced thus far in our lives.

It may assist this understanding if I review how the essence was first recognised and embraced in my own experience. I had known 'about' the subconscious from my early teenage years, from library books about dreams, hypnotism and other psychological matters which interested me. What may also be significant is, I seemed to have a sense even from childhood that there was "something more" than the everyday reality. I could be conscious of that in moments of reflection when I was by myself.

I remember feeling a resentment that 'growing up' meant being confined more narrowly in a three-dimensional world. It was like being enclosed in a small wooden crate where I could hardly move. Then, I know I was using my subconscious to cope with the learning tasks of my undergraduate degree. I would load up my mind with problems, and look to a 'good sleep' to give me answers in the morning. Then, in my early 20s, I started avidly reading true ghost stories. This was apparently to try to get or retain a link with a dimension beyond the limited everyday one. I wanted to directly experience a reality beyond the everyday and obvious, in which I seemed to be increasingly trapped. I also had active religious interests, which finally didn't give me the answers I was looking for. (Or, whatever there was behind religion, I wasn't going to find it from its contemporary representatives and advocates. I looked for indications of 'more'.)

The real breakthrough came with finding Gurdjieff's teaching in the Ouspensky book ISOTM. Here was someone who seemed to really know things. I was relaxing in bed at night with the book, when one thing in particular spoke to me. (I mean, apart from 'remembering oneself' and 'not identifying'.) I remember the night in 1972 when I was reading, and came across the distinction between personality and essence. I can even picture the place midway down the right page where I saw it. It was like something 'jumped' inside me, and I felt blissful and relieved. It seemed to license an ability to carry on my inner life and searches, irrespective of what was happening outwardly in my life. Perhaps this was my "two persons" experience. It gave me a decisive sense of an inner self for which there had been no name or indicator previously. It helped me to identify another reality I had inside me.

This special 'snapshot' remembering of certain experiences earlier in one's life may be related to having "remembered oneself" at the time. There is something that fixes them lucidly in one's memory. My very earliest life memory, as I was sitting in a high-chair beside my mother, who was cooking at the stove, also has the same quality. I can sit and put myself back into those very experiences, so that my eyes now are looking through my eyes at those times. I can recover the 'moment' of them.

Searching back, I can find evidence of some aspects of what I now know to be my essence, displayed from childhood onwards. At times it was coming through, although I did not understand it as such at the time. I know definitely that I wrote to a friend in 1967, when I was 20, and said I realised I had an inner passion to "understand things". (I also remember that in a 'snapshot' way.) That was integral to my essence.

What my 1972 realisation seemed to importantly add to the earlier mix was the identified sense of an "inner" self separate from my "outer" one. (Thus my "two persons" comment.) I was realising there was a part of me inside which I could trust and relate to, and it operated independently of my outer self. It was always there, and I could keep coming back to it.

I did not immediately identify any of the defining characteristics of my essence, or inner nature, when I came across Gurdjieff's personality/essence distinction. It was more a delight at realising I had an inner core to me, something fixed beyond the vagaries of the everyday roles I had to play. To be frank, I didn't particularly like the sort of person I had to be in everyday life all that much. It didn't give me much satisfaction. I was searching for something deeper and more meaningful.

Now the point of "not identifying" with outer life became clearer. It was a great relief, and I found myself deliberately using it when I was confronted with outer things I felt negatively about. It meant I no longer had to "pick up the tab" for behaving within the sociological confines of the outer life constructed from my birth circumstances, or the life options I'd been shunted along in. That wasn't the 'true' me, or the one I felt comfortable and 'at home' with.

It was like, thereafter, I always had the sense of an inner place I could retreat to when the outer world was too much, or uncongenial. In Gurdjieff's terms, I was transferring my belief in what was "real" from the outer personality self to the inner essence self. This process was further assisted when I took up Transcendental Meditation from 1974. The two practices complemented each other, giving me more inner peace and confidence in my inwardly inspired life choices.

**Using the Essence**

One has to start using the essence once a connection is made with it. This is an unfolding process. Gurdjieff told me how he originally envisaged work proceeding at his Institute. He wanted to start the process off for his students, and then he would go off and leave them to work on themselves with it. But he couldn't get them started. He said he could make some progress with them 'one-on-one', but they kept reverting back to their old ways in their groups.

I found 1972 – the year of the personality/essence distinction for me – a water-shed period. I was finding my feet in conducting philosophy tutorials, with personal understanding and communication opening up for me in that teaching role. (That was integral to my essence.) I closed off some incomplete religious studies, put my post-graduate philosophical work on hold, and headed into the education studies area. I was setting my sights on a tertiary teaching position, which I was able to gain in 1975.

The essence travels with the soul, and is part of it for all our earthly lives. We each chose the particular essence we have long ago, before we began incarnating on earth. We have that same essence in each of our lifetimes. Over those successive lifetimes we came to realise more and more of what was in it, and bring more of it into everyday manifestation. So this "knowing of ourselves" - our inner selves – is the way we grow in soul and spirit.

Gurdjieff said this potential is in every human being – it is "inscribed on everyone's DNA". That is why so many people feel an empty, hollow sensation in the middle of their being. They haven't yet connected with that facet of their DNA. They may seek for many, many years through chasing numerous things, like money, power-trips, politics, sexual fulfilment, personal achievement, or whatever. But until they realise it is the "knowing of the self" that is lacking, they cannot find inner peace and fulfilment. A person may have been everywhere, but if they haven't been to "me" (myself), they won't have found it. So, Gurdjieff says, for those on the great search:

> *as far as they need to look, is the "self".*
> *(16/Apr/85)*

The finding of this (inner) "self" is like a "coming home". It is something we knew before we ventured off into the far country. But the inner peace only comes when we 'remember' and reconnect with the soul and the soul's purpose for our life. (Thus my own sense of 'relief'.)

What might be the end of one long search, is then the start of a new direction in life. There is then "purpose", and a way of proceeding that is inner directed. We start to work with "what is our own".

Gurdjieff was concerned that so many people in the present day groups set up in his name aren't making the important step at this point. It is like they are wary or afraid of the subconscious, or trusting it. Perhaps it is similar to learning to ice-skate. People may give us voluminous advice about it, until our heads are full of all the instructions. But at some point we need to just put the skates on and stand on the ice. We may hold ourselves steady at the side-barrier for a while, and test our balance slowly. But in order to actually do it, there must come a time when we venture forth by ourselves, however tentatively. The gliding on the ice is actually done finally by our just doing it. That is the final learning, and then we are actually doing it.

No one has to proceed faster with this than they are able. Balance and equilibrium are always needed for successful performance. But it <u>is</u> necessary to "make a start". The distinctive nature of our essence can, and will, of itself unfold quite naturally. Gurdjieff rarely, if ever, gave more direction to anyone than that during his lifetime. But now the particular characteristics of the essences are to be spelt out like they haven't been before, for the benefit of those reading this book. The process will become quicker and easier, but only because the time is right for it.

## The Seven Essences

The explanation of the essences is actually rather mystically simple and straightforward. Perhaps their very simplicity was why Gurdjieff was reluctant to reveal them. They would probably have seemed too simple for complicated minds, and therefore wouldn't have been given the credence and respect they deserved. In general, people have to earn the right to know certain things, and no one gives away their valuable possessions to those who won't value them. Something misunderstood is quickly misconstrued. But apparently the time is right now for public disclosure.

Gurdjieff gave the biggest clue about the content of the essences when he said they were open to planetary influences. But on the other hand he muddied the issue by telling Ouspensky that there could be either six or seven essences, and some might think twelve. But by following the planetary clue it leads us to the "seven planets of antiquity", which we find in the ancient Greek writings. (This much was grasped and used by Zannos in her recent Human Types book.)

There is a list in the Greek writings of the five 'wandering' planets (Hermes, Zeus, Ares, Aphrodite and Kronos), plus the Moon (Artemis) and the Sun (Apollo). We know them today by their Roman names:

Mercury,
Jupiter,
Mars,
Venus,
Saturn, and
the Sun, and
the Moon.

The number 7, as a 'legominism', is also incorporated into our days of the week. They are also based on the names of associated gods. Monday is "Moon-day", Tuesday (Tiw was a god of war) is Mars, Wednesday (Woden's day) is Mercury, Thursday (Thor's day) is Jupiter, Friday (Freya's day) is Venus, Saturday is Saturn's-day, and Sunday is Sun-day.

But there is a problem with that list. The Sun is not a planet, but a body of a different order. The seventh planet is actually Uranus. (Hephaestus to the Greeks.) It is barely visible to the naked eye in the night sky. But according to Blavatsky it was known in remote antiquity. So our list of the seven planets now reads:

1) Mercury
2) Moon,
3) Jupiter,
4) Venus,
5) Mars,
6) Saturn, and
7) Uranus.

These are the names of the seven essences.

Gurdjieff had me first of all working to establish the elements of each of these planets, according to the sun sign they ruled. He wanted me to work from the bottom up, to get the sense of what was in them and why.

Then he wanted an accurate characterisation of each of them, which he checked and edited. Lastly, I was to place them in a chart, which could be read sideways over two adjacent pages of a book. Then anyone opening the book would have immediate access to all seven, to give the clearest possible approach to them all. YOU WILL FIND THAT CHART ON The NEXT FREE DOUBLE PAGE HERE.

| THE SEVEN | | |
|---|---|---|
| | MERCURY ☿ | The communicator or swift-footed "messenger of the gods" in classical mythology. They have complex and varied abilities, and work chiefly from the head, with mind, reason, intellect. There is a constant urge to communicate. Others look to them to "explain things". Their minds are linked with a finely tuned nervous system. There is an inner compulsion to understand the world and the things in it, especially anything not generally known. Working out life's mysteries and puzzles is a kind of passion and game for them, as they employ their agile minds in quick, subtle, witty or crafty ways. Clear, precise, eloquent in expression. (Scholars, philosophers, writers, communicators.) |
| | MOON ☽ | Their constant fluctuation and movement reflects the Moon's distinctive intrinsic rhythms. Their emotions exhibit their constantly changing moods. They have a natural intuitive grasp of things, based on their inner (third eye) seeing, rather than deductions made from external observation. There is a constant flow between their unconscious and conscious minds. Using this, they have a feel for, and readily express themselves through, psychic activity, poetry and literature. Their energy is cool and subtle, and they may appear to others as cold, aloof, or insular. (Psychics, mystics, poets, imaginative writers and thinkers, soulful actors and performers.) |
| | JUPITER ♃ | Massive energy flows through them, and is linked with a strong urge for large-scale constructive action in the world. They are compulsive organisers, driven by a valid inner sense of their superior grasp of things, or "how things work". Yet they do this implicitly rather than in an overtly controlling or coercive way. They have a grand manner, which need not require verbal expression, but must involve action, gesture and movement. They think big, and move on the broadest scale. (Organisers, controllers, visionaries, jovial mimics.) |

| ESSENCES | | |
|---|---|---|
| | VENUS ♀ | They have a soft, gentle, loving energy. Their emotions are brought into harmony through the affections of the heart. This unity of feeling comes through as appreciation and promotion of aesthetically appealing things. They seek harmony and unity in all things, from co-ordinated room furnishings to all forms of human endeavour. Will stand up against any aggression or injustice. (Unifiers, lovers of harmony and beauty.) |
| | MARS ♂ | Concentrated, combustible energy. Essentially "performers". Mars is bold, flamboyant, assertive and dramatic. They must verbalise. Will fight for what they believe in, champion the underdog. Make firm commitments. Softened by sentiment. Can equally create or destroy when frustrated or crossed. (Performers, actors, motivators, champions of causes.) |
| | SATURN ♄ | Carry a grand sense of order and responsibility, where they feel they must fulfil their obligations above all. Carry "the weight of it all" in themselves, Forebodings of disaster if they don't fulfil their duty. Their commitment to service, which makes them steady, may look sombre and staid to others. Lifestyle and habits made subservient to doing "what needs to be done". (Dependable friends and workers, they order the everyday world.) |
| | URANUS ♅ | Wilful and capricious. Ideas or behaviour can change suddenly, erratically or inexplicably. Lack a stable core within themselves. Stabilised by Saturn people, but thrown into confusion by Moon people. Can 'mirror' any of the other essences for a short time. At best, can be brilliant or inspired, but a worst lapse into scattered or childish behaviour. (Capricious people, unstable or indecisive, occasionally brilliant innovators, or off on tangents.) |

**Identifying One's Own Essence**

Gurdjieff wanted anyone reading the seven essences chart to ask the question: "Which one is the essential me?" That is, it is not a matter of who one might "like to be", or who one might consider oneself to be 'sometimes'. But there will be one of these modes of functioning that will be essentially you.

(We need to distinguish this chart from the lists of offerings sometimes run in popular periodicals. It is not a trivia quiz, or a bit of light-hearted entertainment. People are often curious about identifying aspects of themselves, which is what the popular magazines trade on. But in this chart are characterisations more integral and important to one's life and future than anything else one is likely to find.)

Every person is born with one of these seven essences. We are all born with one, and only one, of them. Gurdjieff says the essence is "born with, and to attain". In most cases, things happen after birth to obscure the essence. Mostly it is the demands of personality – the 'false' personality - that confuse our perception and understanding.

Remember too, the essence is "felt". So, feel which one is you. What sort of person do you essentially feel yourself to be? When left by yourself, which of these ways of operating do you naturally gravitate towards? That is your key.

**Old and Young Souls**

In older souls the essence is easier to identify. Gurdjieff put this to me as "basically, essences are older souls". That is, to have reached the stage where one's essence is obvious and recognised, is to have become an older soul.

With many younger souls there can be complications. Our earliest lives on the earth-plane are spent in most confusion, soul-wise. Circumstances are set-up to teach us life-lessons. At that time we are furtherest from knowing ourselves. There are particular and defined ways in which the essence becomes distorted in a person's self-perception.

That is where the other "types" come in. While it is true that we are all born with just one of the seven essences, the life circumstances of younger souls subject them to distorting pressures. Influences from culture, socialisation and parenting can make their survival depend on wrong expression of their essence. They are learning what is "not-self" by having to experience it. Then by contrast, they can come to recognise the real self when their feeling is developed enough to bring it into awareness.

There are seven essences, and twenty-eight "types" of people in the world. Four of those 'types' are related to each essence. (As Gurdjieff put it to me, "There are four types in every essence".) One of those four types is the "true one", and the other three are law-conformable distortions. The further explanation and elaboration of the twenty-one types who are not true to their essences will be left until the next chapter.

### The Essences and the Chakras

In Beelzebub Gurdjieff talks about "stopinders", which are centres of gravity in his fundamental law of seven. These 'stopinders' are what we know from Indian spiritual teaching and philosophy as the seven "chakras". (That word comes from the Sanskrit for "wheel" or "turning".) They are seven energy/spiritual/psychic centres located from the base of the spine to the crown of the head in our bodies.

Each of the seven essences is connected with one of these chakras. The related PAGE-ILLUSTRATION shows the general correlations which apply.

# ESSENCES AND CHAKRAS

'Chakra' (Sanskrit for "revolving wheel"). Gurdjieff links each essence integrally with one of the seven chakras in Indian lore, and the corresponding nerve/gland function.

Gurdjieff says "the bottom chakra is about nine-tenths of itself, the other tenth divided amongst the other six influences. Lowest chakras are "mostly themselves", with the head chakras becoming more complex. "The top one is a balanced combination of all..giving it it's power."

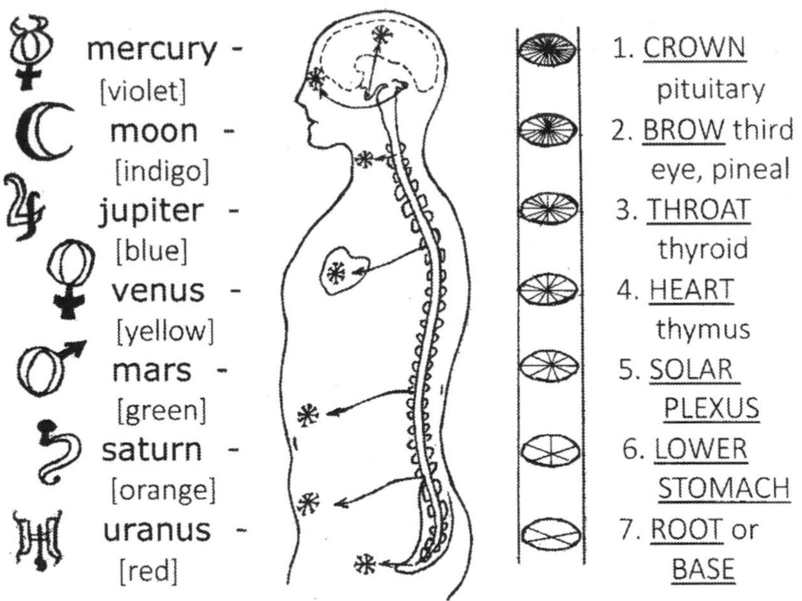


Colour allocation departs from the rainbow sequence in one detail. Yellow and green switch positions. Gurdjieff was emphatic about this, with the sequence given by C.W.Leadbeater, after Blavatsky. He says: "The heart chakra is gold." "Gold is the colour of the (true) intellect. In former times, the intellect came from the heart, not the mind." So green moves to the solar plexus.

This relation between the planetary essences and the chakras in the body was implicit to the work of Franz Anton Mesmer (1734-1815). He discovered certain things in the writings of the sixteenth century Swiss physician and alchemist, Paracelsus. Mesmer said there was a link between planetary influences and the human body. It was a magnetic influence that could be strengthened by passing one's hands over areas of the body to heal physical ailments. He called it "animal magnetism", because it was a kind of magnetism which impacted animal bodies. But his work was ruthlessly attacked and parodied by contemporary medical people who saw their livelihoods threatened. (Isn't it strange that, precisely because his work showed promise, he was denounced as a 'charlatan'! That can happen when you come between existing medical practitioners and their status and income.)

Gurdjieff reviews Mesmer's work in the chapter on "Hypnotism" in Beelzebub. He credited him with having clearly noticed the duality in peoples' consciousnesses. He said Mesmer would have taken his research further if he hadn't been attacked and effectively 'done to death' by the contemporary medical establishment. He was subjected to such ridicule and abuse that his writings weren't even translated and published in English until 1980.

I followed this up in trance sessions, and learnt that especially in those whose feeling ability is activated and working, the magnetism affecting the human body can be readily experienced. If one rubs one's hands together, and then holds them a few inches apart, the energy between them can be felt. Then, if one holds one's hands, palms down, about a foot (30 cm) or so over a reclining person, the presence of the magnetism can be felt at each of the chakra points in turn. It may have beneficial effects for the reclining person, and only needs to be done for a few moments. This is what Mesmer did.

One can also use this on oneself, on one's own chakra points.

**Essence and Individuality**

Individuality is promoted from finding and living in accordance with one's essence. When you find the 'self' that is your <u>true</u> self, then at last you can begin to think and act for yourself, in your own way. Thoughts and actions proceed from something genuinely yours, and not from the recycled directions of others. This is when everything begins to 'gel' as it never has before.

The inner resonance that comes from this gives you confirmation about what you are thinking and doing. Every essence can find the truth about the world for themselves by looking at it and proceeding in it in their own distinctive way. <u>That</u> is the way that truth comes to an individual.

There are certain kinds of interests, and certain ways of operating, that connect each essence to the world. Mercury has an innate longing to work through puzzles and mysteries, and persist until they find understanding. Unresolved things will keep doing circuits in their minds, until they come to see or realise where the answer lies. A Moon has to look to its intuition, and an implicit way of seeing things, to find its answers. A Jupiter dissects how things operate, and implicitly grasps the mechanisms. They then see what is wrong or inadequate, and how it can be organised better. A Venus consults its inner sense of harmony, to understand how anything in the world could be better co-ordinated. Martians concentrate their energies to confront states of affairs in life, and summon a relevant performance to meet the circumstances. Saturns are always looking for the right avenue of service for themselves - a duty that needs to be taken up, or a task that needs to be done, to acquit themselves honourably for the good. A Uranus basically just reacts with whatever it is presented with, and sometimes does it brilliantly.

When operating with the insights of one's essence, one can truly be said to be "in one's element". We don't need to otherwise justify what comes intrinsically to us. It comes with its own assurance. It just "fits".

Ideally, a person in touch with their essence will find or choose a job or vocation which allows them to express their intrinsic abilities. Often though, work choices are made before a person sufficiently knows themselves, or is sufficiently free of family or other influences for making their own decisions. Or, the world forces work choices on us that aren't personally appropriate or fulfilling. But where we find ourselves in personally unsuitable employment, one may seek other avenues of expression in hobbies or after-work pursuits.

A Mars essence may find themselves in an uncongenial or restricting job. They hate not being allowed to talk. Or, if they need to personally concentrate on something, they may like to have the endless chatter of a radio playing in the background. When restricted in some way, they typically react by "putting on attitude", or by making dramatic gestures of discontent or contempt. They're really saying, "I'm not being allowed to be myself".

But they may find a more appealing 'role' for themselves after-hours in a local dramatic society, or being a spokesperson for a community group or interest. Then they can start to "live" in a way perhaps not possible in their job. But Mars people, of course, have a wide range of possible roles presented to them through the media and entertainment industries. That is where "performance" happens. They also thrive on seeing and celebrating the successful performances of other Martians there.

One may find examples of the essences in some people of social prominence, or of characters in film, literature or folklore. Some people who have lived lives of great service and dedication are an inspiration for Saturns. Earlier in this book I referred to Gurdjieff "playing Sherlock Holmes". Sherlock Holmes is a quintessential Mercury figure. If you try to think of someone in fiction, or in history, or in society, who you particularly admire or find to be inspirational, they may well be an example of your essence type.

## The Expression of Individuality

Obviously, we need a certain amount of freedom in order to express our individuality. There are contexts that could restrict that. In some societies and areas there are strong group pressures on people to conform with established community or family patterns of living.

Those contexts have their point for younger souls, who tend to feel "lost" without such "support-structures". Life for young souls is very outer-directed, but finding and expressing one's essence is very inner-directed. You can recognise the younger souls. Even when they don't have to, they will typically identify with structures and groups through memberships, allegiances, formal beliefs and uniforms. Over time, as their soul-realisation grows stronger, they will seek ways of living which give greater individual choice.

Older souls tend to have a problem with self-esteem before they've gained clarity and confidence in being themselves. They can be given a hard time by younger souls, who are more self-assured in outer ways. Typically the younger soul in an uneven relationship will seek to control the older one. This is where an older soul's connection to their inner self must come to the fore, to avoid their being exploited. They need to realise the "ugly duckling" is really a "swan", and assert their right to be themselves.

The knowing of the heart might seem nebulous at times, in comparison with the apparent certainty of everyday knowing. But the quality of heart-knowing is far superior. What the heart knows, the head cannot challenge. It is just that, until a person has found their feet with this subconscious perception, they may proceed tentatively, and can doubt themselves. Apart from general growth in awareness, there is a particular way our heart knowing can be strengthened.

## Strengthening Heart-Knowing

Gurdjieff had an exercise for strengthening our heart-knowing, through which we identify and express our essence. It is the breathing exercise mentioned in chapters 1 and 2 above. He said it originated in ancient India, but he had learnt it from the Sufis. He himself used it throughout his life. It is called "the bow". SEE NEXT PAGE-ILLUSTRATION.

# THE "BOW" EXERCISE

"Bow" (as in "bow and arrow") is a breathing exercise. One breathes in and out in the imagined shape of an archer's bow.

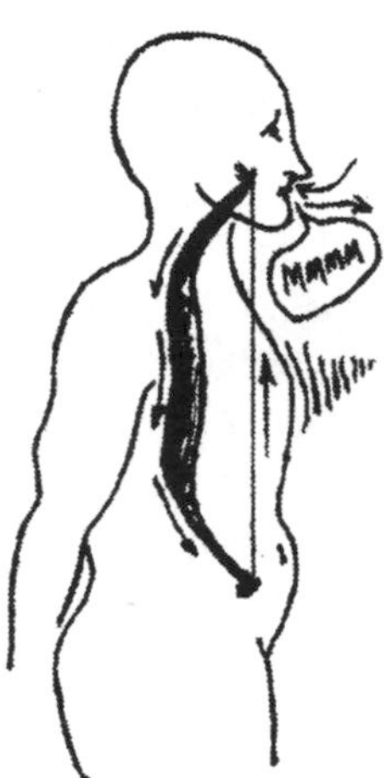

Start by breathing in through one's nose, imagining and feeling the air being taken down around the curved wood of the bow. Take it down as far as possible, to the lower stomach area below the navel. Then one breathes out slowly, while imagining the air rising up the taut string of the bow. As the air rises like this, the feeling of tension in the bow string is emphasised by making a low vibratory hum - "mmmmm" - which is sounded so it can be felt in the chest. Do that until the air is spent.

It should be done with just enough force or gusto as one feels comfortable with, given the size and strength of one's bodily frame. *Don't* over it. Do it, say, two or three times on each occasion. And one should be guided as to when, and how often, to use it by "how you're told to inside". Inner guidance and feeling is the key. It is *wrong* to do it more than one feels the inner urge to do so. Since it promotes a backward flow of energy, doing it too often will bring on a negative response/reaction. Gurdjieff says, "You don't get more just by doing more. You'll end up with less."

Some people need to visualise more strongly. Find what is best for you. "Pushing down" as one reaches the bottom of the bow is a "psychic trigger", which some clairvoyants and mediums use to summon up their abilities. The vibratory hum stimulates the heart chakra, enlivening "feeling". Then one starts to know things in one's heart rather than just in the head or intellect. One *really* knows them then, in one's "being", and can express them fully and confidently. The essence is contacted in this way. Gurdjieff says: "When one knows in the chest, one can tell it forth."

It needs to be emphasised that this "bow" exercise should NOT be overused. You need to listen to "how you feel inside" as to when, and how often, to use it. (I never felt the need to do it more than 2 or 3 times every second, third or fourth day. Sometimes I wouldn't do it for weeks.) I have to highlight this, because people tend to want to do it more than they need to. It will "back up" on you if you do that. You can feel a bit ill or 'strange' if you overdo it, and may want to avoid it then. So just take it slowly and comfortably.

**Other Accounts of Essence**

I was on the lookout for other accounts of 'essence' as the trance work with Gurdjieff proceeded. I found two, and put them to him for his comments.

The first was in E.Wood's book The Seven Rays. (It had been published originally in 1925, elaborating teaching from Blavatsky's The Secret Doctrine.) It traced virtually everything in our world back to seven original and basic impulses. That included people, who were claimed to exist as seven basic 'types'.

In response to this, Gurdjieff told me this kind of information was "out there", if one had the dedication and drive to chase it up, as he had. One needn't think he was the only source for all his teaching. But, he had put it together, as very few others have been willing or able to do. Except that, he had made a unique contribution in the way to combine the three aspects (the thinking, feeling, moving parts) of ourselves into the fourth way. That won't be found anywhere else.

Wood said his book was to aid people in both their career and general life decisions. The problem with his treatment, however, was that his categories were all impossibly abstract. If I said that one type of person was characterised overall by "freedom" - which of the seven essences already outlined would you understand that to refer to? Or, take the Venus essence for example – if you had to choose between the abstract descriptions of 'harmony', 'beauty' or 'unity', which one would you think applied most appropriately there? In fact, Venus incorporates elements of all of them.

So, Wood's categories were very general and vague.

While his work was supporting testimony to the seven-foldness of inner impulses, the details lacked the specific application and usefulness of Gurdjieff's planetary chart.

Gurdjieff rejected the six-pointed star (of David) that Wood used, saying that the essences should be displayed on a seven-pointed star, with the Sun in the middle. (See the seven-pointed star at the end of this chapter.) He did find one of Wood's charts instructive though.

**Introvert and Extrovert**

Wood has a chart of two lists of three rays/types, with the seventh one sitting in a kind of mediating role in the middle. Gurdjieff said this configuration was really about the distribution of introvert/extrovert functions amongst the essences. (In relation to that, Wood talked of inward and outward orientations.) It was Carl Jung who brought this introvert/extrovert distinction to our attention. He had noticed that some people have their attention and interest directed inwards, while living their normal lives, while others have theirs directed outward into the world.

Gurdjieff said three of the essences are inward-looking in their functions (Mercury, Venus and Uranus), and three are outward-looking (Jupiter, Mars and Saturn). But the Moon has the unique ability of being both introvert and extrovert. Moons operate equally in both spheres or directions.

You see, Mars, with its need to be dramatic, to verbalise, and perform, is necessarily "outward-looking". It needs the world "out there" to be its audience. They've got to be performing for someone, to get the feedback they're looking for. They're constantly demanding our "undivided attention" - even irritatingly so – to what they're saying and doing. They can be "in your face" until they get it. Also, Jupiter needs the world so it can organise and re-organise it. If there was no external world, then there would be nothing for them to work on. And Saturn has to have its sphere of service, where it feels obliged to do this or that. It has to have 'others', or the 'common good' to serve.

Mercury, Venus and Uranus can all operate inwardly. "Understanding" is a thing done in one's mind. The sense of "Harmony" is an impulse arising inwardly in the Venus person. Uranus has no reliable or constant modes of outward activity, and all its decisive moves are made inwardly.

The Moon, on the other hand, can be – say – an actor or singer like the outwardly-directed Mars, though of a distinctive quality. (You can pick the difference once you know the essences. Moons are more "soulful", with no less dramatic force. And, they don't need to "feed" off adoring audiences in the same way Mars performers do. Martians have an intense wanting to be liked and adored. Moons just do it, with an almost "take it or leave it" attitude.) Or, on the other hand, Moons can go deep into themselves, either to brood, or to summon up psychic, mystical, poetical or imaginative seeing.

**The "Michael" Messages**

In 1979 C.Q.Yarbro published Messages from Michael – a series of channelled messages from an entity, "Michael", reminiscent of the Seth material. It contains a wealth of advice characterising the different soul ages of people. It also gives explicit advice about 'seven essences'. Those essences are given a series of names identifying 'roles' characteristic of Western medieval society. We find everything from rulers to common serfs, and those involved in fighting, learning or the church.

When I put this to Gurdjieff, he said the information "was from another time". It has a medieval social context. He went on:

> *it wasn't successful because it didn't fit with our time. ..it was given in a retrogressive time, not a future time.* (4/Mar/85)

(Another version of the seven essences appeared in the 1986 publication – written by a Chiappalone, from channelling by the Naylors - Revelation of the Truth. Again we find identifying names - with virtually no explanation of them - which are as abstract as Wood's list, but using slightly different terms.)

## The Point of the Planets

Gurdjieff was also critical of the Wood and Yarbro versions of the essences I asked him about, because he said there was no attempt to have people "align their subconsciousness with their consciousness" there. Only when that is done, he said, is the essence "true". Our two consciousnesses <u>must</u> be aligned.

While further testimony to the fact of the seven essences is welcome enough, I am really wondering why abstract or medieval categories were used in the alternative accounts above. Gurdjieff, if you remember, said in his published teaching that the essences were subject to <u>planetary</u> influences. And he meant that quite <u>literally</u>. They were linked with those influences precisely because those <u>were</u> the affecting influences.

He maintained there was a direct and necessary connection between the planets and their corresponding essences/chakras. Moreover, he said this wasn't just a one-way flow. But, energies flowed in <u>both</u> directions between them. We affect the planets as much as the planets affect us. This was a profound mystical insight. It meant we are directly tied into our solar system. I was told here: "Man is part of the cosmos..and part of the ever-balancing, and fluxing and flowing of the cosmos" (9/Apr/85).

The same numerical cosmic laws operate within us, and on earth, as operate through the rest of the universe. We see this in Gurdjieff's published teaching about the "octaves", where the same pattern keeps recurring at higher and lower levels. He told me this goes on "*ad infinitum*". There is "a universe within each person", and also one "within each <u>point</u> within each person". Each one is "complete within itself", "independent, but being in synchronisation with the other, and everything being tied up" (26/Feb/85).

## The Microcosm and Macrocosm

From this we get Gurdjieff's explanation of the microcosm and macrocosm. This is old teaching that came from the ancient Greeks when philosophy was being developed. "Microcosm" means literally "small world", and "macrocosm" is the "big world". There is held to be a correspondence between these two levels, so that one is always a reflection of the other. Then, by grasping something at the micro-level, we also see how it is present and operates at the macro-level.

In Gurdjieff's explanation of it, we see how "feeling" and "thinking" relate to each other. He says "the microcosm is the feeling", and "the macrocosm is the (mental) knowing". We grasp things first, implicitly, by feeling. That is grasping them in essence. Then the words and thoughts follow that, as we sketch in the particulars.

This applies in all processes of learning. If you grasp something by feeling, you don't initially need the elaborating details to get the overall grasp or picture. They can be filled in later, if needed. But, without the feeling microcosm, it is very hard work, if not impossible, to form the correct overall picture of something. This is why so much "modern" learning is incomplete and open-ended – because people think they can put it all together just working with particular details, by successive hypotheses.

But when we see how our inner essences, and the harmony between them, is a microcosm of the solar system, and then the systems beyond it, we also understand how the same numerical laws govern these processes at all levels. We start to understand what Pythagoras was talking about with the "harmony" and "music of the spheres". And when Hermes said, "As above, so below", we know that within us are the keys to the greater cosmos.

## The Seven-Pointed Star

It is worth drawing the seven-pointed star which Gurdjieff said was the proper way to represent the essences. The Sun is in the middle, and the sequence of the seven planets in their equidistant positions around the outer circle is important. The provided numbering in the diagram merely follows the order of the corresponding chakras in the body, from the top down. (From Mercury at the crown to Uranus at the base.)

The seven planets (essences) are placed in exactly the positions they are, relative to each other, because only then are their energies balanced with each other. This is the "harmony of the seven".

# THE HARMONY OF THE SEVEN

According to Gurdjieff, this is how to present the seven essences in diagram form. It is a seven-pointed star. Each of the essences sits equidistant from the others around the outer circle, and in exactly these positions relative to each other. They must be in these positions. Only then is the whole group in balance and harmony. You will also notice that the Sun sits in the middle of the circle.

The essence numbers show how they descend from head (Mercury) to the base (Uranus) by zig-zag down the circle.

CHAPTER SEVEN

# The 'Combined' Types

We can now look at the rest of the 'types'. Gurdjieff refers to them as human types, or it is just the general or psychic typicality of people. His most definitive pronouncement can be found in HCG (p. 22), where he clearly says there are "28" of them. He also says this was determined in an ancient time.

I asked him how "ancient" this determination was, and he said it went back to Atlantis, or even before that. His guardian told him that. But he himself had worked intuitively to understand and delineate the "not-true-to-essence" types, after he knew the essences. The majority of people are not true to their essence, and he had to find out why.

It was basically the younger souls who were not sufficiently advanced in soul growth. Or, they were "slow learners" who just kept replaying their lessons in successive lifetimes without learning from them. With all the non-true types, something was blocking or distorting the essence at the subconscious level.

So he carried out hypnotic experiments, which are those described in HCG (p. 20). He was able to determine the mechanism of the psyche in those cases. And, as a result of that, he determined almost everything he needed to know. He jotted down notes about it, and his guardian helped him put together the final details while he was writing.

This initial work was done before his teaching phase around 1910. That's how he could recognise that there were only three or four distinct types in his earliest occult groups in Tashkent. That wasn't enough, and was another reason why he needed to shift operations to a more cosmopolitan location.

He needed to closely observe the various behaviours of people across the whole range of types in their normal everyday states. This culminated in his work at the Paris Institute, where he was at last able to attract and observe examples of all the types. He put together a complete picture of human typicality. He had then, in his terms, established the study scientifically. (See HCG, pp. 12, 14, 23, and ISOTM, p. 246.)

There is more to this story, which I will leave until after the rest of the types have been listed and explained.

**Explaining the Other Types**

As I mentioned in earlier chapters, the complete list of the "28 types" includes the 7 essences. Those are the "true" types. But that leaves the remaining 21, which have been called "combined types", to explain. How those types are derived can be seen from the following adapted chart of the "harmony of the 7".

As you will remember from the seven-pointed star at the end of the previous chapter, the location of each of the planetary essences in the circle is crucial. (Balance and harmony.) The derivation of the rest of the types can be shown from this formation.

## LINES OF CONNECTION/INFLUENCE

We use the Harmony of the Seven diagram to then show the possible ways in which the true essence is obscured by subconscious cross-up. This is when wrong belief or commitment pushes through the false personality.

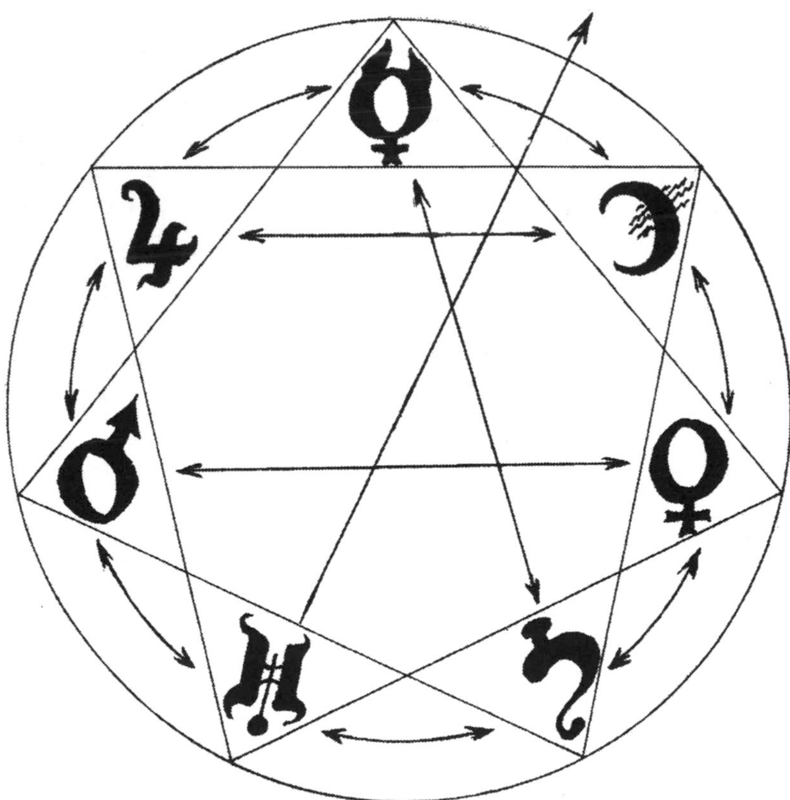

The possibilities for screw-up are shown from the essence placements in this circle. The true essence can be pulled out of alignment by wrong identification with those other essences which sit to each side, or in polar opposition, to the harmonious placement. The arrows in this diagram show the possible influences evident in screw-ups.

Look at the Mercury position at the top of the circle. By itself it stands for the true essence. But it has a relationship with three other essences. It has the Moon on one side, and Jupiter on the other. It also has a polar opposite in Saturn. From this we get the four types for that essence. (Remember, Gurdjieff said, "four types in every essence".)

1. MERCURY
2. MERCURY-saturn
3. MERCURY-moon
4. MERCURY-jupiter.

From there we move to each of the essences in turn, giving us:

5. MOON
6. MOON-jupiter
7. MOON-venus
8. MOON-mercury
9. JUPITER
10. JUPITER-moon
11. JUPITER-mercury
12. JUPITER-mars
13. VENUS
14. VENUS-mars
15. VENUS-saturn
16. VENUS-moon
17. MARS
18. MARS-venus
19. MARS-jupiter
20. MARS-uranus
21. SATURN
22. SATURN-mercury
23. SATURN-uranus
24. SATURN-venus
25. URANUS
26. URANUS-unpolarised
27. URANUS-mars
28. URANUS-saturn

Since it is a 7-pointed circle, one of the essences has no polar opposite. That is Uranus. That is why type 26 is "URANUS-unpolarised".

With each of the "combined types", the planet written first in capital letters is the real or underlying essence in each case. The added planet, in small type, is the wrong or interfering influence.

For example, the VENUS-mars is <u>really</u> a Venus essence, but they think (subconsciously) they are a Mars. Or, the MARS-venus type is <u>really</u> a Mars, but they think (subconsciously) that they're a Venus. Don't assume that VENUS-mars and MARS-venus are the same or similar. They aren't. They are different basic essences, and each combination has its own characteristic behaviours.

## The Wrong Influences

The crossing-up that happens in each case with the 21 "combined types" is only possible because the essence is susceptible to inner misrepresentation (within certain limits), through the relative strength of the false personality pushing into the subconscious. (Remember, the personality is stronger than the essence, which is why, in general, it needs to be made passive to allow the essence to emerge.)

It is like Hans Christian Anderson's story of the "ugly duckling". While the subject of the story is <u>really</u> a swan, it has been alienated from its true being by wrong upbringing and socialisation. That makes it even believe, itself, that it is a duckling, albeit a deficient and ugly one. Then it is not actually behaving like either a real swan <u>or</u> a real duckling, but only as a "swan that inwardly believes it's a duckling". That results in a specific kind of dysfunction. Thus all 21 of the 'combined types' of humans.

## Characteristics of the Types

1. <u>MERCURY</u> (pure essence)(see list of essences)
2. <u>MERCURY-saturn</u> - "A most frustrated, and depressed, individual".

This is the least happy of all the types. When Saturn is added to the essential Mercury, there is no question of a balance between between the two influences. The massive weight of Saturn overpowers and restricts the lighter, finer nature of Mercury. While essential Saturns are quite at home with the weight, pace and rhythms of that planet, essential Mercurys are suffocated by it, and can't get out from underneath it all. Mercury wants to think and move swiftly, but it can't in this combination. Saturn is like a dead-weight strapped to its body, wound around the hips, inhibiting every movement.

This combination is so frustrating, upsetting and depressing that MERCURY-saturns have tremendous mood swings. They are very inconsistent individuals, and are most dissatisfied with themselves and the world. There is constant inner conflict between mental understanding and aspiration, and they have overlaid feelings of worry and responsibility. Because, Saturn makes this type feel they have to put down or deny their own needs for the sake of the needs of others.

The verbal expression natural to Mercury then becomes sharp and angry, with their "hitting out" reflecting the frustration and discomfort of being "boxed-in". This type is often very depressed, and also depressing to be around, because Mercurys can't be talked out of what they know they are experiencing.

They are dogged constantly by ill-health, reminding one of a "cancer-patient". They are altogether very unhappy with their "lot", and feel that there has to be more to life than "this".

3. <u>MERCURY-moon</u> - "Close in essences, the difficulty arises only from an internal tension."

This is the least difficult of the Mercury not-true-to-essence types. It need not be apparent externally that "something is wrong", as it is with MERCURY-saturn. Mercury and the Moon are also much closer to each other than Mercury and Jupiter.

There are no big imbalances with this type. The basic difficulty that does arise is due to the internal conflict or tension between the analytical approach to thinking and working of Mercury, and the intuitive approach of the Moon. This type will tend to want to resolve the conflict by removing the intuitiveness, but with intermittent success. Mercury will still have the words, but the cross-current of intuition will sometimes interrupt the confidence of grasp of mental patterns. Or, the desire to communicate openly will be inhibited. ("I feel it's best not to talk about this at the moment.")

Therefore, this type will sometimes be switched-on, and articulate what it is thinking, and sometimes be switched-off. When switched-off though, the communication will become non-verbal. MERCURY-moons in this situation are capable of giving off a lot of heavy "vibes". They are inwardly absorbed in their own tidal flow, and with their own needs. They will dwell or brood on their thoughts, so that others can feel what they are thinking, when they can't openly express it or get it off their chest.

4. MERCURY-jupiter - "An individual who runs around chasing themselves, achieving nothing"

Since Jupiter is an active, expansive, organising force, it galvanises the physical systems of the MERCURY-jupiter for action. That projects this individual into running around and being continually active. But nothing is actually achieved by all the activity.

Not being an essential Jupiter, this type lacks the natural organising genius of Jupiters. And the influence of Jupiter over Mercury is such as to inhibit its own natural ability for sizing-up and understanding situations. So, with the understanding blocked, or relegated to the farther reaches of the mind, this individual merely goes through the motions of performing physical functions. So Jupiter just scatters the energies of Mercury.

5. MOON (pure essence)

6. MOON-jupiter - "Conscious of the things it's always going to do..one day"

The influence of Jupiter, with its emphasis on organising and doing, very much interrupts the tidal flows of the Moon. So you get a constant impulse towards, and the consciousness of an obligation to be acting and doing. But this person is unable to carry anything through. So they will typically sit and think about what they've got to do. They will get the clearest visual and psychic images. They absolutely know what they are going to do...one day. But they never do them. They never get anywhere. This type may have to reincarnate many times to face the same sorts of situations and circumstances, until it can break through the inaction.

The tension between what it plans to do, and its inability to do it, can create a great deal of anxiety. So they may feel very frustrated, and even cry a lot. They may exclaim, "I can't do it!" or "Why won't it work for me?"

But basically, one can't push against the tide going out, or coming in. This type just needs to realise that the energy and direction of Jupiter is simply inappropriate for the Moon essence.

7. MOON-venus - "A total and complete day-dreamer, content with things as they are while it waits for the world if anything, to change."

The MOON-venus type is locked-up in its own impractical and unrealistic dreams. It even looks like a very dreamy person. It rarely connects with the everyday realities around it.

So this sort of person might live in a bark hut with a bunch of flowers on the table, and pretend that it was something far better and more desirable. It is just "not of this world". It is not practical. It is not self-motivated.

It always wants to sit and wait, believing that things will just improve by themselves one day. It won't take the steps itself to change anything.

8. MOON-mercury - "The internal clarity of its thoughts can't be effectively expressed outwardly."

The difficulties here arise chiefly from the way the intuition inhibits MOON-mercury's attempts to operate effectively in the everyday world through the intellect. The wrong influence of Mercury keeps pushing it to use the intellect, but that won't work.

This is a very internalised person, subject to great internal pulls and strains, and rather unhappy with it. It won't project itself into the environment, and usually won't draw from its environment to construct a sense of itself outwardly. So it tends to lack a "self" in the world.

Internally, it seems to have itself together, because the thought-patterns will form very precisely within the mind. It therefore has an internal confidence in its grasp of the world and life. But the Moon keeps standing in front of Mercury when it comes to outward communication.

Even the most well-structured words in the mind can't be gotten across outwardly. It will get frustrated because it can't explain or communicate its thoughts effectively. This type may gesture a great deal with its hands, or stutter, or launch forth to say something but break off in mid sentence with, "Oh, it doesn't matter!"

It is very difficult to put blame or shame on this person for anything, because they're not participating in an outward sense where blame or shame have a cultural relevance.

9. JUPITER (pure essence)

10. JUPITER-moon - "The frustration of never quite knowing whether they should be active or passive produces obvious anxieties."

The influence of the Moon has a short-circuiting effect on essential Jupiters. Jupiter is an active force, and part of its natural expression of itself is to organise situations and people in an outward sense. It seeks far and wide in the external world for the understanding and information it requires. But the Moon derives its information inwardly, through its natural intuitiveness. It normally intuits the relations that obtain between people and situations. So while JUPITER-moons are driven by their essential Jupiter nature to seek and act outwardly, their need to do so is undermined by what the Moon already knows intuitively.

This type may look like a snake that is poised to strike, but it never does. Or, it may seem full of "huff and puff", but it doesn't go anywhere. All of the action of this type leads it nowhere, like a dog chases its tail in a circle.

As essential Jupiters, they are natural born leaders, but end up being led by others, and hating it.

The Moon has a delaying, inhibiting influence on their organising abilities and purposes, so they end up feeling, "It's best not to do it now".

Being caught between these inward and outward

impulses leaves them with constant and obvious anxieties. They may try to dissipate the anxieties by denying the active outgoing impulses and deferring to the intuitiveness. But since they aren't essential Moons, resolving the tensions in that way only makes them into very lethargic persons.

11. JUPITER-mercury - "Unsubtly verbose, a rather repugnant individual."

As with Mars on the one side here (of the essential Jupiter), Mercury on the other introduces a verbal component that Jupiter doesn't need in its communications. It overwhelms its output. When the outgoing force of Jupiter is channelled into speech, it becomes verbose. Because, their action is translated forcibly thereby into the production of words with insufficient subtle direction to control their sense and point. There is a flow of unsubtle but deadly serious comment about other people, which has a devastating effect on interpersonal relationships.

Others find this type, and their comments, repugnant. Invariably, the JUPITER-mercury is shunned by other people. They become isolated, and experience an alienation that greatly lowers their own self-image. When they try to compensate for their lack of self worth, they cannot help becoming even more overbearing towards others, and so become caught in a vicious circle.

12. JUPITER-mars - "can become quite an obnoxious person, too much physicalness and force."

As with Mercury and the Moon, the essences of Jupiter and Mars are quite close to each other. So the difficulties here result more from over-emphasis than elements which clash or conflict.

Both have a lot of outgoing energy. Jupiter's energy is of the ordering kind. But Mars is equally capable of being a destroying force as it is of being constructive or creative. Jupiter will naturally try to organise situations or people, and it is in this area that difficulties arise. Because, the overload of outgoing energies from these two big power planets, which includes Mars' alternating (constructive/destructive) energies, can produce quite an obnoxious person in the aggressive sense.

This combination is hyper-active, and over-physical. It has too much drive with too little co-ordinated understanding of how and why and where it is being applied, and to what effect.

Also, Jupiter doesn't need the verbalising force and aggression of Mars, because its own natural mode of communication is through actions rather than words. So in this combination there is likely to be an overflow of verbosity and articulated aggression.

13. VENUS (pure essence)

14. VENUS-mars - "this individual acquires for the same of acquiring"

I was given the word "avarice" for this type.

The influence of Mars over Venus in this type is such that, Mars disrupts the natural appreciation of harmony and beauty. Its forcefulness fuels a desire for achieving and gaining things. So appreciation of whatever it is that appeals to Venus is turned instead into acquiring things just for their own sake. Compulsive "collectors" of things are found here.

Mars finds its satisfaction in activity, and it pushes Venus into the active acquiring of things as an end in itself. A VENUS-mars will not normally or naturally steal to gain what it wants, but a MARS-venus will.

15. VENUS-saturn - "Uncomfortable, because however much effort it puts into translating its pleasant visions into reality, they never quite come off."

With this type, there is a lot of striving to achieve tasteful and aesthetically pleasing surroundings. The aesthetic longing of Venus is very much in evidence, but Saturn drags it down to the mundane level of materialistic concern. So all its strivings will be frustrated. It will never be able to achieve in practice what it envisages and hopes for.

Saturn will always spoil this type's efforts by bogging them down with concerns over money and costing. In one way or another, Saturn will ensure that everything the VENUS-saturn does or acquires contains a touch of the austere, the cheap, the nasty, or the inappropriate.

So, one might typically find this individual has a fine crystal vase, even filled with flowers that are beautifully and strategically arranged. But the flowers will be made of cheap red plastic, or something like that.

Whatever the vision is, it won't work, or it won't happen. This type will be out of tune with nature and natural things, however much it might think they are what it wants or desires.

16. VENUS-moon - "Pursues its own good and desires, naively oblivious of the feelings, interests and rights of others."

The VENUS-moon is totally locked-up in its own dreams. So much so, it will constantly run right over the top of other people to gain what it wants or desires. It will not set out intentionally to treat other people like that. There is no malevolence in it or behind it. It can also be very pleasant in doing it. It will simply not realise or notice. It won't see its misuse of other people unless it is pointed out very forcefully, and maybe not even then.

It is primarily in touch with its own bodily needs, and its own aesthetic vision – a self-absorbed hedonist. It simply doesn't consider the rights and needs of others. It is ineffectual at anything but catering to its own impulses.

17. MARS (pure essence)

18. MARS-venus - "Greedy"

When an essential Mars comes under the influence of Venus, in the MARS-venus type, they acquire a good deal of the aesthetic taste and appreciation of beauty of the overlaid Venus essence. But their strong drive predominates over the calm, gentle, loving energy characteristic of Venus. Their drive then is put to service in satisfying the desire to surround themselves with beautiful and pleasing things.

But, the forcefulness then displays itself in greed. They devote themselves to acquiring what they want, and won't hesitate to lie, steal, cheat, or do whatever is necessary, to obtain what they desire.

19. MARS-jupiter - "Always arguing with everyone over everything – externalised, meddling and interfering."

Mars and Jupiter both have a lot of energy, which is directed outwards. This combination produces a very externalised person, with no subtlety. It is in fact, easier to distinguish a Mars from a Jupiter essence, than to distinguish MARS-jupiter from JUPITER-mars. Both types have an energy overload, and are over-active and over-directive. JUPITER-mars is usually obnoxious, because it is aggressively verbose. It tends to be all words and no action though. But MARS-jupiter is all words AND all action.

The most negative qualities of Mars are projected via Jupiter's drive to organise other people. So we find overt aggressive, sanctimonious beliefs and an inability to see any further than itself.

Jupiter normally wants to be leader in any situation. But since MARS-jupiter is not an essential Jupiter, it lacks the grounding and ability to assume natural leadership. So, more aggression and belligerence is summoned up to attain this ambition. The desire is blind though, and the campaign invariably lapses into action for action's sake. They simply lack the feeling and thought to even know what they're doing.

MARS-jupiters don't hear a thing that anyone else says to them. And they don't see what's there to be seen. They bulldoze others, meddle and interfere in their lives, and ride obliviously over their wishes and needs.

They lack the thought or subtlety to even see their own needs properly, and are fighting themselves just as much as anyone else.

20. MARS-uranus - "This person is such an ego!"

Like the URANUS-mars type, this one also has the same mix of centred aggression (from Mars), and the lack of a stable sense of self (from Uranus). The general effect is to see them all "revved-up", but without much idea of where they're going or what they're doing.

MARS-uranus can be quite overt in the strange mistimed and misplaced behaviour it exhibits. Of course, the essential Mars does have a basic sense of self that it wants to project. But add the distorting influence of Uranus, and you get "half-cocked" performances. How they behave may well attract the comment, "That person is such an ego!"

As much of the self as they manage to project in their mistimed and misplaced performances, will lack any reflective subtlety, and be unthinking, unfeeling and non-intuitive.

This type is also far more of a reactor to situations, rather than an actor in them.

21. SATURN (pure essence)

22. SATURN-mercury - "A bit of a verbal bully, committed to organising and telling others what to do."

Unlike the Saturn-dominated MERCURY-saturn type, this individual exhibits a balance between the influence of the two essences. The Mercury holds it own in this combination.

SATURN-mercury is a bit of a bully – a verbal bully. It is full of "shoulds" and "oughts", and telling other people what they should, and shouldn't do. There is a superficial resemblance to Jupiter in this regard, with its attempts to organise others.

This type believes that it has a definite role in life, to say this particular thing or do that particular thing. Saturn's inner sense of obligation is turned outward in this manner. These individuals also take themselves very, very seriously.

23. SATURN-uranus - "Totally inconsistent – firmly committed one minute, and walking out on it all the next."

SATURN-uranus, a bit like URANUS-saturn, comes up as almost schizophrenic. This is because of the combination of the solemn responsibility of Saturn, and the total irresponsibility of Uranus, within the one person.

There is a great deal of moralising, involving "shoulds", "oughts", "can'ts" and "won'ts".

This type can be all puffed up one minute with the sense of its own importance, and pontificating about what absolutely has to be done. But the next minute it has walked off and totally abandoned it all.

It is a very difficult person to work or get along with, because you never know where you are with them. Very split in themselves, and lacking in integration. Totally inconsistent.

24. SATURN-venus - "A bit of a dreamer, unable to give effect to its 'nice' aspirations."

The Saturn-ness overrides here, more heavily than in any other cross combination. The gentle, loving energy of Venus is evident only as fuelling vague dreams and aspirations. So the SATURN-venus type does a lot of day-dreaming about beautiful, comfortable and attractive situations and things. But it cannot give practical effect to what it dreams about.

So, this individual begins to look either ridiculous or pathetic. It might, for example, think it has a responsibility to make things 'pretty' – in the office, shop or home – but simply lacks the flair or ability to carry it out.

25. URANUS (pure essence)

26. URANUS-unpolarised - "The most unstable of the types, and especially when it falls under the influence of the Moon."

Uranus has no natural polar opposite. This is why it is so unstable. Although it can mirror any of the other essences, which it throws up like an illusion, it tends to be drawn to the Moon like a magnet.

This is a most unfortunate attraction, because the effect of the Moon on Uranus is wholly negative. Uranus is the most unstable of the essences, and the Moon least stable after it, because of its fluctuating rhythms.

Uranus is sufficiently capricious by itself, and doesn't need the complication of the stronger lunar tidal rhythms playing havoc with its own subtler rhythms. It causes real problems of fluxing and flowing in the personality which the Uranus person can't control.

When Uranus comes under the influence of the Moon, it makes the person sullen and neurotic, subject to wildly fluctuating ideas of reality, affected by even the subtlest nuances. The mind then becomes completely subjective. Everything is related back directly through a very misguided, and an over-protected and over-protective ego. The person becomes very erratic, unhappy and insular.

This type has great difficulty even living with themselves, and living with anyone else is virtually impossible. So Uranus badly needs to avoid the Moon. They should avoid contact with Moon essence people.

27. URANUS-mars - "An unhappy individual who displays a strange mistimed, nebulous aggression."

The unstable and erratic Uranus essence benefits

greatly from contact with the stabilising energy of someone of Saturn essence. But the centred aggression of Mars is not good for it. It doesn't gain decisiveness or the ability to project and assert itself, as one might have expected. Instead, its instability is accentuated in strange ways.

The URANUS-mars type transmutes the centred aggression of Mars into a strange nebulous aggression. Much of the velocity of the normal Mars essence is lost. This type will "blow-up" or "sound off" periodically, but usually at the wrong time or in the wrong place. It misses those occasions when it needs to be assertive or aggressive. Alternatively, it will "fuse" in the wrong situations.

Because of this, these individuals come to believe that things just keep "happening" to them, rather than that they're in control of their life and circumstances. These are the sort of people who frequently open their mouths just to change feet.

Visually, they seem to be a rather unhappy type of person. They could periodically be reduced to tears in coping with life, or simply display retaliatory bouts of displaced aggression.

28. URANUS-saturn - "Most irresponsible, the outward ordered-ness is a sham."

While Uranus benefits from association with a Saturn essence person, there is an unfortunate effect that Saturn has on top of Uranus in the same person. It institutes a semblance of order, or a consciousness of obligation, but these can never be lived up to.

This type is, also, almost schizophrenic in promising and committing itself to things it never does. It therefore shows up primarily as irresponsible. The overlaid order and responsibility of Saturn just serves to throw the capriciousness of Uranus into high relief.

The URANUS-saturn will typically, while knowing its responsibilities, neglect them, shrug them off, giggle over them, or invariably find some excuse for not fulfilling them. It can be very juvenile in that regard.

When pushed to the other extreme, it can put on a very strong front, vehemently defending the facade of orderliness. But it is only a thin veneer, an illusion, covering internal chaos.

It is very good at "throwing illusions". All its apparent orderliness has no rationale, no foundation, and no consistency. It could not defend its actions in any reasonable terms.

It is a very unhappy soul, having no peace within itself, and it blames others continually for its situation and predicaments. "It's their fault this has happened to me." When a verbal attack is made on its facades, because it has no reason for behaving as it does, they crumble. It can also become very maudlin about its lot in life.

## Concentrations of Types

I asked Gurdjieff about the small number of types he found during his teaching at Tashkent. He said there were only "parts of the Moon, Mars, and Saturn there". In those days, before the First World War, there was a "lack of transmigration", and ethnic groups were concentrated in pockets.

The 1914-18 war changed things to some extent, and Paris was the best place then to find a variety of types. But there was an even greater "melting-pot" effect as a result of the Second World War. Today one can find a much wider cross-section of types in most social contexts.

He needed to review the whole range of types, to complete his teaching, which is why Paris was so valuable to him in the 1920s. Further stages of development in his planned work – which he was never able to get to - demanded gatherings of complete cross-sections of people.

## 28 or 27?

One might ask why, when Gurdjieff declares categorically in HCG (p. 22) that there are 28 types, does he elsewhere refer to just 27? (See HCG, p. 60, and Beelzebub, p. 486.) Well, we know he could sometimes adapt or fudge things to protect his teaching from those who might misconstrue or misuse it. He wouldn't pass things on clearly until he was sure people were ready for it. But he justified "27" later in HCG (in comments to me, 2/Apr/85) by saying his own energies were meant to make up the 28 there. Because, he knew the manifestations of all the types, and could therefore "stand in" for any one of them. (Apart from that, he told me to disregard, or not worry about, what he outlined later in HCG. He said it had been an "abortive experiment" that "led nowhere".)

The reference to 27 distinctive types in Beelzebub (p. 486) could be explained in another way. Perhaps there wasn't that great a difference between the basic Uranus essence and the unpolarised type. The essence itself was unpolarised. The unfortunate effect of the Moon's energies on the unpolarised Uranus would apply equally to the basic essence. In that sense, one could perhaps get away with talking about just 27 types. But it needs to be taken to 28 in a full explanation to make everything complete and whole.

**Seeing and Understanding the Types**

It is important to use one's feeling when trying to identify types in practice. Characterisations in words have been used in this chapter and the last one, for the essences and combined types. But we tend to need the further feeling for the clarity and certainty of identification. They all have a particular 'feel' to them.

Ouspensky records Gurdjieff as saying that it is necessary to recognise one's own type, and then go beyond that, before the others can be seen.(ISOTM, p. 247) So, find yourself in the provided lists first. Then work on how the differences depart from that.

It may have seemed natural when we were growing up to assume that everyone is basically the same. I mean, there are the obvious similarities between people. But, if we thought about it, then there are different sorts of people in the world. A Mars essence person, for example, may have initially judged everyone in relation to themselves. Yes, there were the 'quieter' ones. But maybe they just lacked the drive to be up to the same standard. They might have even thought of telling them to "move themselves", or that they should "get a life". But there are actually differences in abilities between different people. Not everyone has that inner concentrated or combustible energy. The quieter types do more thinking, or "inner considering". And they might also have thought the Martian types too aggressive, brash, or even shallow. Maybe they thought they "used their mouths a lot", and didn't always stop to think things through beforehand.

Gurdjieff said to me:

> *when people are closer to their essence, they're closer to knowing themselves. And that's the object of the entire exercise. And when they recognise their essential self, they can recognise the essential selves of the other six (essences).. (And they) will therefore allow others to be themselves, and who they are, and what they need to be - therefore creating a greater sense of security within oneself, and within one's environment. (This has the effect of) reducing jealousy, fear, greed, prejudice, and the negative qualities that dog society.* *(4/Mar/85)*

As long as people can't see themselves, then their expectations of others are based on a faulty premiss. When you accept yourself as you are, then you can accept others as they are. Or, alternatively:

> *(you will) see others as not being correctly aligned (in the case of the combined types), and therefore (in your) dealings with them, you give them sufficient room. Because, you know some people will lie or cheat because it is their type, and not their essence.*

Yes, as should be apparent from the characterisations above, all 21 of the (not-true) types are dysfunctional in some way.

**The Problem of Dysfunction**

Going through the descriptions of the 21 (combined) types, we see there is a great deal of anxiety, depression, unhappiness, and so forth. The plight of some of these types is greater than others. And, people who have one of these cross-ups can have them in varying degrees. Sometimes the effect can be minimal, and in other cases it is more severe.

When Gurdjieff started his hypnotic experiments to determine the involved mechanism in peoples' psyches, he presented himself as a "healer" of various vices. He was offering his services to remedy undesirable personal faults and behaviours. His subjects were all volunteers who chose to have this done. He was solving real life problems for these people. And he found, as he suspected, that the key was to increase personal awareness and "knowing of oneself". Because, the types who lied, cheated, stole, and so forth couldn't see themselves.

He used "a very complicated technique" to bring self-awareness. He was always careful not to harm the psyches of those in his experiments. He set up a post-hypnotic suggestion in each case to make the subjects overtly aware of their own behaviours. When returned to everyday consciousness, they saw what they themselves were doing, as they hadn't seen it before. They "saw themselves", and the realisation or shock of that effected a conscious change in their behaviour. Thus, he said, he afforded them real relief. In other words, "it worked".

Dysfunctional people, who engage in all manner of strange, self-defeating, inappropriate, obnoxious, abusive or criminal behaviour, have massive mental blocks. They are farthest of all from knowing and being themselves. And what they can't see about themselves, they usually highly resent and deny when it is pointed out by others. (That is, until they're ready to see what's there and advance in their own development.)

It is much harder for the dysfunctional people to recognise their type when it is presented to them. Gurdjieff told me the seven essences could be summarised fairly quickly and easily. Those (true) types are much quicker to recognise themselves. But in the case of the other 21 types, he said "more words" were needed. Thus the longer descriptive sections devoted to those types in this chapter.

Gurdjieff had a special technique or "key" for identifying the types, as opposed to the pure essences, which I will review in the next chapter.

**False Personality and Types**

One might have noticed some correspondences between the "chief features or faults" listed in chapter 2 (above) – where the false personality blocks awareness of a person's essence (from themselves) – and the characteristics of some of the dysfunctional types. This is not surprising, as it is the false personality which pushes into the subconscious to obscure the true essence. The chief fault in not always a reflection of an essence cross-up, but often it is.

For example, someone with the chief fault of "having no conscience" could well be one of the Mars or Uranus types. Alternatively, someone who "has no shame" could be MERCURY-moon or MOON-mercury, or even VENUS-moon. They're so preoccupied with their own internal flows and needs, that they've never allowed the cultural awareness of shame to impinge on them. Also, a "person who appears not to exist at all (won't project a self)" would likely be one of the Moon or Uranus types.

When Gurdjieff said a person can be shown their chief fault many times over without being able to accept it (chapter 2, above), it likely indicates a subconscious block. That is, it doesn't just consist in a belief at the conscious level, which would be open to discussion and modification. But it is installed at a level below the conscious awareness of the person themselves. But the more it can be brought into their conscious awareness, the easier it will be to work on it and dispose of it.

**Gurdjieff's Early Jottings**

I referred at the start of this chapter to Gurdjieff's "early jottings", when he worked out on paper the elucidation of the 'types' from his hypnotic experiments. These written notes were deposited somewhere in Moscow, and never recovered by him. He could never return to Russia safely after he left during the throes of the revolution prior to 1920.

This came up as I went through some biographical details from MRM with him in 1985. In that book he refers to some 'hundreds of songs' which his *ashokh* father sang, as being recorded on phonograph rolls, which he said may still exist amongst possessions he left in Moscow. (MRM, p. 46)

I wondered why he would have been so concerned about those songs, even given his respect for his father and the *ashokh* tradition. He then revealed that these records were actually his early jottings about the 'types'. They were written on the backs of the phonograph rolls.

He told me in 1985 that the rolls were still there then, with "wooden battens on either side of them". I do not know his connection with the people at the Moscow dwelling. (Could it have been one of his 'marriages'?) Anyhow, if someone knows about this location in Moscow, the records may still be recoverable there.

## CHAPTER EIGHT

# More About Types And Essences

The managed 'shocks' or 'social insults' that Gurdjieff used on many who came to him (see chapter 1), were not just for the awakening and aligning effects. They were certainly for that. But they also assisted him to determine if a person was true to their essence or not. Or, in the case of the combined types, it showed him what the true essence was.

### Harrying People

I once put to him that I'd heard a person will display their essence when they're hungry. He said:

> *No...not hungry. (It is) when they're harried! It's a key.* (4/Mar/85)

Having given me this "key", he went on to explain how it worked:

> *We're dealing with very delicate balances..with the essences. (That is, those who are true to their essence.) But the types are far less immediately responsive, simply because they are types. The types will display their (true) nature when pushed. But the essences will draw into themselves every time when they're harried.*

So, very little hassling or harassing is required to see those who are true to essence draw back into themselves. That is, if their status wasn't already obvious before anything like that was attempted. But for Gurdjieff to talk of "harrying" the types, they must need a good serve before you can get a worthwhile response from them.

So these were the ones, obviously, where Gurdjieff

set out to stamp on their largest corns! It had to be harsh enough to bypass the distorting influence of their internal identification with the wrong essence. But the real essence is always there, underneath. The shock of the harrying obviously brings the two consciousnesses into alignment, and the true essence must display itself then. We just need to know the typical modes of response of the seven essences to pick it.

Gurdjieff went on:

> *An interesting experiment on paper would be to harry the types into finding their essences, by recognising themselves in stress situations. They can be pushed through into finding their true essences.*

I wasn't sure whether he was recommending this as an ongoing method for reducing the types back to their essences in this way, or not. Since he said it was an "experiment on paper", then probably not. But at least we know this mechanism and its potential now. Perhaps it is enough to do it once or twice to display to the person themselves how they respond when upset or under stress.

This technique wasn't necessary with the two groups I ran during 1984-9. Although of different soul ages, or spirit levels, all the participating individuals in those groups were fairly readily aware of their true essences. At least, they were able to recognise their essence when it was presented to them. Or, they trusted and were ready to consider the guidance for this group they chose to be part of, and then saw it for themselves. And this was confirmed by the ongoing work with those of different essences around them.

And, of course, one only has permission to use the harrying technique where someone is seeking and choosing their own development. (It is not something to take out into the world and use on people in general. You'll hardly be 'thanked' for that. This kind of development is not to be <u>pushed</u> on anyone.) But those who are 'seeking' are more willing to trust and work with advice from those they see or sense are more advanced on the path they want to travel.

When I asked him, Gurdjieff saw no problem in accepting 'types' for work in a group of seven. This is possible. But a group can't complete its work until each member has reached the point of feeling their true essence. So the reduction from dysfunctional type back to essence must happen for those people during the work of the group. (The shock of the spinning 'dance' technique – to be explained later – also assists that.)

**The 'Meddling' Types**

It is characteristic of those true to their essences to 'accept' others as they are, as a correlating effect of their having come to "accept themselves" as they are. (This is "live, and let live".) The contrary effect is apparent amongst the dysfunctional types in general. When a person can't see or accept themselves as they are (in their true subconscious being), then they will actively try to interfere with others. It's a kind of (less than conscious) 'cockamamie' attempt to justify themselves in their ruling dysfunction by wrong-footing everyone else. (Like, "I'm not the one out of step. Everyone else is.")

As Gurdjieff said:

> *They're all people that will meddle with other people. They're all people that have got to say and do, or put their ideas or their perceptions onto others around them.* *(9/Apr/85)*

We've all run into people like this. They're everywhere. It's the neighbour that wants to tell you what you should or shouldn't be doing on your own property. It's people in the street or at the supermarket who want to tell you you're doing things the wrong way. They seem to flock into bureaucracies or anywhere where they can assume a mantle of petty authority to lord it over others. They will obstruct you, abuse you, or generally waste your time and energy with irrational and stupid demands. And it arises solely from a subconscious cross-up in these peoples' psyches.

In general, there's not much mileage in trying to fight

this. They're so irrational, and fortified by their mental blocks. You usually can't put a sensible case or argue convincingly with them. One learns over time to just avoid them as much as possible. They can be basically "too stupid to talk to".

Gurdjieff says:

> *your essential types are far more self-contained, and can step back and see (what's really happening)...*

He himself was very good at "taking no crap" from the dysfunctional types. He didn't go looking for confrontations, normally. But where they arose, he had the know-how to quickly assess the psychic mechanisms and use them, to walk through or past such people. For the rest of us, his advice is to basically step back or around those who want to meddle and interfere.

Apparently it is part of the soul growth of the dysfunctional types to carry on as they do, until they eventually realise it earns them nothing but unhappiness, misery and frustration. It is all outwardly-mediated false personality stuff, and relief will only come when they start to look inward.

**The Prospect for Types**

The prospect for 'types' depends upon the relative mildness or severity of their cross-ups, or how far they are "lost in" their dysfunction. It may be how 'young' a soul they are. And, of course, their willingness or unwillingness to consider and pursue a way out of where they are. There are the exercises they can perform on themselves, which provide a 'shock' for aligning the two consciousnesses. Or they may seek the help of someone who understands the essences and types. That is, if they can come to see they aren't just "okay as they are".

Younger souls can, if they choose, develop quite quickly. Gurdjieff says they don't have to resign themselves to waiting for more deaths and rebirths to make advances. He says the transition from type to essence

> *can be short-circumvented in one lifetime.*
> *(26/Mar/85)*

But they have a much greater battle to do this, with more karmic lessons to learn on the way:

> *the more karmic lessons a young soul learns in one lifetime, the less personality it will carry, and the more it will shard off – or slough off – to get down to the essence, for the maturation of the soul to occur.*

Even with the 'shocks', he says the advance an individual will make depends more upon the readiness of the soul to grasp what is happening, rather than the size of the shock. It can be a matter for some of "the right trigger" coming "in the right lifetime". But, "it can come at any time".

The only exception that he mentioned was people born with a condition that ruled out the possibility of development. He said:

> *(There are) people who are born with psychoses. Some people are born with them. There are some people who are born to be sick – some physically and some mentally. That is a life-long karma. But people who are born with all the normal faculties (can develop their essence).* *(26/Feb/85)*

Where even the hard karma that some people have to face has been socially mediated – or set up by circumstances after birth – they can still develop awareness through the essence. They can come to understand what they are going through, and why. Where this increased awareness doesn't lessen the karma, it still gives greater peace in working through it.

And,

> *Once (a person) has finished a karma, they can change their personality.*

That means a person is free to then tap their genuine

essence, and to thereby change their false personality into the true one.

**Two Fortunate Types**

The two most fortunate types, who have less distance to travel than the others, are MERCURY- moon and MERCURY-jupiter. Gurdjieff even ranks them amongst what he calls the "advanced psycho-spiritual types". There are five such types, which are the three essences of Mercury, Moon and Jupiter. But also, it includes MERCURY-moon and MERCURY-jupiter.

(Remember, from chapter 1, I said that 5 of the 28 types were better placed to benefit from 'shocks'. These are those 5. They react more positively than negatively to them.)

It is because they sit, as it were, "at the head of the totem-pole". The proximity to Mercury is the decisive factor. In the case of these five, there is a force that can readily combine the "intellect and the soul". They are all 'head' chakras. It can be just a short step to development. It may not even take shocks to get them moving.

It does not mean these types will automatically develop their potential. But it's a shorter, easier step once they start moving in the right direction.

**Types and Compatibility**

In ISOTM Gurdjieff is recorded as talking about compatibility between the sexes for the purpose of partnership or marriage (p. 254). In Beelzebub he said that astrologers in bygone days in ancient Egypt knew which men and women were compatible with each other (p. 289).

I wondered if there were guidelines for this, such as when zodiacal astrologers today tell us about increased compatibility between those born under certain Sun signs. I asked Gurdjieff therefore to expand on his ISOTM claim that, people who know their essence will always choose the right partners for themselves.

But, he said, there is no list of which essences couple best with which other essences. He explained it as:

> *It is not a matter of right or wrong coupling. When people are in their essence they will automatically find (the other) essence. There can't be a wrong when there's a coupling of essences. It won't occur. (9/Apr/85)*

What he is saying is, when someone knows their essence, they will choose a partner that also knows their essence, no matter what essences are involved. 'Wrong' unions happen when the other, dysfunctional, types get together. Or, if there should somehow was a union between an essence and a type (Such as when someone marries before they've come to an adequate appreciation of their essence.)

Unions based on (false) 'personality' factors are mismatched, and inevitably lead to so much time and energy being tied-up with the incessant nagging from the other part. (Beelzebub, p. 289) It is the mismatch of inward and outward factors in each person which sets up that tension and conflict.

**General Incompatibility**

What applies in sexual unions also applies to jobs and occupations in the everyday world. If the choosing of a marriage partner is based on inappropriate 'personality' considerations, then so also will be the preferred form of work.

It is precisely this choice of a wrong partner or occupation that was thrown into high relief by what became recognised and known in the 1970s as the "mid-life crisis". People in their 30s and 40s started to realise in sufficient numbers that they weren't really where they wanted or needed to be in their lives. It was an age where people could assess where they were in the light of an inner longing. It wasn't too late to "change things". Something inside them said, "Enough", and they charted a new course. There was enough time to get out of something that wasn't what they really wanted, and to work more closely with the soul's purpose for their life. (People will typically say, "It's like

I grew, but my partner didn't. And I realised we were no longer compatible." Or, "What originally took me into that work area, was no longer meaningful or satisfying.")

In the way the world 'works', or doesn't, too many people are in the wrong jobs. They are trying or pretending to do things which they are not inwardly fitted or suited to do. This is one reason why outer reality is in such an "upside-down" state, or the world is in such a mess.

## Topsy-Turvy Land

Truly, it is the 'types' who live in "topsy-turvy land". Thus Gurdjieff's references in Beelzebub to the topsy-turvy state of peoples' perceptions.

He links the topsy-turvy state initially with the blocking effect of (what he calls) the "kundabuffer" organ. But that "organ" is basically a metaphorical way of referring to "whatever stops the kundalini rising", or what keeps people in their unenlightened, dysfunctional condition.

It can specifically be the wrong use of sexual energy, or just an absorption in the pursuit of pleasure which distracts us from real life questions. It can even be the right use of sexual energy at the wrong times. (Sometimes sexual energy needs to be redirected, with awareness, to assist stages in our inner development. That entails drawing back for a while from normal sexual expression. If you're sensitive to inner prompting, you'll recognise this.) Sexual energy is the chief factor strengthening hypnosis or sleep in everyday life. (There are passages in ISOTM about this.)

But the "kundabuffer", he says is

> *more than just the sexual aspect of it. It's the shutting of the third eye, the lack of introspection, the lack of self-awareness, the lack of 'knowing thyself'... It's because (people) don't know themselves. (10/Jan/85)*

The screwing-up of the subconscious is right up there for the 'types' - the chief obstacle to the knowing of themselves. They are the most locked-in of all people who see reality upside-down.

Look especially at those types who are subject to the wrong influence of their polar opposites. (See numbers 2, 6, 10, 14, 18, 22 and 27 in the list in the previous chapter.) They literally have their perceptions turned upside-down.

## The 'Types' Problem in Beelzebub

There are various characterisations and clues in Beelzebub about the 'types' problem. For example, look at where he talks of happening to see illogical or irrational behaviour in oneself or others. These displays are said to be put down to peculiarities of character, because what governs typicality isn't known, by the people themselves (p. 560). There is also Gurdjieff's categorical claim, based on his research into this matter, that abnormality in the human psyche comes chiefly from the subconscious area (p. 530).

Even in Atlantis – remember he told me that the understanding of the 'types' went back to that time or earlier – it was clear that there was something other than what it should have been in some peoples' psyches (pp. 819-20). But they evidently had ways of addressing that then and remedying the problem.

Gurdjieff's most detailed account is found embedded in a trivial treatment of something unrelated, where the merits of catching pigeons by their big toes is being discussed (pp. 31-2). (This is how Beelzebub was written. Sometimes gems were mixed with the rubbish.) The treatment here virtually defies all attempts to summarise it. He starts by referring to something hard to get a grip on, but which also yields easily to the touch. There are all the elements of his talk about laws – what conforms and yet is disordered, and a presence that transfers. The centre of stability of a whole working system transfers itself for a while elsewhere. And, due to that, something not expected issues in behaviour open to ridicule to a very large extent. We might just call the outcome "ridiculous or idiotic behaviour".

Having read about the 21 non-true types in the last chapter, we understand the kind of dysfunction Gurdjieff is talking about here. It flows naturally then into his other teaching about 'categories of idiots'.

## Feasts, Toasts and Idiots

As we saw in chapter 4 (above), Gurdjieff introduced his 'Master of the Feast' toasts in 1923. It was a time of great frustration for him, as he constantly looked for ways to impact the psyches of his students. How could he drive them to a point of breakthrough, or breach the impasse in their comprehension?

We now know that "harrying" was the major tool in his arsenal for confronting the 'types'. Short of hypnotising them all, and installing the post-hypnotic suggestion that they should start to see their own ridiculous behaviours, the next best thing was harrying. It had some potential for getting them to display their true essences under stress. General teaching, of course, couldn't be carried out by hypnosis. He was actually trying to shatter the hypnotic effect of the everyday world on them, which wouldn't be assisted by more hypnosis. He could, though, find new ways of doing the harrying, and the "toasting of the idiots" was an ingenious form of that.

Of course, the 1924 car crash was a severe warning to him to stop the unrewarding ego-interplay with his unresponsive students. He did get on with his writing then. But the feasts and toasts resumed later, after he'd done his writing substantially, in the 1940s. He couldn't resist trying as far as he could to harry people into breakthroughs.

There are a number of accounts of Gurdjieff's "toasting of the idiots", but possibly R.Zuber's small book, Who Are You Monsieur Gurdjieff?, contains the best. Zuber didn't meet him until 1943. But he was treated, or subjected, to these weekly experiences on several occasions from that time.

## Harrying the Assembled Company

The 'toasts to the idiots' began with the drinking-glasses of the gathered group being filled with strong spirits – vodka or armagnac. Then Gurdjieff, or his nominated toast-master, would stand and propose each of the toasts in turn. There were said to be 21 'gradations', and therefore potentially 21 toasts to be made.

Gurdjieff didn't name, or give characterisations specific to, the 21 types though. The 'idiot' qualities incorporated in the toasts were more generalised. Perhaps to be more specific about his identified types would have needed him to explain far more of what he wasn't ready to publicly divulge.

So, mostly just single and nebulous qualities like 'ordinary', 'hopeless', 'round', 'square' and so forth were coupled with 'idiot' in the announced categories. Zuber includes one amusing example which refers to a person who doesn't confuse themselves with being the tail of a dog! When each toast was announced, Gurdjieff would identify by name or nickname those at the table to whom the category applied. Everyone was then meant to down their drinks in one gulp and place their glasses on the table for refilling.

Zuber doesn't remember the toasts ever getting anywhere near the whole twenty-one. After one or two drinks, people would start cheating or find ways of avoiding the refilling. The alcoholic intake was a trial for everyone. And we can only imagine how the public naming of each person's "idiot" went down, with the people themselves. Even given the genial good cheer of the master of the feast throughout the procedure, it was unsure to the group exactly what he was celebrating, and why.

Some commentators have suggested that Gurdjieff was merely lampooning his assembled followers as prize idiots. And that, perhaps they weren't quite smart enough to see that. But that is superficial and totally misses the point of the man and his work. He also included himself in the announced toasts as the 'unique' idiot. The harrying had a very real point, as did his highlighting of the 21 categories. All of this was meant to speak to those (at least) in the future who would at last understand what he was trying to do, even if the assembled company couldn't.

### Seeing the Idiocy

He desperately wanted people to see "the idiocy of it all",

in themselves, and in the world at large. He wanted them to see the idiocy as he saw it. To be able to see that, meant awakening to it, and moving out of the hypnotic sleep. He wanted to transform peoples' consciousness.

Everyday life is conducted with a seriousness where people generally don't see, or see through, the nonsense which passes for 'normal' in the public world. That is the "illusion". Some advance may be made with satirical assaults. The Hans Christian Anderson story of the "Emperor's New Clothes", or the Monty Python humour, are cases in point. But the great mass of people draw back, and take things seriously as they usually operate.

Gurdjieff went far beyond what anyone else could hope to do in assaulting and outraging the public personas of people. He just "got away" with so much in that regard. He did it because he could. No social pretence was 'out of bounds'. He was so "unattached", he could denounce or 'send up' just about anything.

**Looking for Someone Developed Enough**

He told me he was looking for someone – anyone – who was sure enough of their own individuality and perceptions to stand up to him. He said that's what he was looking for all the time. He wanted someone who could say to him:

*"Gurdjieff, you're a bullshit artist!" (19/Feb/85)*

Then, he said, he would have rolled around on the floor in hysterics. He would also have asked his challenger, "In what way?" The person would have needed to specify, "That isn't so!" or "This is not the case!" He said he would then have fallen down, and shaken their hand. He just wanted someone else to be able to see the ridiculousness of it all.

He didn't want to always have to be the "unique" idiot. Even if one other person was to join him, he would no longer be unique.

He told me there were no "humble" people at his Institute, only cringing ones:

> *There's a difference between cringing, with a massive ego behind it, and a true humble person.*

So people played the 'cringing' game there, and simply deferred to him. All the time they were waiting for him to tell them "what to do". So they just endured his verbal assaults. He hadn't told them to do anything else! They wouldn't think and feel for themselves, or take charge of their own lives. (He once said the closest to being a humble person was de Hartmann.)

One incident during one of the "feasts" is worth mentioning. (J.Webb, The Harmonious Circle, p. 321). He reports that only once did one pupil, Rachmilievitch, dare to insert his own toast amongst the official ones. He raised his glass and wished Gurdjieff the blessing of God to continue his unique work. There was a silent, awkward moment, which drew only a mildly pleasing glance from Gurdjieff, before the official toasts recommenced. It was a momentary challenge of sorts, but not enough.

(Rachmilievitch was an unusual case, bearing comparison with Fritz Peters, and a bit more needs to be said about that later.)

**Waiting for Individuality to Break Through**

As reviewed in previous chapters, only when a person is sufficiently in touch with and listening to their own essence, will they have the confidence and direction to be their own person. They can then break through the social conditioning, and say and do things others are neither equipped nor game to do. This might be hesitant and partial to begin with. But it increases over time with the inner clarity of one's perceptions.

Gurdjieff illustrated that well, though to an extreme degree. He was certainly doing it with his sending-up of "idiots". It was like, "Call it if you see it!" But he never missed the opportunity to make a teaching point. We are not expected to imitate him in his extreme behaviours. But it is part of our development to know the illusion when we see it, and mark it in some way. In that way the clarity of our inner perceptions is enhanced, and we grow our individuality. So also we come to use our essence as a sufficient and trustworthy guide.

(In my own case, the taking-up of Transcendental Meditation from 1974 assisted that. I gained a lot of inner clarity through this practice. And it seemed to dissolve the 'static' which makes one hesitant to do or say just what one was thinking in everyday life. The clarity and peace I found while meditating started to transfer itself effortlessly into action, before my usual cautiousness could apply any brake. It coupled with and assisted my "remembering of my self".)

When you read ISOTM, you get the impression that developing through the ideas there is only possible if you join a 'school' or put yourself under the direction of a competent teacher. Neither was an available option for me in 1972. I just felt grateful therefore for what I had learnt from the book, but believed I was "on my own" for any further advance.

I can see why Gurdjieff was so insistent in his earlier teaching that those attracted to his ideas should come and put themselves under his tutelage. It was why he didn't even want Ouspensky rushing off and publishing anything until he could check it and approve it. Until the essence was properly contacted and operating within a person, they couldn't be trusted to use or disseminate the teaching competently. You could end up with partial and distorted versions of it. So Gurdjieff would just see himself being "misquoted" again, and that would undermine his work and benefit no-one.

This was another reason why Gurdjieff was always looking for anyone amongst his pupils who had developed the necessary confidence in their own individuality and perceptions. He looked for it as the outcome of his teaching. He was also waiting for someone developed enough to whom he could pass the rest of his teaching. But they never came.

### "Don't Change Anything!"

We find the warnings in ISOTM that people should constantly observe themselves, but not try to change anything there. Of course, it was both unnecessary, and would have been counter-productive, in the early stages of working on oneself. But the caution was never released. We don't know from that early teaching when a person can start to change anything. When I asked him about that restriction, he just said:

*For you to do it for yourself!* *(10/Jan/85)*

That is, he was never going to say to anyone, "Okay, you can start changing things now". He was never going to tell anybody how and when they should do that. There must arise a confidence within each person as they activate their essence, to know for themselves when they're ready to take their own steps. Then, what anyone else says, doesn't really matter. Gurdjieff was clearly able to see when people weren't ready for that, and would puncture any deluded hopes or efforts. Someone who was ready, he would have just let go.

Overall, he saw his role as only that of "pointing the way", or "putting people on the path". He believed intrinsically that he had no right to override the will of anyone else. He might berate and insult you, and point out your 'idiot'. But it was always your choice as to what you did with that. As to exactly what might be changed, and when, it really needed to come from the choice of each individual. It must come from the prompting and readiness of an individual's own soul, which only that individual was properly in a position to recognise.

He knew there could be no general rule at that level. He said he was

*always aware that (different people) were at different cosmic places.*

The clarity of his own perceptions as a tremendously advanced Mercury essence couldn't be imposed directly over the essence perceptions of others. That would have fused them inwardly or thrown them into disarray. They had to translate what he gave them into something inwardly appropriate for themselves. This is where individuality must be sovereign, and that only comes from the activated essence.

**Reality and Illusion**

I once asked Gurdjieff what was the best direction he could give to people in general. He said it was for them

*To see themselves in reality.* *(10/Jan/85)*

Of course, to see oneself as one "really is", is intrinsic to "knowing oneself". But he here put it in terms of our ability to see what was "real" in us and for us. This is a big issue for the essences versus the rest of the types. It is also for those carrying false or unhelpful convictions and beliefs formed in the false personality. In the 1970s they started to call this "baggage". People can have all sorts of 'pet' illusions or "hang-ups". They can be expending energy on things that don't really matter. So Gurdjieff was saying we should aim to "get real". That advice can be appropriately given to anyone, at whatever stage of development.

Strangely, everyone seems to think of themselves as "normal". ("I'm just me.") I say strangely, because, even the most abnormal people still seem to have the same belief. (Just as, even the most vicious criminals have this belief within themselves that their behaviour is justified.) There is a massive lack of awareness, or self-awareness, in so many people.

This is where Gurdjieff expended so much time and energy, to try to display the elements of delusion in those whose behaviour was anything but normal. He once told me it was very difficult for him sometimes not to burst out laughing at the illusions apparent in many who came to him. But nevertheless, he devoted himself constantly to teaching and trying to point out to people what they needed to see and know.

It is a gift, attained at the more advanced levels of 'knowing oneself', to be able to just see through others' illusions and fears. One is then in a position to give accurate aid and advice to those who need it. It must entail being detached enough from a particular outward identity, such as Gurdjieff was. Only then can one see clearly, straight-off, how the mechanism of the psyche is working in others.

(Of course, many of the dysfunctional types will readily tell you "what's wrong with you". Such advice is usually offered freely, and constantly. But Jesus had a saying about this. He said that before people tried to remove a speck of dust from someone else's eye, they should first remove the much larger block of wood from their own.)

**Seeing One Self "in Reality"**

Our sense of "self" is our vehicle for the long journey from sleep and illusion to enlightenment. Ultimately the self is "all one". But it is confined and limited in various ways on the stages of the journey. What most people think of as their 'selves' is only part of the full spectrum of what is there. In this respect it is like the old parable or story of the person who owns a large house, but is confined or shut in just a small portion of it.

Gurdjieff mentions this briefly when talking of 'four rooms' in the preamble to his fourth way teaching (ISOTM, p. 44). It is taken up and elaborated by R.S. de Ropp in his book, The Master Game. He there talks of a crazed king, who lives in the dingy cellar of his palatial residence. While others tell him of the glorious rooms above, he insists that the dingy cellar is the extent of his domain.

There has to be a change in consciousness, and an expansion of awareness before the king will even consider the other rooms above. But we typically construct our sense of self from what surrounds us where we are. Or rather, we see our selves as limited according to the confining possibilities open to us in our perceived environment.

As we journey through increasingly expansive changes of consciousness, our sense of 'self' is constantly renovated. We might be still "just me", but new possibilities are opened up, and we start to feel better about ourselves. This is one way to check how we are progressing on the path. Ask yourself, "How do I feel about myself now, compared to say, two or five years ago?" Is there a noticeable change?

And, there are items of personal functioning we can also refer to in assessing the progress of the self. Am I still locked in circumstances that won't change (karma), or can I advance and develop? Is my life still unhappy and unfulfilled, or am I able to achieve more satisfaction? Am I locked into a series of unavoidable roles, where I have to keep pretending to be who I don't like being? Or, can I relax more and be more of the self I like being? Does my life lack meaning, or am I finding more of it? Does the everyday-ness of living still seem paramount, or can I see and sense possibilities for personal expansion and fulfilment beyond that?

## "Everything is Already Present"

In his recent advice to me, Gurdjieff used another version of the 'room' story/parable. It was no longer a case of being confined to one room of a larger residence, but everything happened in just the one room. This room is still the "self", but over time we become aware of more features and aspects of it. We just see more of what is there.

His main claim about this "one room" of the self was that, "EVERYTHING IS ALREADY IN The ROOM". Everything we need for all stages of our progress and development is already present for us. We're just not seeing it. We don't need to change our location then, just our awareness, to see more of what is "there".

The state of our 'self', or what we currently see or realise about that self, is always reflected in the room or environment around us.

Before we have taken the relevant steps to connect with our inner self, our understanding of who and what we are is constructed from the physical world location in which we were born. If we want to change that, once we sense it can be changed, we are still thinking in 3-dimensional terms initially, and therefore think of changing location to find a more congenial one. The self is still seen as subject to its environment. That understanding is turned upside-down when the essence and intrinsic self is tapped. With our 'centre of gravity' inside us, we now see we don't have to travel anywhere else to change things. The room itself will change around us. Because, the environment always reflects the state of the self, and not *vice versa*. All real changes start from within.

## **Back to the "Pivot Point"**

We find ourselves back at the pivot point reviewed in chapter 1, and the Copernican revolution of the psyche. We saw there how the subconscious ought to be the real consciousness in us, rather than the consciousness typical of everyday living. What is usually "active" in us has to become "passive", and *vice versa*. Then we saw how that worked through the 'personality' and 'essence' as the vehicles of the 'switching over'. The subconscious isn't a help for the dysfunctional types until they can return to the place where their essence is 'true'.

We can restate the switching mechanism involved here, with regards to the 'self'. It involves moving from an outwardly constructed sense of self, where its potentials are based on the surrounding environment, to an inwardly felt one. The 'centre of gravity' has moved from outside to inside.

The discovery and use of the (true) essence is the most important step on this path to self-realisation. It is no wonder Gurdjieff identified the tapping of the essence as the key to tapping the intrinsic self. The psyche itself is vast and complex, and Gurdjieff told me he could write 10 books just trying to explain the connection between, say, the essence and the conscience. But the tapping of the essence is the sufficient trigger for setting the whole complex inner 'mechanism' in motion. That's what starts it all moving.

## **A Curious Aspect of the Enneagram**

Gurdjieff introduced a new symbol in his teaching, not previously publicly known. You will find it presented in numerous accounts of his teaching. He claimed it had been a kind of close secret in certain quarters, but he was revealing it to the world. Supposedly, a person can show their level of development from its features.

# SYMBOLS OF NINE AND TEN

An intriguing symbol from ancient Greece is the Tetraktys or "sacred tetrad". Ten balls or dots are arranged in four stacked layers – 1, 2, 3, 4. It is numerologically suggestive.

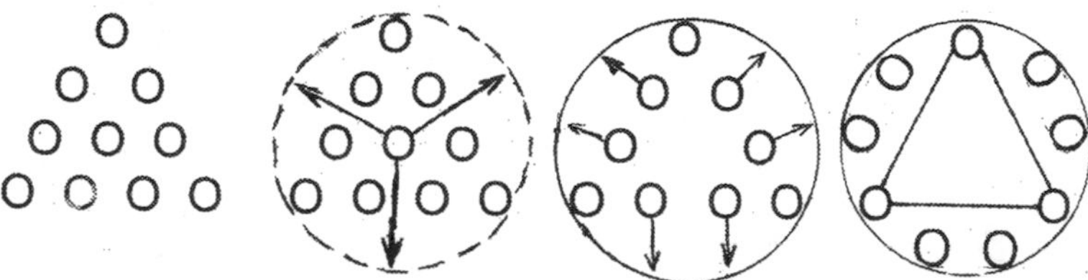

The tetrad will transform into Gurdjieff's enneagram in the following way. The middle ball/circle expands outwards then to enclose everything else within it. The triangle structure remains inside. The three triangle ends expand to the circle, giving one inner structure. The other six move equidistant with all balls around the large circle, so nine spaced points are in place to form the enneagram. A second structure is drawn from six.

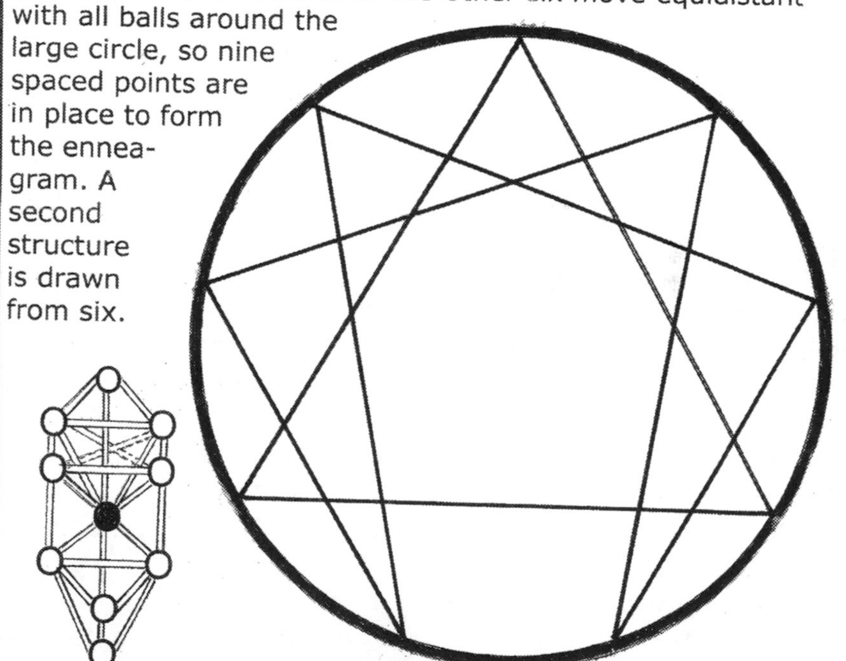

We can see how the traditional Cabbalistic "tree of life" will likewise transform. "All and everything" is then "One".

"Enneagram" means literally, a writing or drawing of 'nine'. Nine equidistant points are marked around the enclosing circle. Then we have internal lines joining each of the nine points, which form two distinct or separate structures.

There are some sketchy explanations of the significance of the enneagram in ISOTM and elsewhere. None that I have seen seem to give an essential or definitive account of it. Numerologically, of course, nine is the number of "completion". It could be that it lends itself to many different applications. What always struck me about it was, the relation it bears to other diagrams of 'nine'. Look, for example, at the further symbols of the 'sacred tetrad' or Tetraktys of Pythagoras, and the traditional Cabbalistic 'tree of life' (included in illustration number 6).

Both the 'tetrad' ("four-lined", or "group of 4"), and the traditional 'tree of life', are 9 or 10 place figures, depending what significance is given to the innermost circle. We could call them "9 + 1" figures. It is what happens to that additional "1" that intrigues me.

The important difference between those traditional symbols and Gurdjieff's enneagram is, the inner circle of the older symbols has expanded and grown. In the Gurdjieff symbol, the 'nine' are enclosed by the 'one', instead of sitting around outside of it.

In other words, what was "innermost" has now become "outermost". Or, the outermost now sits within the expanded inner sense of 'one'. It corresponds to how our inner selves, once found and embraced, move to "take control of the externals". (The 'externals' here can be seen as, firstly the "3-in-1" triangle, and secondly, the blending with the other six essences. [More about that presently.] All are inclusive to the new expanded self.)

When Gurdjieff encouraged me to use the enneagram diagram at this point in the book, he did so with one caution. He said the switch that takes place, where the inner circle becomes the outer circle, doesn't happen in one quick move. But it transfers slowly over time, as a result of growth and fullness.

**The Big Switch**

So, amongst the many aspects the enneagram may have, there is at least one very central feature. It acknowledges the "big switch" in those following and being transformed by their essence. As to the further teaching which explains how all seven essences are related to each person, with only one essence within themselves, the following chapters will address that.

CHAPTER NINE

# The Moroccan Episode

We have now reached the point where a journey that Gurdjieff made to Morocco can be explained, along with what he learnt there.

In all the published material about Gurdjieff's travels, there is no mention of Morocco. Yet he travelled there in 1899, at age 32, and found something integral to his work with the seven essences.

His account of that journey was given in a special trance session, where he involved the medium in the various sights, sounds, smells, thoughts, feelings and impressions of his travelling. It led up to a meeting with a mystical teacher, and his initiation into the cosmic importance of 'seven'. It gave him a new technique and way of proceeding, beyond anything he had read or learnt to that point.

I asked him if it was connected with the "Seekers of Truth" group he talks about in MRM. But he said, "No. That was later." At this stage he was very much working by himself – alone, aching, and driven by his guardian.

## Setting Out

The medium was given a picture of him crossing a bridge. She said, "It's a curvature, like Sydney harbour bridge. The place starts with a 'T'." I mentioned Tiflis. (It became Tbilisi in 1936, the now capital of Georgia. And it has a bridge with a curved top.) Tiflis was just a few miles north of Gurdjieff's birthplace and home in Alexandropol. It would have been his connection with the main roads for his travel.

The medium said he was off on a pilgrimage. He needed to "meet and talk with a man somewhere. It's very important." (Trance session, 17/Jan/ 85). He's 32, and on foot. It all seems such a long time ago. The only mode of transport was horses or donkeys. Or, you just walked. The description went on:

> *He's already in books now. He's already in papers, and using papers, but he's still following an old tradition... He's still not working on his life works. He's still sorting through philosophies and ideas from the past. He has shed the cloak of orthodox religion. ..He's got papers in a carrier on his back – a crude sack. And, he's going to see a man.*

But the fighting he will have to pass through on the way worries him. He thinks he maybe shouldn't go, because of that. But he's "under direction" from his guardian. At this stage he has started to talk with, and listen to, his guardian. He hasn't mentioned this to anyone else, but has recognised this communication within himself. The guardian says he must go.

He's passing people coming from the opposite direction who have been in fighting. It's nasty. He's tired within himself of the conflicts he's met everywhere he's gone in his life – skirmishes, rifle shots, murdered horses and people. He's sick of people being hurt. He feels it all very deeply, and pains a great deal. He can't understand any of this – why it has to go on.

## The Start of His Longer Journeyings

This was the start of his longer journeyings. He feels very sad. He's leaving the shelter of his family, and his group, and starting out alone. All of this weighs on him as he crosses the bridge in Tiflis.

He's heading for north Africa. He's very strong physically, with a very rugged constitution, and has been raised with a great deal of physical exercise. But he carries some scars on his face. It is his inner softness he must confront as he starts off with a sense of mission in dangerous environments.

He's heard of this man that he is going to see. But it is his guardian telling him he must make the journey.

Both his father and his uncle gave him some money for the trip. It all added up to a thousand roubles. He also sold some of the books he'd collected since he was 17, which were a rare commodity in those days. Most of the money is in roughly-minted gold coins, with a few of lesser metals. They're attached to his body in a pouch.

He travelled on foot, trying to avoid the main towns. He felt sickened by people, by society. He made his way roughly around the top of the Mediterranean and through the Pyrenees into Spain. We find him next waiting for a boat at a Spanish port.

He is sitting on the quay, near an embankment. The medium sniffles as she feels his emotion. There are a number of children around him. They're dirt poor and in tatters. It must have been a hard economic time. His heart goes out to the children. They're dressed in rags, made from a home-spun sack material.

He can hear his father saying to him, "Don't give away your riches". Of course, this meant to not just give away what you are, or what you know. But it also applied to his money. But he feels deeply for the children, and says "humpph" to his father's caution. He starts to give some of his smaller brass and copper coins to the impoverished children.

(He was always generous, and couldn't keep much money together. He worked in demanding and ingenious ways to collect funds sometimes, but he kept giving it away on others. He never had much sense of, or respect for, material things. At this stage also, he had no sense of a future to be saved or prepared for.)

**Travel by Boat**

He boards the wooden punt-like boat. It's got sails made from animal hides, with many holes in them. There are supplies of salted fish on board, and they stink.

His fellow passengers are a group of Mauritian workers, with black shiny skins, returning home. And there are a number of Arab-looking people. There are also animals on the boat. Gurdjieff stands out with his lighter skin, and wearing his Cossack-type suit. People start to talk to him, but he doesn't understand the language.

Wherever he goes, he attracts people. He has that charisma about him. He's actually an isolate, but his self-containment emanates a kind of energy. The energy makes people curious.

I was not given the name of the Spanish port or the place he arrived in Morocco. But it was a short trip. The two countries are only about 15 miles, or 25 kilometres, across the Mediterranean at their nearest point. It would make sense for the ferry to operate there.

## The Moroccan Atmosphere

Getting off the boat, it is just very, very hot. He's never experienced heat like this before. His clothes make him very hot, and he doesn't know what to do with them.

He then walks into a bazaar in a walled city. Everything is the colour of sand – all the walls and buildings. Everything is built with blocks of mud-bricks, with a slurry over them. And there's straw everywhere, and it smells like donkeys, pigs, chickens, everything in together.

His spirits start to lighten, and he's feeling better. He can hear music, made by tiny bagpipe-like instruments. They are "wailing" away.

Inside the walled city there are palm trees, people, and a lot of noise. Black figures are walking around everywhere, and women totally covered with veils. Even their eyes can't be seen.

He is now totally taken by the whole scene. He thinks he's finally found something that is "real". He's starting to feel alive.

## The Meeting

The man Gurdjieff was looking for is not hidden away in a back-room somewhere. He is sitting in the middle of the bazaar in the middle of the city. He's sitting under a cloth awning. The area is spread with tables and chairs, where people come to drink coffee and smoke their hookahs.

In the far right corner Gurdjieff sees the man. He is smoking hashish from a hookah. He's a mystic. He has big black eyes. Gurdjieff yells out "Me!", and is motioned to come and sit by the man.

He finds himself totally within the aura of this man. He says to himself, "The wisdom of the East", and feels he is going to get a great deal of wisdom and information from this man. He relaxes with the smell of cooking lamb wafting around.

**The Man**

The man's name is "[a]Ho-shu-ma-al". (That's how it sounded.) The medium said, "They're telling me I haven't got the first bit right. With the "Ho" I'm being told to roll my tongue under the teeth to get the gutteral sound. Anyhow, it's more like an 'ahhr'."

He is a large man, dressed in a white robe. He's wearing gold somewhere around the hands. His hair is up. He doesn't cut it. He has the hair-do of a Sikh, and the robes of an Arab. This man has been to India. He is an Eastern mystic, but of Arab or middle-eastern descent, from Morocco.

This is Gurdjieff's first real encounter with a total mystic.

(Gurdjieff was a Mercury essence, but mystics have the Moon essence. I presume the recounting of all the sights, smells and details of the trip leading to this encounter have a special significance in their "picturing". They are the currency of the Moon and the 'mystical', and will appeal with more force and validity to those of the Moon essence. The trance medium, who was obviously a 'Moon', was delighted with this trance session, and often asked why we couldn't have more like it. Gurdjieff was in charge of what was transmitted during our trance sessions. He brought in more 'pictures' and impressions later when explaining his frustration after the Paris Institute was set-up.)

**The Hashish**

I asked about the significance of the hashish, and the part it played in this mystic's teaching and practice. I was told it was "part of the cult". It was what the groups following this practice engaged in. However, everything could be done without it, and that was "up to you". Gurdjieff took it up.

The spinning exercise which Ho-she-ma-al gave to Gurdjieff reminded one of the "whirling dervishes". When I later asked Gurdjieff about the significance of his visits to Turkey, he said that "Morocco and Turkey were virtually one". It was a continuing episode for him. He was inducted into this "Dervish type learning", and the "Sufi traditions", in Morocco, and he went to Turkey to continue that learning. It was a "group" experience or 'religion' rather than solitary one, and they also smoked the hashish together in Turkey.

(Although not aware of Gurdjieff's Morocco visit, J.G.Bennett comments that the Naqshbandi Order of Dervishes were known to have spread to Morocco and beyond. <u>Gurdjieff: A Very Great Enigma</u>, p. 51.)

**<u>The Importance of 'Seven'</u>**

This is where the importance of the number 'seven' came in strongly for Gurdjieff. They talked about the cosmos and the number seven, and planetary conjunctions. What Ho-shu-ma-al had to say was a total and complete revelation to Gurdjieff. He'd known about it and thought about it before, and read about it. But he'd never seen it previously with such incredible clarity.

The man drew diagrams on the table with his finger. Gurdjieff attempts to unload his sack, to bring out his papers and drawings. But the man says, "No, no. That's not it." He already knows what is in the writings, and tells him not to worry about his books any more.

Gurdjieff is trying to explain to him what he already knows. But the man says,

> *No. Don't know your wisdom, but <u>feel</u> it. If you know your wisdom, write it down. But it's too long for you to write it down now. You've got to know it (inwardly?) first.     (17/Jan/85)*

This approach sparks Gurdjieff's mind, and becomes the catalyst for much travelling, wandering and seeking in the years ahead. It all came from this encounter.

Then the man told Gurdjieff about the hashish. He had, in fact, known something about it and used it before. But this man told him more particularly how to use it, and explained its "mysteries". It was intimately connected with the spinning exercise, and "knowing through feeling", and developing the heart chakra.

**Using the Spinning Exercise**

I'll detail the spinning exercise in a moment. When Gurdjieff was given the understanding of it, he started to perform it himself according to the recommended timing and cautions. (Once a month when the full stage is reached.) But he told no one else about it, and wouldn't pass it on to anyone else until he had assimilated it properly and knew its point and worth.

It is not the sort of practice one can immediately employ to its full extent, or necessarily expect to see immediate results from. It can take time. Gurdjieff also wouldn't pass teaching on to others until it "fitted" with other things in his overall understanding. He used it by himself for just over 5 years.

Then I was told that "something happened" after those 5 years, when he was 38, which triggered off the effect. Then he "got right into" the whole mystique, or mystery, of the hashish and the spinning.

He reiterated to me again that the hashish is not necessary, for me or others, to use the spinning exercise. He entered into that side of things as part of the cult that came with his learning and teachers in Morocco and Turkey.

**Spinning**

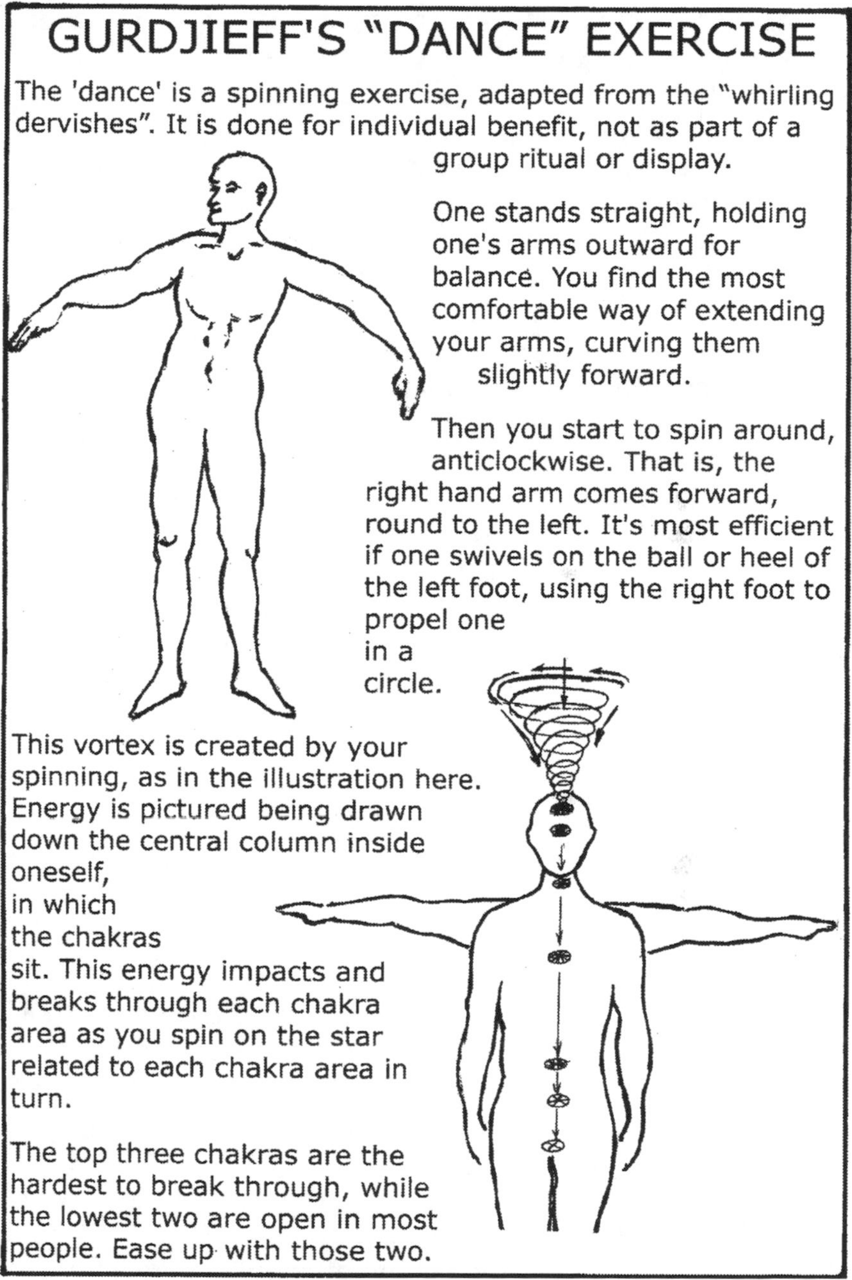


I'll explain the spinning exercise – known as "the dance" - in sequence, to cover all the elements.

First you take up a stance with your arms extended outwards, and curved slightly to the front – as if you were embracing the trunk of a huge tree. The arms need to be extended to assist your balance when spinning.

The right balance and 'feel' are important, to make the movements as smooth and harmonious as possible.

Gurdjieff talked of having himself performed the dance in a heavy overcoat, of the sort he was accustomed to wearing. It flared out during the spinning to provide a further counter-balance for his movements.

He told me I could get the same counter-balancing effect by using four lead weights, of a few ounces. They are attached to four cords of about two and a half feet (75 cms) in length, spaced equally to hang from a cord belt around the waist. (I found some suitable lead weights amongst my fishing tackle.) The lead-weighted cords should hang to about the level of one's ankles.

When spinning, the lead-weighted cords flare out. This gives a smooth momentum. Then one can lose oneself in the sensation of the spinning, and concentrate on the other things that need to be kept in mind.

Gurdjieff said it is best done with bare feet, for grip and steadiness, and on the ground outside rather than inside. The spinning is done most efficiently by swivelling on the ball of one foot, while the other foot is used for propelling oneself in a circle.

**Anti-Clockwise**

The spinning is done in an anti-clockwise direction. That is, your right hand comes forward round towards the left hand position. You proceed in sets of seven turns at a time. That progression is via seven spaced portions of a small circle.

Then you take a step to the right, to begin another set of seven turns on another small circle.

It is best for a start if one completes only one set on each occasion. Concentrate on mastering the basic movement and sequence in that one set. Get the technique right first, before attempting any prolonged spinning.

**Warnings**

No-one is ready to attempt the complete sequence of spinning straight off. It is simply too much for the body to cope with. You may have a heart attack if you ignore this. So we start off with just one circle, not more than once per week.

Then we graduate, after several weeks, to doing 20 to 25 turns at a time, no more than once per week. (Even the full 'dance' sequence should not be done more than once a month, when we've reached that stage. And the full dance is best done at the time of the Full Moon.)

It is simply not necessary to do the full dance more than once per month. There will only be a negative effect if you do it more often than that. The body has to cope with, and recover from, the backward flow of energies that it induces. So, be conscious of the powerful effect of the technique and treat your body with respect, not over-taxing it. If on any scheduled occasion you don't feel like going ahead with it, then DON'T DO IT. Give more time and space.

Also, you MUST use the "bow" exercise (explained earlier in chapter 6) over the same period of time as you're attempting the 'dance'.

The spinning exercise is best done at night, when you're shortly to retire to bed and rest. If done during the day, you should not engage in any physically demanding activities for a few hours afterwards.

**Absence of Dizziness**

One surprising feature of this spinning exercise may be noted. Ordinarily one might expect to feel giddy after spinning around a few times. Children typically do a bit of spinning like this, and find themselves dizzy, and inclined to fall and stagger about afterwards. However, as long as you approach the practice of it in the recommended way, and don't try to stop abruptly after you've been in full flight, giddiness need not be evident. When I allowed myself to taper off the pace and relax as I finished, I found I could walk away with an almost absence of dizziness or discomfort. Of course the body was drained and tired, but I did not end up in a screaming heap. Probably this was also due to having worked my way through slowly to the stage of doing the full dance. So, take it slowly, and avoid any big reaction.

**The Full Dance**

The full dance consists of seven sets of seven turns – a total of 49 in all.

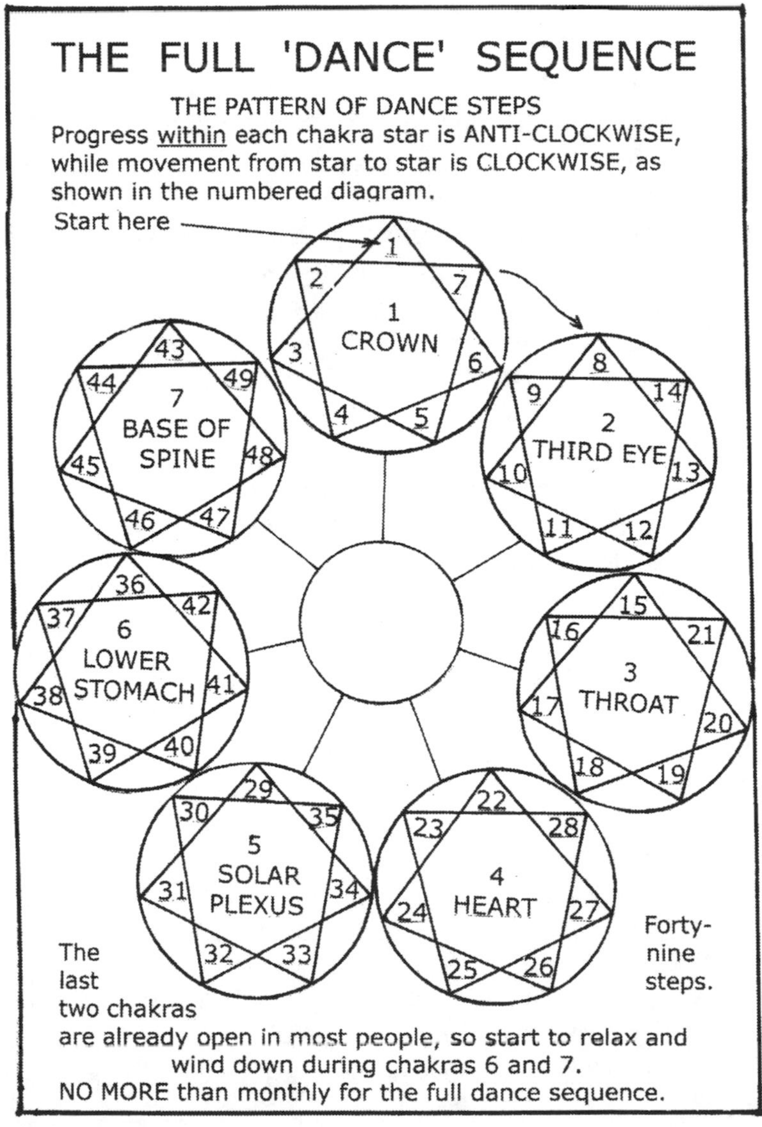

They are arranged according to the included diagram, where all the steps are numbered. Here we have sevens within sevens, and stars within stars. Each smaller star is a junction point in the larger star.

You will notice that, while each individual turn is anti-clockwise, and you progress around each small circle/star in an anti-clockwise direction, the progression around the larger star is in a clockwise direction. (You can see all this from the numbered steps in the diagram.)

You will also see that, each of the smaller circles/stars relates to one of the seven chakras in your body. You start with the uppermost crown chakra, and work your way down in sequence. (See chart of the chakras in chapter 6 above.) Imagine the chakras situated along a circular tube that runs down through the middle of your body.

It is important to know roughly the location of each of your chakras. Because, you need to think about, or picture, the effect of the spinning and the energies invoked by it, on each of those specific chakras in turn.

This is one reason why it is important to master the basic spinning and the sequence of steps prior to attempting the full dance. You can then concentrate on the other aspects of what is happening in the full sequence.

**The Energy Vortex**

An energy vortex is created by one's anti-clockwise spinning. It draws energy down from the cosmos through the chakras along the central inner column/tube. (A depiction of this is included in illustration number 7 above.)

As you spin, picture and feel this downward spiralling energy, boring into and breaking through each of the chakras in turn. Concentrate for the first seven turns (of the first star) on getting it to come through the crown chakra. Then the turning on the second star is working on getting the energy through the second – third eye/Moon – chakra. And so forth.

Gurdjieff said most effort and practice is required for the top three, head, chakras. The fourth and fifth (heart and solar plexus) still need clearing. But he said almost everyone today has the sixth and seventh chakras already cleared. So little effort or concentration is needed for those final two.

You still need to go through the whole 49 turns (when doing the full dance), but you should use the last two stars for starting to relax and slow down. Once the full pattern has been completed, you get the maximum benefit.

(As additional advice here, Gurdjieff said to picture and feel the energy being drawn from the 'outside' as we work our way by spinning through each of the chakras. That is, when working on the second ('Moon', third-eye chakra), see the energy still coming from outside, and going through the first (crown) chakra in order to impact the second one. And, so on, through the rest of the chakras. This reinforces the impact on each of the chakras.)

**"Don't Forget the God"**

It may take a while to get your head around all that's involved in performing this exercise. That is another reason why the slow lead-in practice is important. It gives the body time to adjust to the demands being made on it. But it also allows you to get a grip on all that needs to be kept in mind. But there is one further part to be added.

Gurdjieff said, "Don't forget the God", or "Don't forget the prayer". We ask for assistance in what we are trying to do. This reference is deliberately vague as to who or what one is asking for assistance from. Basically one is acknowledging a power or intelligence greater than oneself. It may be "the Absolute", or "the Source", "All That Is", or whatever. That's up to you, and what you're comfortable with. Certainly Gurdjieff clearly acknowledged in many ways that he knew there was a power greater than himself behind everything.

When he told me to start the spinning at our very first trance session in late 1984, he said I should picture the face of my guardian. That will do. The guardian is your connection with all things higher. He said, "When the God is remembered, you will feel an energy arising in your being".

He said not to forget this request for assistance, because without it one wouldn't get the spiritual benefit and breakthrough. (But this request is made just prior to performing the exercise, rather than being something else to remember while doing it.) There are, of course, purely physical benefits that come from the spinning exercise, which you will get anyway. He said it acts to eliminate toxins from the body, and it also balances a meridian system that we have. (There are points on each of our shoulders and hips. The spinning aligns them horizontally with each other. When that horizontal balance is achieved, the vertical meridian flows can work properly. He said that gives "total alignment of the body".)

## The Effect of the Full Moon

As I mentioned earlier, when one has reached the stage of doing the full dance, at the Full Moon is the best and most advantageous time to do it. This is a useful reminder both for doing it, and for not doing it more than once per month. (It doesn't have to done on the day when the Full Moon is 'exact', because the Moon is basically "full" for 2 or 3 days both before and after that.) It won't hurt to do it at other times of the month, but you won't get everything you could from it. The Full Moon gives one additional benefit.

As you know, the Moon has a pulling effect on bodies of water, or liquids, on the Earth. This is what causes the swelling and ebbing of tides in the oceans. I was told it has an effect on the fluids in our meninges. (These are the membranes which envelop our brain and spinal cord.)

To get this benefit, one needs also to take up a particular yoga position for ten to fifteen minutes shortly after doing the dance. (Oh dear – so much to remember!) You kneel on the floor, or ground, and lean forward, extending your arms out in front of you on the ground. The head is tucked down.

At the time of the Full Moon there is a greater possibility of these increased meningeal fluids dispersing, especially after the spinning. The yoga position gives maximum likelihood of their "moving", putting pressure on the pituitary and pineal glands, for "awakenings that can happen around the brain". That will stimulate further insights.

## Using this Technique

Gurdjieff said it took him "5 years to smash open all the

chakras by using this technique". That was by using it in its full form every Full Moon.

It is a "clearing" of the chakras. That is to enhance their functioning, and especially for the one associated with one's own essence. It also prepares the way, from the top down, for the rising of the kundalini. (But it only prepares the way for that. It does not, of itself, stimulate or trigger the rising of the kundalini. One need not be concerned that anything will be set it motion prematurely in that regard by performing the dance. The soul will protect you and not allow that to happen prematurely. The timing of the rising of the kundalini lies properly with the choice of each person's soul.)

A further specific claim he made to me here was – the downward spiral of the spinning "physically changes the molecular structure of the brain".

Gurdjieff recommends its use, always in conjunction with the "bow" exercise, for those working in a "group of seven". (I will explain that group experience, as Gurdjieff led us through it, in the following chapter.) The dance exercise also applies the necessary "shock" to our systems for bringing the conscious and subconscious minds into alignment. It is also important for any "type" in a group of seven, for bringing them back into touch with their true essence.

At other times, Gurdjieff also said this technique works to explode, or implode, the outer ego. That is, it disrupts its dominance in one's life, and brings it into balance. And it promotes one's individuality.

**Importance of the Technique**

One can see from its many functions, and the part it played in Gurdjieff's own development, that this is an extremely important technique.

I had previously taken it that Gurdjieff had worked with the "feeling" aspect of knowing from the time of 'grandma's advice', when he was 13. He must have. When one never does as others do, and doesn't automatically trust advice from others, then one is only left with a knowing that has to come via one's own inner feeling. But there is obviously an even stronger, ramped up, more developed sense of working from one's feeling, when the input from the subconscious becomes much stronger.

Apparently Gurdjieff hadn't been applying this "feeling-knowing" to his "book learning" around age 32. If he had been, the advice from his Moroccan teacher wouldn't have been so illuminating for him. He had resorted to trying to figure out the general teaching mainly by intellect. So the importance of how one knows one's wisdom was impressed on him from that time.

When I looked for background information on the dances of the Dervishes, all I could find was a solitary reference in one book on dance. It said that the Dervish form of dance originally had an astrological significance. Gurdjieff told me that was all I would find in any book published in English. Apparently though, more could be found in books published in other languages.

Gurdjieff's trip to Morocco had been crucially important for his own 'education'. It changed everything for him from that time onwards. It gave him far more than he could have found in Turkey or with any other Dervish group. The mystic teacher he met had put together elements from both Indian and Middle East traditions, in an original and highly independent way. Gurdjieff could not have got that anywhere else. But neither would he have been capable of grasping what he was given in Morocco if he had not been sufficiently advanced in his own development when he went there.

## Subconscious Connection

In one way we could see the happy coincidence of factors here as "chance" or "accident". That's the way Gurdjieff often presented his breakthroughs to his pupils when explaining how things had happened or come together in his life. Those who came to him weren't sufficiently aware of how the subconscious worked. It wasn't until later that Karl Jung brought the notion of "synchronicity" to public attention. What looks like 'coincidence' to the ordinary everyday consciousness, which only operates with linear causal links in physical reality to explain things, is actually far more. We need to get into the subconscious to understand how things really work in the world. The links between things are far different, and operate in different connective ways, than simple physical conjunction.

So, the 'mystical' Ho-shu-ma-al had linked important elements from two spiritual traditions, and found how to stimulate subconscious thinking and perception to a high degree. (It was apparently his "master's-piece".) This alerts us to how 'fragments' of the truth can be found in diverse spiritual traditions, and await those who have the perception and insight to put them together productively. In his own life and experience, Gurdjieff went on to put together the elements of the "fourth way". (See chapter 5 above.) He achieved that himself. Almost certainly, Ho-shu-ma-al's own contribution had importantly enabled that.

In his general teaching, Gurdjieff said to take the wisdom from the East, and use the methods of the West, and then 'seek'. He was inviting people to start putting even more spiritual insights together. This is something our subconscious minds can do, once we get into them and start working seriously with them. We can start productively with the "spinning", and the tapping of our essences and intrinsic selves. There is no doubt an intriguing parallel between unifying the fragmented parts of our 'selves' and starting to put together fragmented parts of genuine teachings spread throughout the world. We will start to "see" how they fit together. The level of knowledge that we can individually attain depends upon the level of 'being' recognised within ourselves.

## The "Special Oath"

Gurdjieff did not mention the oath he took in Morocco when he led the medium through the details of that episode in 1985. It was not until two months later, when I asked him about the special oath he mentioned in HCG (p. 11), that it came to light. He told me then

*G: That was in Morocco.*
*DH: Can you tell me exactly what the oath was?*
*G: No. ...And I won't.*
*DH: It was something personal and private?*

*G: Yes. It's not written. There are several reasons why I can't impart the oath. It was in a different tongue to the understanding of English, that – should it be translated – it would lose its essentialness. That, it was a strict secret when it was given. It's an oral oath, not a written oath. Very, very few people know of this, and it's made by a soul. It's made from a soul to a soul. And it's nothing that will benefit anybody by reading the information. But it's very valid that the oath was made. I'll tell you briefly and very succinctly what the oath was about. (One) commits (one's) life to the task of aiding lesser mortals in the process of "knowing oneself".*

*DH: Am I allowed to publish this?*

*G: You can print that material, but no more. (2/Apr/85)*

In fact, he didn't give me any more than what he told me I could publish.

I wasn't expecting an explanation like this. I was just gathering background information on the oath, or oaths, he refers on other occasions to having taken. He links it usually with a decision he made to live an "artificial life", to promote his teaching for the benefit of others.

A number of references might lead one to infer his oath was made around 1910-12. In fact, in HCG (p. 11), written in 1932/3, he says he made it twenty-one years earlier (= 1911/2). Obviously these references were meant to obscure the place, time and content of the oath, while acknowledging one had been made, because it was a strict secret.

I cannot tell you whether such an oath was required, or voluntary, or might even have been a condition for Ho-shu-ma-al to tell or show him certain things. But the fact that it was made heightens the mystical nature of the interchange between the two men. And it underlines the importance of what Gurdjieff learnt and has now passed on from that meeting.

CHAPTER TEN

# The Group Of Seven

We saw earlier (in chapter 3) how a "group of seven" played a significant role in ancient Mesopotamia and ancient Greece. In the Epic of Gilgamesh there were said to be seven sages who laid the foundation of the city of Uruk. In ancient Greece the tradition of the "seven wise men" was maintained for hundreds of years. Chosen political and civic leaders there, always kept at the number seven, met periodically. It was openly for administrative purposes, but the underlying reason for such a grouping was spiritual.

"Seven" was the pre-eminent number of the wisdom tradition, or the "ancient wisdom". Wisdom is the knowing or understanding of the heart (or feeling, or subconscious), as opposed to the 'head' or intellectual knowing. We now know, through Gurdjieff's work, that these groups of seven were a collection of the seven essences. Or, they were composed of men (in those days) chosen to contain one of each of the seven essences.

(Essences of both sexes are equally valid here, there being no spiritual reason for distinguishing male and female in this matter. In practice, in the modes of essence expression, there may be some differences in the abilities exhibited. The medium once said during our trance sessions, "The female Moon can do things the male Moon can't". True. (Female Moons make the best mediums.) And also *vice versa*. But both are equally "mystical", holding the same energy. There is just some variation in the expression of it. And you also get a 'drift', with some women displaying more typically male qualities, and some men displaying more typically female qualities. So there is overlap. The same applies in the case of all the essences. In all genuine group work however, there is no distinction of gender.)

It wasn't until I began to research the ancient sources

that I saw the wider social functions these groups of seven might have. It was a dimension that wasn't highlighted or revealed in our trance guidance for the two groups of seven I was involved with in 1984/5 and 1988/9. Both of those groups formed, ran for a number of months, and then quickly disbanded. They were 'pilot' groups, experimental in a sense. Their focus was on another crucial function or culmination of the gatherings. We'll come to that presently.

I have often wondered why these two groups were of such short duration, but they fulfilled the reasons we were given. Things moved on in other directions. More recently, Gurdjieff has intimated that much of the point of them was to assist my understanding and give me material for this book, to pass on to others.

**Forming a Group of Seven**

It is quite clear, of course, that you simply require one of each of the seven essences to form a genuine group of seven. They must be people who are either at the point of finding or knowing their true essence, or close to it. The proper culmination requires that every member be able to 'feel' and know their essence, and then extend that.

Recruiting the Uranus person into such a group may be a problem. Their orientation differs from others, and they won't see the point of the group in the same way. Some kind of subsidiary motivation for them will help solve any problem. This may come naturally from them, with their own inner guidance giving them a reason to be there. Or, thought may need to be given to how they are invited, in a way that appeals to them. You may even find that, even when they are being true to their essence and expressing it, they won't recognise it! Such is Uranus. Take this into account.

Recruitment (in general) was not a problem in our 1980s groups. People just sort of "turned up" or obviously presented themselves. It was clear that it was being arranged or orchestrated somehow "from the other side". There are forces on the other side who are committed to advancing this work, including the guardians of the people involved. Inclusion in such a group was a rarely offered opportunity for personal development.

There were two minor problems with these first two groups. With the first, one more person than was needed wanted to be part of it. They had to be turned away. With the second, there was one reluctant attendee. We had to take the group to them briefly to include them in it.

It is always useful if one of the attending seven has a psychic gift for providing guidance or messages for the activity. The Moon in my first group was the medium who was channelling Gurdjieff and others about the project. Guidance, when needed, was always at hand. With the second group, I had the Mars essence from the first group, whose abilities as a clairvoyant and seer subsequently opened, to guide our activities. But we were told that extra help was given to us to establish these initial groups.

**Reference to Groups by Gurdjieff**

We know that Gurdjieff moved from Russia to France in order to – amongst other things – locate the full range of human types. He was still studying the 'manifestations' of all the types, and conducting experiments with them. But he was certainly moving towards some sort of group work with his students, as apparent from the plan he outlined in HCG. For those he described as heading towards self-development, he announced the future formation of three kinds of groups (p. 38) – an outer, a middle, and an inner circle. And of course, Gurdjieff's depiction of the work of Ashiata Shiemash, in Beelzebub, involved a group, or groups.

I picked up the reference in Katherine Mansfield's Letters to one group of seven at the Institute in 1922. It wasn't amongst Gurdjieff's English students, who weren't ready for it. But it involved the cooks in the kitchen. Mansfield said that Gurdjieff asked her to sit in the kitchen with the cooks, and just watch. She was placed in the corner. And there were 6 other people working there. (Letters, p. 680.)

This was done without any explanation of the purpose for such a gathering. The cooks just got on with their cooking, and Mansfield sat and "watched". When I asked him about this combination of seven, he said:

> *It was more personal for (Mansfield), because she was too heavily imbalanced in the intellect. I wanted her to witness people who were fairly in-depth type people while they were doing natural everyday type things. It was a lesson for her. ..But yes, it did make up the seventh energy, and she was (the) Uranus (essence). (10/Jan/85)*

So he was using this group of seven for correcting a personal imbalance. It is not clear if Mansfield replaced another Uranus essence who normally worked in the kitchen, or if Gurdjieff took the opportunity to provide one through her to simultaneously assist the cooking group.

He was always experimenting and "trying things". He obviously understood something about the dynamics of groups of seven when he put Mansfield in the kitchen in late 1922. But it wasn't until the following year he went off to observe the Basques in the mountains of Spain, to try to understand more of the dynamics of group work. Those people were working with an oral tradition that went back thousands of years, and had used the groups as "survival cells" in circumstances of stress and threat.

As I mentioned previously (chapter 4), most of the advice Gurdjieff gave us for our 1980s group work came from his Basque experience in Spain.

## The Set-Up for a Group

Basically, you need a round or oval table for the seven to sit around. It could be done with just a circle of chairs, but the table seems more convenient. Such a table had come to me, by 'coincidence', a few years previously. When my maternal grandmother died, an oval cedar-wood table built by my carpenter grandfather had been left to me.

You need the circular formation for the energy work, where all seven are included in the circle and facing each other. It also underlines the "round table" principle of King

Arthur. There, all players are equal participants in the proceedings.

When the Mars essence person and I ran our second group, we sat outside the circle. We were present in the room, but not included in the energy proceedings of the circle.

The order of seating for those in the circle is crucial. It follows the sequence shown in earlier diagrams of the seven essences in a circle.

Certain basic information needs to be circulated to those participating. I ran off copies of those important things, and it is all reproduced in this book. The "bow" exercise should be started straight away. The "dance" exercise can be started when people appear ready for it. But it is more for individuals to do on their own, rather than as an organised group activity. Each will choose to do it, and advance with it, at their own pace.

**The Proceedings**

Much of the 'work' of the group is very informal, and needs to be to fulfil one of its crucial aims. Of course, many things are reviewed at the table in relation to the purpose and ongoing progress of these meetings. Everyone's views and contributions are welcomed, and there is much free discussion of what is happening in peoples' lives in general. Intrinsic interest is inevitably aroused by the interplay between the seven very different people who now face each other.

There are constant discoveries about how each of the seven sees, reacts to, and handles a range of life circumstances. There is constant comparing and contrasting, where each gets feedback about how others see them, and realises how others' orientations are different. There were processes of discovery in the first group before I had the characterisations of the essences on paper to distribute. We were initially all given a task to perform (choosing and potting a plant), and then we had to report back as to how we handled it. That started the realisation of differences.

This is a crucial process in coming to know oneself – as the essence one is – and to equally see how the other essences are distinctly different. We tend to grow up in life assuming everyone is basically the same. Or, we interpret differences as weaknesses or failures, or just oddities. But in crucial aspects they aren't. We need to come to the realisation that there are just different, but equally valid ways, for people of different essences to operate in life.

Mars types tend to want to jump in and become the "life of the party". Poor old Saturns tend to sit back and think, "Why can't I be as assertive as that?" But they will take their obligation to attend meetings very seriously, and won't miss one unless another unavoidable obligation intervenes. Uranus may inject a comment that goes off on a strange tangent, leaving everyone wondering where it came from, and where it's going. Venus will try to smooth over any hint of conflict. Mercury will be sitting there, taking it all in, and trying to work it out. They will address any request for further explanation of anything. Jupiter will try a manoeuvre or two to steer the proceedings in certain directions. And the Moon will either make a few ponderous comments, or try to give a differently inspired picture of where it's all heading.

That's just a selection of possible behaviours, and many others are just as likely within the known orbits or motions of the planets.

**Gurdjieff's Comments on Such Groups**

He said, quite early:

> *It's very important..that each of the planets – and therefore each one of the people – have the opportunity to interact with the other planets in some sort of concerted way. Because, the whole basis of the group - the whole reason for the group – is to get people to become whole. (They need) to accept every facet of their personality. And that is what this does. (3/Dec/84)*

Group members, then, know the point of the activity in these terms.

If there is a problem with people who want to dominate the proceedings or ride their hobby-horses, this itself is something that other group members should openly address. It is all part of coming to see and accept all aspects of our selves. (Gurdjieff commented that, if there is something a person can't accept about themselves, it is most likely to be a dysfunctional-type behaviour. Highlighting it helps to jettison it.)

In the first group, at some point, in order to avoid shallower interplay, we were told to "count to ten" before saying anything. This gave people time to think whether what they were about to say was worthwhile or not. It avoided some less-than-helpful comments and distractions.

There were a couple more exercises given to us. Everyone was asked to try to identify their "chief fear". Recognising and working on that is a big advance in anyone's life. Also, once we were asked to (anonymously) write down what we saw as the strengths and weaknesses of the other essences in the group. This was meant to be constructive, not a complaint process, or one of praise or blame. The assessments were read out, to assist everyone in seeing themselves from another point of view. It was to help everyone identify and accept every facet of themselves.

## The Harmony and Energies

When I included the diagram of the seven essence placements at the end of chapter 6 (above), I called it the "harmony of the seven". That is the only sequence or formation where the essences/planets are all balanced with each other. That gives harmony.

Occasionally someone would say, "Something doesn't feel right". Almost certainly we would realise someone was out of their normal sequence, for some reason, and correct it by moving back.

When a group of seven people are placed in this harmonious order, certain energies operate through those sitting to the left or right of each person. There is another kind of balancing energy between polar opposites.

At the conscious level, each essence assists the essence to its left, and is assisted by the essence to their right. For example, the Moon can handle its own constant fluctuations better when assisted by the precision and orderliness of Mercury. Mercury is assisted by Jupiter to organise the outward details of its life. Mars gingers and reinforces Jupiter in its plans for action. Uranus trips Mars into asserting itself. Saturn calms the capriciousness and instability of Uranus. Venus softens the austere commitment of Saturn. And the Moon sparks imaginativeness and change in the unified, self-contained world of Venus.

You will also find this complementary coupling of essences in the natural friendships that people tend to form in the everyday world. People who are "best friends" are most likely to be those who essences complement each other. (Like, a Moon and a Venus, or a Mars and a Jupiter. These essences sit next to each other in the harmonious circle.) Although, people of the same essence gather for group projects that further their shared interests and passions. (Martians gather in dramatic societies, and Mercurys in research projects.)

The complementary subconscious force works in the reverse direction. The Moon sparks the imagination and intuition of Mercury. Mercury makes Jupiter consider the details and implications of its planned actions. Jupiter alerts Mars to the broader framework. Mars shows Uranus how to be more decisive. Uranus shows Saturn how to be freer and less restrictive. Saturn gives Venus strength and determination. And Venus gives the Moon more softness and co-ordination.

## The Polar Opposites

Here we have the classical opposing energies, balancing each other. The Mercurial temperament (active, spontaneous, ever-changing) is in balance against the Saturnine one (grave, gloomy, heavy). Mars and Venus are the archetypal contraries of male/female, active/passive or forceful/soft energies. While Jupiter is outwardly jovial and forthright, it balances the cool/cold inward fluctuations of the Moon. Uranus, of course, has no polar opposite, which is why it is so unstable.

We see with these complementary and contrary influences how each essence – where a person knows their essence – is part of the harmonious whole. There must be sufficient confidence in 'knowing oneself' through one's essence here. The very energies which modify, enhance and balance each of the essences in this group, are those which cause dysfunction in the 'combined types'. That is when people aren't secure in their essence selves, and wrongly identify (inwardly) with a different energy.

Of course, dysfunction arises because of other socialising factors during upbringing, and won't arise during group work. But the confident identification of one's true essence is necessary to participate properly in, and benefit fully from, the work of the group of seven.

**Another Enhancement**

We were told about another enhancement to try during the time of the first group. Before each group meeting I would chart the positions of our seven planets, at the time of our meeting, from an ephemeris. Then, before we took up our normal seats, we would stand around the table in the formation of the actual planets at that time. This was just for a few moments. It emphasised our link with the actual planets, and connected us with them. "As above, so below."

**Spinning the Energies**

Later in the work of groups, when everyone is quite confident of their own essence, something else can be done. It involves "spinning the energies".

Now, the energy can be pushed around the circle in two ways - clockwise or anti-clockwise. I've heard some pretty strange explanations in other kinds of groups about "what is best" or "what should be done" in this regard. (For example, some 'bright spark' said a group should be guided by the direction in which water swirls when going down the plug-hole in one's bath!) The basic explanation that Gurdjieff gave here was, it depends whether

> *the energy is being subconscious or conscious. And whichever way you send the energy, it's going to affect you on a different level. Sending it anti-clockwise, it will affect how you interact with other*

> *people. Send it clockwise, it affects how you see yourselves.* (19/Feb/85)

He then said that the clockwise movement was "not so necessary". It gives some enhancement to how we see ourselves at the conscious level, but it doesn't change very much. However,

> *If you push it anti-clockwise then it will be consciously much more beneficial for your lives.*

The anti-clockwise direction is working with the subconscious. So by pushing the energy in that direction, it impacts everyone's subconscious. Further, he added:

> *you won't see it actualised there (in the subconscious). You'll see it actualised in the conscious area.*

This practice supplements the explanation I gave just above, of the effects of the complementary positioning of the essences. Everything I said earlier remains valid, but the spinning ramps it all up.

It is necessary to have a preliminary understanding of how each of the adjacent essences can supplement its neighbours. That learning takes place during the conscious interchange between group members, via verbal exchange. But once what is happening there is realised, it can be done quicker and more effectively by the spinning of the energies.

## Gurdjieff in a Group?

I was curious about whether Gurdjieff had himself been part of a group of seven, at some time. I asked him about it. The answer was "no". That is, not in the sense of the kind of gathered group we had in 1984/5. What he had done was, "type people in their natural essences" over a long period of time. (He observed and identified them.) It took many years. He had "watched them closely, and had the interplay" with them. And this was "not knowingly to the souls themselves".

But he was learning, and putting it together, by that means. He said it took him "a long, long time". And he was doing it with a view to developing his teaching about it. Only after that did he apply it inwardly to himself. The awareness he developed as he carried out his observations was in a sense also being referred inwards to himself as he did it.

What is interesting about this is, anyone who wants to develop this aspect of themselves can do the same. I mean, if there is no immediate prospect of finding or being part of a deliberately formed group of seven. One can always look closely for the behaviour characteristics of the seven essences in people one knows and interacts with in daily life. Becoming acquainted with the list of essence qualities from chapter 6 will give you a flying start. But don't forget to "feel", to get the sense of who is what essence. See if you can put together the complete set of seven.

This will expand one's awareness. When one is working with awareness like that, it short-circuits the need for so many "shocks" in one's life. When one can see how the essence functions "out there", it is an important part of coming to know more about oneself.

Within a group, each person's gathered awareness of how all seven essences function in life, is crucial to its natural culmination. We finally need the 'feel', not just of our own, but of all seven.

## Further Effects of Spinning the Energy

Four months into the work of our first group, Gurdjieff came out strongly, urging us to consciously send energy anti-clockwise around the whole circle. It was like, "You have to do this. Get it all moving." We were told to discuss how the subconscious flow would affect everyone to their right, and then embrace it with gusto.

He said:

> *this is the prime concern, for Mercury to give (its energy) to Jupiter. It is (then) Jupiter's bound obligation to give it to Mars. It is Mars' bound obligation to send her essence, her energy, her*

*aggression, to Uranus. It is Uranus' bound obligation to send almost capricious sort of tendencies to Saturn. It's Saturn's responsibility to send her staidness to Venus. And it's Venus' bound obligation to send her affection to the Moon, because the Moon is notoriously cold. That's what it is – silver, aloof, cold. And it is the Moon's obligation to send her intuitive vibrations to Mercury. And we're working (here with) the very verbal, right through the gamut to emotion. From intellect to emotion. (19/Feb/85)*

It then became clear we were moving into "something else". After the accentuated subconscious pushing of the energy to everyone's right, the effects were discussed and noted. Behaviours were being changed or modified.

But Gurdjieff was intent on pushing if further. The spinning had to progress with gusto. This was then to affect not only the person/essence to everyone's right, but go much further. Everyone's energies had to go round and round the whole group, until there was a further merging. The whole group was melting into an extended version of "all seven in one". Every essence was to take on board the qualities of <u>all</u> the other six.

I was told, "This also is melding". (You may recall that in chapter 5 above, Gurdjieff explained the process of combining our three outward functions into one as "melding". They were to melt and weld into one unified, harmonious whole.) Then, as an extension and complement to that, all seven essences where to be melded in each person. This was the second aspect of the "complete person".

The complete person is "3-in-1" in their outward functions, and "7-in-1" in their subconsciously driven functions.

## Another Exercise in the Second Group

Another exercise was given to us to speed up this outcome in our second group of seven. We were told:

*It's too slow to wait for everyone to come into harmony together.*

This was almost 12 months after the second group had formed, and they were being pushed to the culmination point. We were given the picture of seven gateways.

> *Gateways... behind the first gateway, about 10 paces back, is another one, and then another, and then another one. There are seven. And these are symbolic... They must be walked through. They must be gone through... that's part of the initiation. .. As one goes through each gateway, a change takes place. (28/Jul/89)*

Each gateway represented the essence characteristics of one of the seven, going from Uranus to Mercury. Group members were being asked to exhibit the characteristics of the corresponding essence as they walked through each gateway in turn. This wasn't just during our group work, but for people to do in their everyday lives outside the group.

Obviously some members of the group were "dragging their feet", holding the overall progress back. So each individual was asked to take the steps themselves, to exhibit their grasp of the other six essences. I asked how this was possible prior to the overall melding of the group, and was told:

> *The melding..takes place above, once (they) go through. It's too slow a process (otherwise, with the way the group is going). Once somebody has gone through the seven (gateways), they're melded with the others that have gone through. .. It's too slow to wait for everyone to come into harmony together.*

That was an interesting variation to the melding process. It still required the "learning" that had come from the group participation, for each person to have acquired the feeling and knowing for expressing the other six essences.

**The "Seven in One" State**

The melding of all the essences in a person brings them

to a state of wholeness in themselves. It creates a "new type" of person. You will find Gurdjieff's reference to this in HCG (p. 27). He there talks of how modern 'civilised' life today has taken away peoples' ability to advance naturally to this new type, by disrupting the path of natural essence expression for getting there.

It is possible to advance to this new stage – of becoming the "new type", without work in a group of seven, as Gurdjieff himself had done. But so much is against it in the outward organisation of human life at present. At least, without knowing where one is heading, and why, the possibility seems extremely remote. But with the understanding now given, a person may follow the steps just outlined – in the absence of a 'group' to join - and achieve it for themselves. The point of joining a "group of seven" is to greatly speed up the process, with full awareness, with six other willing participants.

**The "Eighth Nature"**

This new type can also be found in the writings of Hermes, where it is called the "eighth nature". Look in the book of the "Pymander".

It is called the eighth nature, obviously, because when all seven essences have been combined into "one", it is the further stage, and therefore the "eighth". It can be represented diagrammatically by extending the drawing of the seven chakra points in the human body upwards. The eighth chakra is found in a straight line up above the human head. (You will find pictures of a chakra, or chakras, up above the human head in many Indian spiritual philosophies and manuals.)

In explaining how the seven essences are melded together, Gurdjieff said "you still always do it in your own essence". That is, your original essence remains your original and primary essence. But the other six parts are "invited in" to supplement that. So, if you like, the original essence then functions like a director or chairman of the board. But we will feel more "complete" than we ever have before, and be able to function in a far more adequate way in everyday life.

When I asked for further explanation of the changes the melding and eighth nature would bring to people, he told me it approximated to "a state of total well-being". Previous feelings of alienation or separateness would dissolve. It was like being "enlightened into person-hood, but not Godhood".

He said there would be "subtle physical changes" in a person. This might be noticeable in photos after 3 or 4 years. Each person would become more of the way they saw themselves internally. Or, they would manifest more of the way they would like to see themselves.

It would have been handy to document this in our case with photos. But when each of our groups culminated, people just went off in all directions to other things.

## Some Research about the Melding

When the first group disbanded in mid 1985, I had to wait until 1987/8 for the next important advance in teaching about it from the other side. In the meantime, I had plenty to work on and research from Gurdjieff's messages and our group experience. I also had many other things to cope with at a tumultuous time of my life.

I put a lot of things together at that time, and later, which help to explain the melding in other ways. For example, I found the correspondences between the human eye and the harmonious positioning of the essences in the group of seven. Both are circular. If you're looking for something circular in the human body, it is obviously the eye, our organ of 'seeing' or visual perception.

I went to Iridology books. The charts of the eye all show the distribution of bodily parts and organs in the same basic pattern as that of the essences in a circle. Look at the left eye. The thyroid, Jupiter's gland, is shown at the Jupiter position. The heart is at the Venus position. Mars corresponds with the autonomic nervous system. And so on. It was a surprisingly perfect match-up.

The significance of the left eye was that, it corresponded with the "right brain", which is the path into the subconscious. The essences arise from the subconscious.

# THE EYE, TRIANGLE, TWO LAWS

Iris diagnosis charts typically include features listed below in this free-hand left eye map, where bodily parts or functions match essence positions.

Osiris

MERCURY
MOON
VENUS
SATURN
URANUS
MARS
JUPITER

FRONTAL BRAIN CEREBRUM MENTAL/SPEECH

POSTERIOR BRAIN CEREBELLUM SENSORY

HEART UPPER BREAST

SPLEEN LOWER ABDOMEN

PROSTATE SACRUM COCCYX ANUS

AUTONOMIC NERVOUS SYSTEM

THYROID THROAT

Starting once more with the ancient Greek "tetrad", we see the resemblance to the older Egyptian form of the "eye in the triangle". It is a representation of the two important laws in Gurdjieff's teaching ('3' and '7'). Triangles are demonstrably "3-in-1", and the eye gives us the melded "7-in-1" of the essences, inside it. 7 + 3 = 10 = "1".

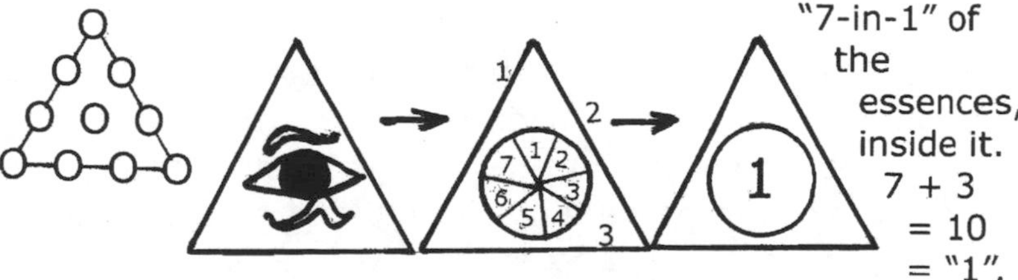

Beyond that, I began to look at the representations of the 'eye' in ancient Egypt, of which there were many. It was one of the most important symbols there. Then there was the god Osiris, the most well-known figure in the Egyptian line-up. Look at his name – Os-iris. It is taken to mean "place of the eye", "seat of the eye", or even "sits in the eye". It is written in hieroglyphics with an eye and a throne-seat.

Then it appeared to me that the old and familiar symbol of the "eye in the triangle" was a representation of the two aspects of the melding in Gurdjieff's teaching. It was sort of apparent in Pythagoras' "tetrad" symbol I included earlier, at the end of chapter 8. But the "eye in the triangle" gives more definition to the central circle included there.

We needn't be concerned with later uses of this symbol, whether they might be deemed to connect with other things either positive or negative. If the eye situated in the triangle seems a bit "sinister", look at its meaning, as "being of the left side". We <u>are</u> working here with the left eye. In ancient Egypt it had a distinct meaning from the right eye.

Notice that the triangle has three sides, joined together. These are the three aspects of a person (the mental, emotional and physical) unified into one structure. The circle of the left eye represents the harmonious positioning of the seven essences. They are melded together into one when all seven parts are contained in the one person. The symbols are "mystically simple" once one knows what is being referred to.

Gurdjieff highlights two fundamental laws in his writings. They are the laws of 'three' and 'seven'. They are of prime importance for anyone engaged in his work. They are the keys to the rest. In order to become a "complete person", there must be the melding of the three outer parts, and the seven inner parts, in an individual.

The simplified symbol of the circle inside the triangle could be taken as representing the melded and complete person. Once the significance of the two parts has been realised, the simpler symbol can suffice.

**And Then Osiris**

I wasn't expecting the next development in the unfolding of the work with the seven essences, but it was perfectly logical. It began in December 1987, at the lesser of the two important astrological conjunctions of that year. (After the major "harmonic convergence" of August.) The ability of the Mars essence person (from the first group of seven) opened as a clairvoyant and seer, after we'd attended a hill-top meditation together.

When she had settled into her new role, a few weeks later, two things happened. Firstly, people started "turning-up", and I was asked to form another group of seven. Secondly, as that group was coming together, a new guide appeared and introduced himself as "Osiris".

I subsequently came to understand that, the successful melding of the first group of seven had "awakened Osiris". Osiris is the embodiment of the "complete person", the "spiritual man", and the "eighth nature". This was integral to what had been going on in ancient Egypt.

I hadn't expected that dimension of things to open. Gurdjieff had given no prior warning about it before the trance sessions stopped. When Osiris "arrived" in May 1988, he took over proceedings for the second group. He did not present himself as superseding the Gurdjieff teaching however, and sometimes referred me to passages in <u>Beelzebub</u> to explain things. But we had already gone further than Gurdjieff was able to in his lifetime. (Only with his help and guidance, of course.) We had a melded group of seven. And that brought Osiris into play.

Of course, I was now asking myself why we had a "god" to guide us. But it wasn't that unusual. When you look at any of the seven essences, their names are also those of the planets <u>AND</u> of the gods of antiquity. The 'god' element was intrinsic to the process. If you look at the 'gods' Jupiter (Zeus) or Mercury (Hermes), or any of the other essence personages, the accounts of them in ancient times illustrate to a large extent the qualities of the essences. That meant they could at least be taken as teaching models for the essence characteristics. But, more than that, they were also the embodiment of them. And they had a definite independent existence.

The same gods and characteristics crossed cultures. The Roman Mercury was the Greek Hermes, the Thoth of the Egyptians, and Odin/Woden in Scandinavia. Likewise for all the essence gods. Over time I came to see the 'gods' as "powers of the subconscious". To the Egyptians the realm of the gods was the "tuat" or the "underworld". It doesn't take much imagination to see the underworld as what we call the subconscious today.

Beyond that, I asked Osiris a number of questions about ancient Egypt. One would've expected him to know the answers if he was indeed Osiris. He gave me interesting and illuminating answers which went far beyond anything I could hope to find in books. But he said he wasn't there to "prove himself", and he told me he only works with people who are genuinely seeking their development. Anything else is a "waste of time".

## And the Ninth?

If there is an "eighth nature", then one might also expect there would have to be a "ninth". Nine is the completion of the numerological series. Gurdjieff had sometimes said the law of seven was also the law of nine. (He had nine points marked around his enneagram.) Somehow, eight and nine both grew out of seven. We saw how that operated with the "eighth nature", when the seven essences melded to give us the eighth. Beyond that I was still searching in 1988.

Then I found a Gnostic tract attributed to Hermes, in the published Nag Hammadi library. Its original title in the manuscript was missing, and it had just been called a talk about the "eighth and ninth". Inside the tract was the claim that the eighth would display the ninth! There was no explanation in the writing about what this eighth and ninth were. But how could it be anything else than the eighth nature referred to in that other Hermetic writing, and its logical extension to the next place?

When Osiris was available, I asked him about it. He confirmed the existence of the ninth nature, saying:

*You're on the right track, but don't try to delve too quickly.* *(27/May/88)*

I had to experience the eighth, and at some point it would direct me to the ninth. But I don't necessarily expect that any time soon.

**Further Gurdjieff Input**

Thankfully, Gurdjieff's further contact with me this year (2012) gave me the opportunity to gain his direct comments on the eighth nature and Osiris.

He said Osiris was like all the gods, who operate in a different reality to the one we know in the everyday world. We could see them as "symbolic". But there can be an interplay between us and them. Don't assume though, that everything in that area operates like a kind of super-computer. It was accurate, however, to see the gods as "powers of the subconscious". That's exactly what they are.

He confirmed the "eighth nature" was indeed the "new type" he spoke of. As he put it: "It is a reality". None of his pupils (during his lifetime) ever reached the stage of the eighth nature. And he said that he himself, when he was here, "wasn't fully into it". He was still working with it. (So the melding of the 7 essences opens the door to it. But further work on oneself is necessary to experience or realise all there is to it.)

It intrigued me that Gurdjieff himself wasn't fully into the eighth nature. But then I remembered the claim in the 1984/5 trance sessions, that he hadn't gone as far as he might have. He had trudged a long, lonely, gruelling path, and there was no company or supportive understanding for him to continue on at such a level. He couldn't even get his students to take the simplest steps with the subconscious. So, who could he tell or pass the information on to, as he went further into the eighth nature? This is one reason, probably, why his last book is smaller and less complete than the first two in the "All and Everything" series. Of course he had to record and mark that stage somehow, and give some characterisation of it. But the explanation wasn't complete, because his own experience of it wasn't.

**The "I AM"**

In fact, you will find that his last book, LIROT, is about the eighth nature. (No wonder he had said to me that "no-one understands it".) Look at the strange 'evaporation' of previous abilities and certainties that he talks of there. That is transitional as one moves into the new way of operating. And the "I AM" is central to it – finding and understanding what that consciousness involves. One's attention needs to be focused in the "now". ("I am" is an acknowledgement of oneself in the present moment.) One needs from there to find the "ableness" within oneself to proceed and take control of the various elements in one's life, like a "master".

He says it was "hard work" for him, along with everything else he had to cope with in the 1920s and beyond. So he "took rests" occasionally from it, and indulged his "vices" at times. His work on it was slower. So not much more can be said about it here.

He had talked at times, during his lifetime, of putting together a collection of sayings from previous Masters in his final book, but didn't get that far. It does give us a clue though, as to where to look for further information about the eighth nature.

# CHAPTER ELEVEN

# Beelzebub

Gurdjieff wrote four books. Beelzebub was the first, the longest, and the most important of them. He described it to me as his *piece de resistance* - the best and most substantial of his offerings.

During our trance sessions, the medium described how his eyes lit up at the mention of it. They literally twinkled whenever it was referred to. It was his great joy and consolation – the greatest product and record of all the long gruelling years of his efforts to pass on his message.

It is a massive work, with 48 chapters and almost 1240 pages. All and Everything was the overall title that Gurdjieff gave to the "three series" of his writings, of which Beelzebub was the chief part. I asked him (in 1985) if that meant he had indeed included "all and everything" in it. He affirmed that he had. The medium also said "most of what he wanted to say" was in it.

(In a later, more recent message [November 2012], he now says that the book is "only the tip of the iceberg". From where he is now, there is no doubt much more that he could say. But during his lifetime Beelzebub was his best effort to record what he knew for posterity.)

The big difficulty with Beelzebub, however, is that it is impossibly obscure and demanding in its presentation. One has to "read and read", and "dig and dig", to begin to get anywhere with it.

## Why He Wrote it as He Did

He told me he wanted it known why he had written Beelzebub in the way he did. Much of that has been explained already, mostly in chapter 4. There, I recounted his constant frustration at being unable to communicate the simple steps his students needed to take for their real development. They were constantly looking for more and more involved intellectual guidance and illumination. They were so "locked in their heads" they effectively wouldn't credit, and refused to follow, his simpler personal development instructions to them.

Some intellectual grasp of his teaching is called for. We need to be aware enough of what we are doing, and why, when we follow his instructions. But we cannot advance spiritually by just extending and refining intellectual comprehension. Something more, something different, is needed. The students at the Institute were extremely resistant to Gurdjieff's attempts to get them moving in that area. This is why so much was ignored or "misquoted", or recast or reinterpreted, to suit already fixed understandings of their conscious minds.

After years of torment and frustration, which eventually drove him to his unbalanced state in 1924, and the car crash, his only real way forward was to write an obscure book. He had to somehow record what he knew for future generations, which was his "life mission". But it was presented to his existing students as a great puzzle and enigma for them to confront and solve. He told me he wrote it (as he did) "for the smart-Alecks at the Institute". Like, "They wanted complicated, so I gave them complicated". But it was more complicated than they could handle.

Gurdjieff had wanted to show them his genius in presenting the steps to spiritual development in the simplest peasant-like traditions he had come through. His preference always was to use very few words, and to exhibit the essence of any matter in the most concise way. In himself he combined these two main elements of a pretty rough and raw peasant upbringing with an absolutely genius mind. (It was also greatly assisted by the comprehension of his feeling-perception and the direct input of his guardian.) So he could understand the most complex things far ahead of the intellectuals of his day, and yet the "real" explanations for him were always the simplest. In a sense, it was just as easy for him to talk in the most complicated way as it was to put it all simply. But the simplest explanations were the "real" ones.

**The Putting Together of Beelzebub**

Gurdjieff began working on Beelzebub as soon as he was able after his car crash. The first draft was substantially written in the three years from 1924 to 1927. Then there were important revisions from 1930/1 and afterwards. He completed and signed-off on the final drafts shortly before his death in 1949.

Copies of some of the earlier drafts were circulated in Gurdjieff groups in Europe and the U.S. But the work was not published and available to the general public until 1950, shortly after his death. Translations in other languages followed.

**The Method of Writing**

The book is virtually incomprehensible to most people. In his last book, LIROT (pp, 4, 5), Gurdjieff describes his observations of those listening to readings of Beelzebub. He says that only those people previously familiar with his ways of thinking and talking grasped a few fragments of what he was saying. Others without that background got virtually nothing from it.

This gave him pause to consider whether he should re-write everything he had produced prior to that point, to make it more accessible to a wider range of people. But he was too "locked-in" at that stage. He didn't have the time it would require. In 1933 he dashed off the more reader-friendly booklet, HCG. Unfortunately he got nothing but a horrified reaction from his existing students over it. It just proved it was impossible for him to "go simpler" and get anywhere with it then.

So he had to "protect" his teaching both by recording it somehow, and at the same time cater to those who would have charge of it when he was no longer here. He couldn't push credibility beyond what his existing students could bear, but simultaneously had to give them something they judged to be worth preserving.

Ouspensky, apparently, said that Gurdjieff was an excellent speaker, but hopeless as a writer. They all seemed to have their opinions about how and what he wrote. Even if they understood how difficult it was to try to convey precise ideas across several languages, his trying also to cater for the different 'types' and their levels of mental and soul development was a hugely complicating factor. Add to that their lack of comprehension of the 'soul' aspect of things, and you start to appreciate how many dimensions he had to encompass when putting pen to paper.

Gurdjieff was firmly up against the limited mentality and understanding of his most devoted pupils, and still couldn't bridge that impasse. His dubious health would hardly permit any attempts to work around that by the mid 1930s. His guardian wanted him to get as much as he could on paper, however obscure. So he persisted with Beelzebub as the main vehicle of his message.

**Half-thoughts, Locks and Rubbish**

Over time he explained to me his method of putting Beelzebub together. He was playing an intellectual game with the people who couldn't get out of their heads. He said he wrote "gobbledygook", sending-up the ways in which his followers kept embellishing what he told them. There were "words between lines", and "lines between other lines", and he often really only wrote half-sentences, half-thoughts. You may find, as I used to, that one would struggle to hold the sense of all that was being said in a long, involved sentence, only to find I hadn't grasped the ultimate point being made. You'd get to the end, and then re-read it, to try to find what had been missed. But it just wasn't there!

Certainly there are many passages where he writes "normally", and the literal sense of what he is saying is clear. But the relevance of much of that is hard to see. It is also difficult to grasp "what is linked with what" in the broader sense. Some of his clear passages seem superfluous and irrelevant to anything of importance. You ask yourself, "Is this leading anywhere, or not?" In general, we can't get a flow of comprehension to put together a conscious grasp of his overall message. So, if you asked someone who had read it: "What was Gurdjieff essentially saying in Beelzebub?" they couldn't tell you. The conscious mind was nonplussed.

He told me, the reader had to "extrapolate out by a very complicated, convoluted thinking pattern". Maybe every fifth sentence he would "throw a key into the whole five sentences". Only "very, very complex minds could cope" with that. Most people hardly finished reading his introduction to the book, and never went further with it.

Then he talked of the "tricks and keys, locks, padlocks, chains, and God-knows-what" that he included. He excelled at this in his most creative period, in the revisions from 1930. This is when he sometimes talked of "burying the dog deeper". (Or sometimes it was burying the bone deeper, to make it harder for the dog to find.) But he was burying the dog – his readers – in a mass of irrelevant, contrived and pompous verbiage. They might indulge their intellectual curiosities in following this or that 'clue', or even imagine that they were "getting somewhere" with the book. Maybe many of the insights gleaned were genuine. But show me anyone who has got a firm grip on the underlying message.

Then there was the "rubbish". He included a lot of that. There were "red herrings" (distractions and 'dead-ends'), and what he called a "calibration of rubbish". There was "ultra rubbish, little rubbish" and otherwise just plain rubbish. It was there to "catch the mind off-guard". He said that behind every rubbish point there was something really fundamental to his teaching. So the mind had to keep adjusting itself to try to cope with that. Just when you were thinking, "What the hell was that?" he would hit you with something shooting off on another tangent. Most people don't know where they stand when confronted by such tactics.

Not the least of his befuddling tactics are the "made-up" words used throughout the book. He gives clues about the meaning of some of them by direct comment, or some of the component parts are suggestive. But many of them contain allusions from numerous languages the reader may not be acquainted with. Or, some are totally "made-up" in a way that gives us no point of reference for deciphering them.

All of this might have been a kind of revenge on the "smart-Alecks" in the 1920s, but it also worked to deflect the misunderstanding of critics and debunkers. They couldn't grasp anything sufficiently to mount even a half-cocked attack on it. They risked exposing their ignorance by doing anything other than claiming to be insulted by the manner of writing. Most of all though, Gurdjieff wanted the simple steps to spiritual development preserved for those who could use them later. And he packed a lot of the accrued wisdom of his life in there. It is just a pity that, to date, it has been too tedious and off-putting for ordinary seekers, who need something simpler and more up-front to work with.

**Finding the Sense in It**

Overall, he was still following the great dictum which guided his life from teenage years, to 'not do as others did'. No one else had ever written a book like this. He had done it completely in his own way. But it still remains for us to find the sense in it.

He affirmed that there was indeed a central core of absolutely crucial teaching in the book. He greatly regretted that he couldn't have stated everything he had to say much clearer from the start. But it was simply beyond the bounds of what he could write and get away with in those times and circumstances. He knew no-one would have believed him if he'd done that. He would have lost his credibility with his current followers, and the teaching wouldn't have been transmitted for future generations.

In 1984/5 he told me that the thrust of Beelzebub had to be changed. He wanted the book "taken out of the hands of the intellectuals" and given to "more everyday people". In that regard – (much to my horror) - he told me it was up to me to

> *get the keys, and undo it all, and turn it into simple language (5/Feb/85)*

He obviously had a higher estimation of my abilities than I did! It would be a monumental task to completely revise that book. (His own estimate in LIROT was that, it would have taken him just as long to simplify his first two books as it did to produce the complicated versions. That would be years, when he knew exactly what he was doing.) He did, however, provide me with a number of comments and clues for unlocking the meaning of the book, which I will explain here. There were some main points he wanted to make in Beelzebub. Everything else of importance there is claimed to relate back to them.

**Seven Salient Points**

Gurdjieff told me there were "seven salient points" in his book. I cannot find any published reference where he said that explicitly. He did refer at times, during his lifetime, to there being "keys" in the text. It is worth noting, also, that in the introduction to his second book, MRM, he talks of acquainting people with, and clarifying, seven sayings there. He claimed he'd collected them in his travels, written on ancient structures, and they expressed the highest, profound truths. The first one is spelt out for us (p. 4), but the rest have to be searched for.

He then explains parallels and differences between MRM and his first book Beelzebub. In particular he is talking of his ability to hide serious ideas behind an externalised form of saying things. In Beelzebub he had done it by sheer volume, but intended to do it in another way in MRM – by the intrinsic merit of his expression. This at least acknowledges that there were serious ideas hidden in Beelzebub, and probably by direct implication also seven of them.

Of course, the "seven salient points" were the simple but profound truths, or directions, he had wanted to communicate to his followers for some time. He had been working on "writings" for this even before the Paris Institute was set-up. He had a bundle of papers, either on the desk in his Institute study, or he carried them in a rucksack on his back when he went travelling. But he could make no advance in getting people to "work on themselves" with that kind of guidance, no matter how much he rewrote them in that form.

Eventually, as J.G.Bennett and others tell us, he was seen burning a large collection of papers at the Institute around 1930. When I asked him about that, he said:

> *Leave that. Nobody would have understood it. (5/Feb/85)*

He disposed of all his previous writings in a bonfire after Beelzebub and MRM were well under way. There was no-one he could have entrusted the older writings to.

His description of the seven points in Beelzebub as "salient" is interesting. That could mean 'prominent', 'conspicuous' or 'striking'. But it can also have the sense of 'leaping' or 'springing' or 'projecting in an outward direction'. Later in the channellings he said that, as I worked through the seven points, I'd find each one was a "locale" or "hub":

> *Each salient point is a hub. And..there's..rays of information coming out of each hub. And as you get to that salient point the other rays will come in around it and support it. ... It's a thing in total. ...It will work for you, not against you, this information. (2/Apr/85)*

So, here is the way to penetrate Beelzebub, as provided by the author.

**How to Find the Salient Points**

It should be perfectly clear by this stage of the teaching in this present book, that meaningful learning only takes place when our subconscious is stirred and engaged. When Gurdjieff worked directly with people, he would employ his preliminary antics to jigger and disrupt their everyday complacency, abrasively summoning the subconscious. When it came to presenting his teaching in written form, there had to be other ways of catering to and stirring the subconscious.

This was a big problem for writing Beelzebub. There, Gurdjieff had an audience willing and waiting for teaching from him. But they were so locked in their conscious minds, something radical had to be done to impact their subconsciousnesses. So you can see why he used all the tricks and devices he did for stalling the conscious mind in its tracks. He needed them to think subconsciously, and use their feeling-perception.

When the normal settled flow of everyday understanding is disrupted - for example, by something insulting, cryptic or enigmatic – we have to look beyond it to re-establish sense and meaning. It's like the conscious mind shouts "Help!", and a distress message is immediately despatched to the subconscious. We are so used to the mechanical predictability of how things flow in everyday life, the intrusion of something unexpected or indigestible provides a kind of shock.

So, if you like, Gurdjieff was extending his strategy of the 'shock' to the printed page. He was quite explicit about this in Beelzebub (pp. 24,5). He said he was deliberately expounding his ideas in a way that was rationally affronting, so that he could thereby impact the subconscious of his readers through their conscious minds.

So there was trivia, rubbish, insult, exhaustion, and any number of conscious-mind-disabling antics to activate the deeper minds in people. If they expected to find any sense in what he wrote, it could only be by the usually delayed deliverance of a response back from the subconscious. So later, after having read something, a time-delayed thought or realisation in connection with it may suddenly pop into one's mind. (He described his concealed ideas in the MRM introduction as capable of being 'made out' only with that characteristic time-delay. They won't strike you straight away, but come to you later.)

This is one reason why his friendly word to the reader at the outset of Beelzebub suggested the book should be read three times. That repetition increases the strength of the mechanism for delivering realisations back to the consciousness from the subconscious. In respect of the genuine ideas he was trying to communicate, the oddness of anything out of character or of a different nature in the text would have more time to gel and resurface.

All his "salient points" have that character. (But of course, there are a great many more significant points spread throughout the book than simply the 'salient' ones. The salient ones are just the 'hubs'.) Those with a functioning – non-sleeping – subconscious may see them sooner. They may even start to feel the oddness or conspicuousness as they actually read them, and be given cause to reflect directly upon them. The subconscious has a vested interest in all the salient and genuine points made there. (It knows.) It will, as far as it is able in a given person's life, kick back on them, to shoot them back into a person's conscious awareness for further attention.

You may find, for example, that hours or days after reading some of Beelzebub, an odd or illuminating thought will suddenly surface in your conscious awareness. It may come while you're buttering your toast, soaping yourself in the shower, or heading off to the toilet. They tend to come when you've relaxed your normal concentration in some way. The subconscious can then bypass one's tightly-held conceptions or preconceptions, and shoot a different kind of thought into the mind.

Gurdjieff also confirmed recently that he

> *wrote Beelzebub in such a way that it affects the mind at the subconscious level.* (17/Sept/2012)

**The First Salient Point**

Gurdjieff said he would expedite my identification of the salient points by directing me to the areas in which they were located. I still had to read through those sections though, and not until I asked directly about a particular claim or passage would he confirm it. He wanted me to "feel" the point first, and thus know it myself.

The first point is in the introductory chapter. I had read that chapter many, many times. There had always been two items of particular interest to me there - "grandma's advice", and the "two consciousnesses" claims.

Grandma's advice (reviewed in chapter 1 above) always gave me inner joy. The claims about the two consciousnesses (also prominent in my chapter 1) gave me a definitive conscious grasp of how Gurdjieff's whole teaching enterprise was set-up. But I'd also done a lot of reflecting on both points over time to get a deeper sense of them.

Grandma's advice was for "me", while the consciousness claims were for "the teaching". Obviously, grandma's advice was the first salient point. (He had said as much when - as recorded in chapter four above – he lamented the failure of the Institute students to grasp that starting-point.) Once you see it, it looks like a dead give-away. How could it not be grandma's advice? I mean, for Gurdjieff himself it was the prime datum, the lever which set everything else in motion in his life. It was the most pivotal advice you could give anyone for their own development. Here was the very practical basis of individuality through subconscious contact – be your own person and do your own thing!

If Gurdjieff hadn't followed grandma's advice, then he never would have got to the point of seeing and expounding his teaching about the two consciousnesses. He couldn't have written Beelzebub in his own way.

## The Second Salient Point

The second point comes in chapter 3 of Beelzebub. It relates to why there was a delay in the progress of the spaceship *Karnak*. In terms of the outer story-line here, a problem had arisen that would delay the spaceship carrying Beelzebub from reaching its intended destination at the original time. The intersecting path of a comet will force the ship's captain to either stop or make a detour to avoid it. You would think the captain would be capable of automatically calculating the best alternative to take here, and make the decision himself. But he brings the problem to Beelzebub, and it then becomes the subject of some general teaching.

Beelzebub relates it back to his experience on Earth, and then draws on the wise advice of his "guide", the Mullah

Nassr Eddin. He says nothing can be done when we are faced with something controlled by powers greater than we are. We can only defer to it and go along with it. And all we can do in the meantime is, make the best of the time and circumstances we're left with.

When Gurdjieff confirmed this as his second salient point in 1985, he added further explanation. Firstly, he said that when confronted by a delaying force in one's life, one needs to face it, and see it for what it is. Secondly though, we need to distinguish between the force itself behind the delay, and the actual problem we've been presented with. We can't fight the force, and just need to accept it for what it is. But any problem we're presented with can, and should, be worked on. That is, we battle the problem, and not what was behind it.

He said to me:

> *We must face problems, or the source's forces higher than our own. We must face them. We must come to terms with them. The soul will not evolve until it confronts the teacher..the source.* (2/Apr/85)

In the face of a karma that we may be facing, or a delay to other life-plans, sometimes we need to experience these in their entirety before any action is taken. Once seen though, the soul always has a way open for grappling with them. So, when Beelzebub talks of using the delay with the spaceship to do something useful, he is not just talking of occupying oneself in a different pursuit. It is not an excuse for a holiday. Any opposing force that stops our progress is still there to be worked with, or the problem it presents. We employ our time working usefully on that.

In this regard, one might consider Gurdjieff's 1924 car crash. He was impacted by a force that couldn't be resisted. He had to learn the lesson from that, and then find the way to proceed around it. He had to get on with the task essential to his life-mission of recording what he knew, even when that meant resorting to enigmatic writing.

So, we don't stop working when we meet a set-back.

Certainly we shouldn't "give up". There will always be a way through or around it.

**The Third Salient Point**

The third point is in chapter 7 of Beelzebub. Look at the chapter title. Awareness must develop of what is there called a 'duty' we have. In the story-line here, Beelzebub's grandson, Hassein, becomes sorrowful, depressed and dejected. The thought has just occurred to him that all the benefits and conveniences he currently enjoys, are entirely due to the dedication and work of people who lived before him. They didn't just "happen", or come ready-made.

Others who lived before him had to invent, produce and provide such things. They might have laboured long and hard, or even suffered to produce things beneficial to him. He could have lived his life without ever giving a thought to their contributions. But when this realisation comes to him, or 'hits' him, he starts to feel he may be under some obligation for what others have provided.

Really, Gurdjieff is talking here about the spiritual accomplishments, teachings and benefits provided to us by those who came before us. And he objects to the word "duty" used in this passage. This is a translation issue. It wasn't translated to express what he meant. He told me it was an "obligation", not a "duty". He also wanted it made clear that this obligation wasn't to those who provided the benefits we now enjoy. It is, rather, an obligation we have to ourselves, to our own being. He said:

> *You have an obligation to your own psyche to investigate what preceded your time. That, much wise information has been accrued, from persons walking the earth. And that, it's to be looked at and assessed – that a great deal of information can be gained, not simply from our (own) life experience.. but from the life experiences that have preceded, by the Masters. .. (The obligation is) not to them, (however), but to the self.* (2/Apr/85)

He also said it was of great benefit to one's soul to bring another person to the same standard as one has reached. It both reinforces what is already known within oneself, and the channels are cleared for new information to come in. Seeing it taken up and used by someone else, lightens what one needs to remember within oneself. More progress can then be made, while always working – of course – from the remembered foundation within oneself.

We can note that Gurdjieff spends a great deal of time in Beelzebub reviewing advice given by those who came before him. He also there gives us the benefit of so much of his own life experience. This is part of paying for the fact of one's own appearance on Earth, which he refers to at other times.

**The Fourth Salient Point**

The number seven was so important to Gurdjieff, he included a second salient point in the same small chapter 7.

As regards the (previous) third salient point, Beelzebub counsels Hassein (his grandson in the story) that he is not yet old enough (at 12) where he needs to involve himself with the obligation to his being. Time enough for that later, when he will become aware of questions relating to essence. But when he reaches that later time, he should also see and grasp the nature of the obligation he would then be under to himself.

But, there is something else more important he should do, even at his present age, to equip himself for his future. He is told he must, unavoidably, be up when the sun rises every day, and forge a link then between his conscious mind and the unconscious parts of himself.

That seems like a very tough regime for a 12 year-old! But Gurdjieff is overstating the requirement to highlight its importance. This is actually something he is recommending that everyone does. But, it is not necessary every day. Once per month is quite sufficient. It is best done on the morning after the Full Moon.

As he went on to explain it to me, Gurdjieff is talking about

> *meditating on the central core of the self...bringing it together at sun-rise... (This is) not metaphorical, it's literal. ...This is the time of day for the consciousness to meditate on itself, where it will find these shattered parts of the self and bring (them) together. ... The rise of the sun after the night of the Full Moon is a very beneficial time for the psyche to fall into pattern by itself. ...      (2/Apr/85)*

It is a kind of meditative introspection. He goes on:

> *Go into the navel, into the solar plexus, rather than the heart chakra. Centre the energy, just concentrating on the radiating energy behind the navel, with the breath pattern... (This will) give many answers.*

## **Grabbing One's Attention**

What initially drew my attention to Beelzebub's advice to his grandson here as a possible salient point, was its being described as an unavoidably necessary practice. Further, its potential for linking the conscious mind with all the unconscious aspects of one's being was a "big", compelling, prospect. To do something like that in a relatively easy way – apart from the onerousness of getting up at sunrise every day – certainly interested me.

Then Gurdjieff's further explanation of it made it even more intriguing and enticing. I'd never been an "early riser", and had always done my best work through the evenings and into the early morning, at least for most of my life. So only having to engage in this practice once a month was a big plus. It was more do-able, at least for me. The meditation, concentration on the solar plexus, and breathing to effect the result, which Gurdjieff added, all opened up new dimensions to what was happening here.

The "centrality" of what was happening also hit me. Here was the fourth – and central – point of the salient seven. We were being asked to concentrate on the solar plexus as the central point of ourselves. (Not the heart, as might have been expected.) And if you picture yourself meditating with the rising Sun on one side, and the setting Full Moon on the other, you realise you are then centred between them.

The "centring" of oneself was clearly integral to the practice. Often we talk of "centring ourselves" as the way to come back into equilibrium. This fitted with the idea of "falling into pattern" by such a means.

Putting one's attention on "the radiating energy behind the navel" invoked another aspect of what was happening here. Commonly we think of the Sun radiating energy, and since we have a solar plexus at the middle of us, this had to be the Sun within us. (Remember the correspondence between the planetary essences within us and the planets of our solar system. Well, we all have a Sun "in here" which corresponds to the Sun "out there".)

From there, all sorts of things started to "fit into place", and I found that it was also a key, and a "hub" for other information in Beelzebub to gather around. (Thus the "many answers" he spoke of.)

**The Solar Plexus and the Sun**

Of course, Gurdjieff had also told me that, when the circle/star was drawn for situating the seven essences/planets in their respective positions, the Sun sits in the middle of them. (See diagram at the end of chapter six.) I had wondered if the Sun there represented the emerging "new type" - the melded person who embodied the 'eighth nature'. It must be connected with that. This is the "new person" who has their own "I Am". The meldings give access to our centre.

In Gurdjieff's previous teaching, the 'heart' was more central to what was happening than the 'solar plexus'. In everyday terms, the 'heart' has always been synonymous with the core or central feature of anything. (As for example, in "getting to the heart of the matter", or identifying the innermost or vital part of anything you care to think of.) But now, in his advice to me, he talked of the "central core of the self" as being in the solar plexus. That is an important change of emphasis. We might ask, "Why?"

There is teaching about the solar plexus in relation to the heart in chapter 17 of Beelzebub. There is a story to be told about that. It happens to be included near the end of that strange chapter which radically challenges the accepted view of our physical Sun.

("That's absurd!" you might say, as you read what he has to say about the Sun there. But he knew that. He even titled the chapter to reflect the overarching absurdity of how it would appear to anyone today. The trouble is, it's seems too obvious to be just part of the "rubbish" he certainly included in Beelzebub. He presents the surety with which the nature of the physical Sun is held today to be something that has never been doubted since mid-Atlantean times. And, strangely, it is by the "instinct" a person can access for sensing reality, which comes from the solar plexus core of their own selves, which enables us to distinguish truth from fantasy. I suppose that means the truth about the Sun "out there" must also be sensed from the Sun inside ourselves.)

I had puzzled over the colours that Gurdjieff allocated to the heart and solar plexus (see the 'Essences and Chakras' chart in chapter 6 above), where he switched the natural sequence of rainbow colours for those two chakras. Yellow "fitted" well enough with the knowing of the heart, and green the autonomic nervous system. But why were they switched to give that result? The answer must lie in his explanation of how the functions of the heart and solar plexus were originally located in a single mass in the breast area. (Beelzebub, pp. 146-7.) In the natural order of the seven chakras in the body, we would assume the heart chakra (number four) would be the centre. But with the separation of functions, we're told we now need to look for it in the solar plexus.

## And the "Shattered Parts"?

He said the sunrise meditation was "literally" for finding and bringing together the "shattered parts" of the self.
In the salient point he mentions the conscious self and

some unconscious aspects. We know from the very start of this book that the subconscious had been separated off from the everyday consciousness. That must be one of the unconscious parts. But there would be at least one more, which so far has been unaccounted for in his teaching.

To somehow bring all the "shattered parts" together is a monumental reunification of the self. If it can be done by these monthly sunrise meditations, then we could hardly ask for a simpler way of doing it. Moreover, if it could be done by a boy of 12, then how much later agony and work that would circumvent!

We are pushed to see a parallel between the shattered self and the account of the shattering of the Earth by the comet Kondoor. (See chapter 9 of Beelzebub.) When that happened, we are told that two bits of the Earth fractured and flew off. They are identified as the Moon and a smaller piece called Anulios.

**The Physical Shattering**

There have been a number of 'scientific' theories about the origin of our Moon. The most widely accepted one today is that it was formed by the impact of a large cosmic body on the Earth, and is composed of materials from both bodies. So Beelzebub's account of the comet catastrophe has an everyday feasibility. But, what about the second fractured piece, which Gurdjieff called "Anulios"?

By reversing the first four letters of Anulios, we get "luna", which suggests it is a second, smaller moon of the Earth. But, no such second moon has been found by modern observation methods. Later in Beelzebub we are told that the Moon and Anulios are further, self-sufficient planets of our solar system (p. 181). While the Moon itself was halted in an orbit around the Earth, Anulios might have ventured further out before being caught in a wider orbit by the Sun. There are hundreds of sizeable small 'planets' in our solar system, and literally thousands of tinier ones. In relative proximity to the Earth, close enough to experience some magnetic attraction from it, we might look at Toro, Eros or Hermes. (They are called "earth-crossers".)

Toro was presented as "Earth's second satellite" in a 1970 publication, after its rediscovery in 1964. That was apparently said, however, to highlight the fragment's unusual orbit. But, Toro is in fact a satellite of the Sun, not the Earth. It travels in space roughly between the Earth and Venus, approaching at times within several million miles of the Earth. But Hermes is only half the size of Toro, and occasionally comes much closer to us, within half a million miles. No other planetary body comes closer to us, except the Moon. So, there are possible explanations of 'Anulios' here.

But nothing of consequence seems to come from further pursuit of these physical facts. If Anulios was identified with Toro or Hermes, what would follow from that? They simply don't have the significance for us that Gurdjieff was suggesting Anulios had. (Some even smaller fragments have also recently been found circling the Earth – at least 4 or 5 of them. But none are big enough to even be classified as a "small planet".)

We wonder what Gurdjieff's reference to Anulios was about. But let us try another tack. It may be more important to concentrate on the shattered parts of the human self. The Moon must surely stand for that large part of our unconscious which we call the "subconscious". But what then of Anulios? Gurdjieff says it hasn't been generally known about or seen since Atlantean times, and people today are accustomed to seeing nothing that is "real". How can we then identify it? We have two clues.

## Another Possibility for Anulios

Maybe the reversing of the first four letters of Anulios, to get "luna", was a happy or contrived distraction. (If so, we needn't torture ourselves still trying to find a second 'moon'.) That would make it easier to accept Toro or Hermes as the body in question. But it's not clear that leads anywhere. Another possibility with Anulios is that just the first three letters are important - "Anu". In the pantheon of the gods of Gurdjieff's beloved Babylon, Anu was the highest god of all. He was the "sky-god" and dwelt in the highest heavenly realms. He was a kind of "god above the gods". That's starting to sound promising.

As our second clue, we can look for what is still missing in the human psyche once the subconscious is re-blended with our consciousness. Since the functions we know about in the subconscious (conscience and essence) all involve "feeling", we might identify this Moon aspect with what Gurdjieff elsewhere calls the higher emotional or feeling centre. But he also talks of a higher intellectual centre, the characterisation and recovery of which are not detailed in other places in his teaching. Anulios might be smaller than the Moon (at least in one sense), but linked with a more exalted function.

This runs parallel with Gurdjieff's designated third and fourth states, or levels of consciousness, outlined briefly in our chapter one above. Through the subconscious we achieve self-consciousness. But in the fourth, higher, state we are said to come to objective consciousness. There seems to be an affinity here with a "god above the gods". If the "gods" are, as affirmed in chapter six above, "powers of the subconscious", then the "god above them" must be of a higher, different order.

## Objective Consciousness

Actually, in Beelzebub Gurdjieff does tell us that the possibility of acquiring objective, and also divine, reason, comes only after we have achieved the facility of the two cosmic laws of "7" and "3" in us. (See p. 244.)(Those are the meldings of the "7-in-1" and "3-in-1" states.) If the sunrise meditations allow us to identify and bring together ALL the shattered parts of ourselves, they must have the potential to take us both through the meldings and right up to objective consciousness.

Then, what could that fragment Anulios be, aligned with the possibility of our acquiring, or re-acquiring, objective consciousness? Here things seem to twist and turn a bit. If we took the most obvious course, we'd see a parallel between the poor, barren lifeless Moon – which needs vibrations from organic life on Earth to 'feed' it – and the

Sun. Gurdjieff also described the Sun as a poor benighted body, cold to freezing like the proverbial hairless canine, and badly in need itself of a bit of light and heat from elsewhere (p. 135). Do some kind of vibrations from the Earth also 'feed' the Sun? Perhaps. But identifying Anulios with the Sun also has its problems.

Anulios was clearly said to be a smaller fragment than the Moon, but the Sun is enormously bigger than that. But, to the "Moon religions" of antiquity, the Moon was certainly more important than the Sun. Perhaps "smaller" then refers to "importance in the scheme of things" rather than physical size. Gurdjieff also says that Anulios was known as Kimespai in the final stages of Atlantis – a name supposed to indicate that it deprived people of the ability to sleep peacefully. How could it do that? Was there a fear it might crash back into the Earth, which constantly disrupted everyone's ability to sleep? That's not so likely. Or could it be, that it was the Sun, and therefore its daily shining made it difficult for people to keep sleeping after it rose in the morning?

Some of the best mysteries are hidden in plain sight. Could it be that obvious then, that Anulios is our (physical) Sun? It half-fits, but surely must be a bit of nonsense. After all, the Sun is the prime body in any solar system. Without the Sun first, there couldn't be a solar system, and there wouldn't have been an Earth and other planets here before the Sun was in place. What would the planets have been attracted to and revolved around? So, how could the Sun be formed as a fragment that flew off the Earth? No, it won't work.

It would appear instead that, Anulios (as a physical body) must be just a fragment of the story-teller's imagination, part of a "tale" that a grandfather was spinning for his grandson, but with another point to it. That doesn't mean there weren't other fragments which flew off into space when the Moon was formed by an impact on Earth. (Maybe Toro, Hermes and Eros are all such fragments.) But looking for Anulios "out there" may be a fruitless quest. It may have its point in the story by drawing attention to the internal sun we all have "in here", in the solar plexus. And maybe we all had the potential of objective consciousness in the "oneness" which existed before the psyche was fragmented. Could we reconnect with that through concentration on the solar plexus, to recover the function of the Great Central Sun?

There is an analogy with the spiritual quest of Everyman, who starts by looking "out there" for what can only be found "in here". In a substantial sense, none of us sleep as deeply and peacefully as we could until we find how to reconnect with the unified potential of our highest selves.

## Pulling the Plug

At this stage in my writing, Gurdjieff conveyed a message to me. He said the elaboration of his seven salient points could fill a whole book in future. He told me then to leave the rest, and they would remain secret (if enterprising readers couldn't find them in the meantime) until that later book. Apparently I have just been conscripted to write a further book for him! I welcome his confidence in me, but that will have to be considered.

I thought it important to demonstrate how his salient points operated as 'hubs', to draw other information in around them. But one reason he pulled me up at this stage was, he wanted the present book to be a "basic introduction" to his teaching, without too much elaboration. He said people have to be given time to digest what is presented, before they are given more.

I can only apologise for not being able to present all seven salient points here, and the overall key to Beelzebub.

If I ignore Gurdjieff's advice over this, I may not be given further teaching. I can, however, round off by saying a few things about Ashiata Shiemash.

## Ashiata Shiemash

Finally, a word about Ashiata Shiemash seems appropriate. Remember, in chapter one we looked briefly at this very important figure, who was able to transform a whole area of Central Asia in ancient times. He had a method for restoring the proper functioning of the human psyche, which led to an amazing social transformation. For a short time, before other factors intervened, human beings began to function as they should, like all other three-brained beings in the universe. Details of that episode are recounted in chapters 25 to 28 of Beelzebub.

Gurdjieff presented Ashiata Shiemash as an historical figure, and that invited us to speculate as to who it might have been – someone we've heard of in ancient times (under a different name), or a person unknown in modern history? I tended to assume it was an incarnation of Hermes, because surviving Hermetic writings testify to the seven essences and the eighth nature. Whoever was behind that teaching knew the process for restoring the human psyche to the level of the "complete person". That's what must have been involved in any social transformation exhibiting the characteristics Gurdjieff described. J.G.Bennett, of course, believed it had been Zoroaster. He had his reasons for that.

But this approach was seriously impacted by Gurdjieff's later claims, when he declared more than once that he was Ashiata Shiemash! On another occasion, when asked exactly when this hero lived, he said rather confusingly that it could have been "not yet"! This was what I wanted to clarify when I recently had contact with him. It was apparently the kind of confusion that only Gurdjieff could create, and resolve.

**The Gurdjieff Answer**

He began by affirming that all the elements of his depiction of Ashiata Shiemash were "historically based". (He said, he "didn't just make it up".) There had been the teaching close to Babylonian times which had, for a short time, fuelled social transformation of the kind described by restoration of the true functioning of the psyche. But he also maintained that, we shouldn't put this down just to the work of one man. He had given the name "Ashiata Shiemash" to a central figure, but such a movement always depends upon a whole group of people incarnating together with the same purpose. The group supports the individual leading it.

He used the word "amalgam" to describe this grouping. (This amused and delighted me. Since, an amalgam is, by definition, a blending of Mercury [Hermes] with another metal or metals.) But then again, leadership of such an enterprise will inevitably devolve to a person, or persons, with the Mercury essence. Mercury is the most able of the essences.

Beyond that, apparently, is the same idea connected with the legendary King Arthur in Britain. (This is my example, inserted to explain what Gurdjieff went on to say.) The legendary elements of that episode are based in a kind of historical enactment of certain things, whose significance transcended what we might think of as just another ancient king and court. Something from the 'otherwhere' breaks through, for a short time, to exhibit a reality – subconsciously based – which goes beyond 'normal' everyday experience. And, King Arthur became, thereafter, "The once, and future, king!" It embodies a promise for the future.

This is why Gurdjieff could claim he was Ashiata Shiemash, or that this individual might be still to come. If there had been the right group of willing and able supporters around Gurdjieff, he could have begun the social transformation process. He had the teaching and vision for it. But it wasn't to be, at least during his lifetime, because the time wasn't right.

Gurdjieff said that his depiction of Ashiata Shiemash's role was "absolutely crucial". That hope, that vision, that expectation is integral to the coming and future good we all need to hold in prospect. It will happen. And its coming into being will be facilitated by those who embrace the vision and look to its manifestation on the Earth. In this sense, as he said, "Just the possibility is crucial". And that's why he was compelled to include the account of Ashiata Shiemash in his book. Those on the path needed to hear it. It gives "people access to their own subconscious thoughts", which is the bridge to the outcome of a restored humanity in the everyday reality. (See also his comments on "aspiration" in the final chapter.)

**Mission Sufficiently Completed**

Gurdjieff died in 1949, shortly after signing-off on the final drafts of Beelzebub. That was significant. He had "done enough" to complete his life's work.

The medium told me that for

> *the last 3 or 4 years (of his life)..just every day he wanted to go. And he really dragged the chains. (19/Feb/85)*

The autopsy after his death apparently puzzled doctors, because his organs were in such a condition that they wondered how he could have lived so long.

He had been concerned as he wrote LIROT in 1934 whether he would sufficiently fulfil the various aims of his life to merit a peaceful end (p. 6). He did. I know from my review of his kundalini experience in Beelzebub (p. 38). He said there he had experienced such a peacefulness from the kundalini experience as he had only one other time in his life.

When I asked about that second, later experience of profound peace, the medium said it was "when he came close to death". It was when he knew he had completed all that he had been goaded, guided and directed to do during his lifetime. The important writing had been done, and groups organised to carry on his legacy. His successor had been appointed. After that, the burden lightened. He found a state of great well being. It must have come to him in time to revise the text of Beelzebub and insert the reference to his second experience of great peace.

The question arose during our January 10, 1985 trance session, as to whether Gurdjieff had reincarnated to Earth again after his death in 1949. The answer was, "No. .. He doesn't need to."

CHAPTER TWELVE

# Conclusion

It is now over 40 years since I first read ISOTM, and over 30 since Gurdjieff made initial contact with me through the medium. In 1984 he told me he'd made the big mistake during his lifetime of "trying to go too fast". That's how he

> *got ahead of (his) time. And why (he) didn't complete even what (he) should have completed when (he) was here. (10/Dec/84)*

So he wanted the work with me to go "very slowly", to get it right. He said he didn't have a "pacing mechanism" in himself during his lifetime, and that's why it all got "too complicated and too intricate". The timing was out. He also tried to advance to later stages of the work before he'd properly laid the foundation. It had all been too much of a rush. He was "pushing, pushing" constantly. He even deferred or ignored work on himself, and his "life's work" on the writing, to try to get things moving outwardly with his students.

We see here how even those advanced in mastership can have problems in coping with the dense conditions of living a life in the world. Even when he'd returned to the "other side", his original timetable to me of "nearer to 2000" for publication of this book was out. Timing depends crucially on the flow of events, and actual dates have to be moved back or forward to co-ordinate with them.

But everything was in place for my work on this book in 2012, and as I write this conclusion we have now reached 2013, past the celebrated marker of 21.12.2012. Apparently we are now decisively in the "new age", which so many see as the time for monumental changes on Earth.

Some months ago Gurdjieff sent me the message that

many thousands of people were "poised" for significant spiritual development. It could indeed be an exciting time on the planet. So many people watched like spectators to see what would happen in December 2012. But St Germain had said it would be a day when "nothing much happens", and "everything changes". It will be chiefly by inner changes and realisations that a new way of life will emerge. The driving force will be awakening individuals.

According to Gurdjieff, the world will change by "one individual at a time". And, "the thing that we can do" to assist that, is to work on changing ourselves. He said he himself had proceeded "with himself, in the moment".

**Observations on the Groups**

In his messages communicated to me over 2012, Gurdjieff often commented on the "groups" set up in his name. He originally organised such groups, before his death, and left them with specific instructions. He chiefly wanted them to preserve and transmit his intact teachings to the rest of the world over time. They had a very important role to play in that regard, and they have certainly fulfilled it. The writings are still available.

But he's been disappointed by other aspects of what he's seen there for some time. Remember, he told me in 1984/5 not to bother with the groups, because they'd already lost most of their meaning. He was talking about their grasp of his teaching. More recently, he said my work was important because I'd managed to put so much together outside of the groups. It showed how his teaching could be passed on directly to people, who could now use it without the group structure.

Yet, with his constant checking of "how the groups are going", he obviously has been rather concerned about them. Could he have been so disappointed if he didn't still have expectations of them? I can't be sure exactly what his plans or expectations have been. But I presume he gave me the comments he did for passing on in this book. He never told me not to use them, and provided comments for the book foreword in line with them. Surely those in the groups can only benefit from his feedback, critical as so much of it is. If there is anyone with the right and ability to give relevant advice here, it is him. After all, these kinds of groups were originally set up by him, operating in his name, and claiming to pass on his teaching. So I present the various comments he's made to me about them for consideration.

By this stage, over 60 years after his passing over, there are none of the people he originally appointed to run his groups still there. There is no-one who had direct contact with him to inform the running of the present groups. A completely new generation are now the 'elders' and leaders of these movements. Unfortunately, this is when less desirable changes can start to appear.

From what he said to me, there is still the old problem which he had in the 1920s to 1940s. People are reluctant to find and use their subconscious. This is absolutely pivotal. That's why the emphasis in this book is so strongly on understanding and embracing it. Certainly those in the groups know about the subconscious in themselves, but they are rather reluctant to <u>trust</u> it.

> *People in existing groups are afraid to confront themselves. The step to actually trusting and working with the subconscious is one they're scared to make, and draw back from.* *(7/Mar/12)*

A fear here is that, they don't want to lose conscious control. They imagine that, if they open themselves to the subconscious, it will be like a "gushing well". So they don't want it taking over and getting out of control. But, he said to me, the subconscious <u>doesn't</u> "take over". It doesn't run out of control. It will sit non-threateningly within the confines of an ordinary life, and bring transforming moments to it. So when this fear is faced, and dissolved, it can only bring great benefit.

## Finding the Basis

Earlier in this book (chapter 5) I included a 1985 comment from Gurdjieff that the groups "can't give you the basis" or "foundation" of the work. He was talking – again - about the emphasis on intellectualising there, and the avoidance of the subconscious, and feeling, and how individuals might connect with it. People who are afraid of their own subconscious aren't well placed to show this basic step to others. It is the crucial step each individual must take to start the transforming process within themselves.

(There is teaching relevant to this in chapters one and two above, where the approach to conscience and essence is also outlined. Further explanations about the essence, from chapter six onwards, should also greatly assist those ready to venture productively into the main work on themselves.)

Of course, those still struggling with buffers, negative emotions, chief features or faults, or restraining fears, may be assisted in understanding and dealing with these through the work of the groups. But then again, maybe enough has been explained about those in this, and other books, for self-starting individuals to make their own way.

## Groups that are "Stuck"

Gurdjieff talked on another occasion about groups that are "stuck". He put this down to two things - "timing, and exercises".

The timing issue is when groups, or individuals in them, aren't ready to be "disabused of their illusions or delusions". They're not ready for the buffers or blocking personality features to be removed. So, this just has to be allowed to continue, as he told me he "had to do for Ouspensky and others" when he was here.

The problem with the "exercises" is, there is no-one like himself in these groups at the moment to direct what exercises are appropriate, and when "shocks" should be given. So, people are being given the wrong exercises, or at the wrong times. This is counter-productive.

## Ouspensky

Ouspensky only went so far with his own development, and it wasn't appropriate for Gurdjieff to push him any further. He had basically recorded and written up the early teaching, which he was meant to do. But he was hung up on a "chief feature or fault" which blocked his further progress. (See the section on those 'features' in chapter two above.)

It is rather strange to see Ouspensky explain the chief features or faults in ISOTM (p. 226). He even cites the propensity to talk too much as the first example of it, but never ever related it back to himself.

Gurdjieff "sort of suffered Ouspensky", but found him hard to take in some ways. He lampooned him to me as going on like, "Da-de, da-de, da-de-da..." He said he had

> *too much to say about too little. .. If he'd said less, he'd have known more. (10/Jan/85)*

He acknowledged he was "very intellectual", but lacked empathy, intuition and psychic insight. He was rather neurotic in some ways, and tended to see himself as "a bit of a monk". He was hopeless at relationships or being able to relate meaningfully at a personal level to others.

The incessant talking was obviously the axle around which his false personality revolved. He "needed" it to function in the everyday world. He had written up all he needed to know about this in ISOTM, but wasn't ready to look at it in himself.

Gurdjieff even tried further to get him to confront this. He asked him from the mid-1920s to re-write the teaching in a form accessible to more people. That wasn't only because Gurdjieff wanted the teaching in a simplified form. It would also have led Ouspensky to transcend his fixed manner of verbal elaboration, which he was locked into. It wasn't appropriate for Gurdjieff beyond that to try to directly disabuse him of his illusions. Because, we must all see any chief fault or feature we have by choosing ourselves to see and confront it, in our own time. Until we choose to see it, it can't be moved beyond.

If Gurdjieff had intervened to strip Ouspensky of "all the talk", he would have overridden his will, and taken away the choice of his own soul. That would have prematurely stripped him of what was holding his false personality together. He would have been left in a total mess. That is why removal of the chief feature of fault can't be forced on someone by anyone else.

**Certain Groups**

On another occasion, Gurdjieff went into an animated 'rave' about "(certain, current) groups". He said they were "misrepresenting and changing things" in his teaching. And this was becoming "negative" and "dangerous". He said they needed to do three things:

1) *Read Beelzebub three times.*
2) *Read Fritz Peters' Balanced Man. And,*
3) *Remove from their eyes the illusion that they know what they're talking about.*

This may be linked with some other comments he made about "belief structures". He said we need to get rid of our belief structures. The mind builds them up, and they become an obstacle to our ability to progress. He said the subconscious has no belief structures, and neither should we.

The reference to Fritz Peters' last book is interesting. It seems most people never understood Peters, or why Gurdjieff named him publicly as his successor.

**Fritz Peters**

I didn't understand at first why Gurdjieff was so insistent on referring me to Fritz Peters. It was certainly interesting background. But I couldn't find much in Peters' writings which directly assisted the explanation of the points at issue in this book. Then, as I sat down to review what he said slowly, with Gurdjieff's prodding, I saw how he embodied the teaching rather than verbally expressing or expounding it in the same way as the others. He had more "inner access" to what it was all about.

Peters had been brought to the Paris Institute when he was 11, and did some important "growing up" there. He was treated as a boy rather than a student of the teaching, and received crucial tasks and guidance for his "upbringing" directly from Gurdjieff. It was how he developed in that relationship which determined what he went on to become. Gurdjieff, of course, knew peoples' essences, and adapted his dealings with them to cater to that.

In his early 30s, Peters visited Gurdjieff at his Paris apartment shortly before the latter's death, with a group of people. Gurdjieff then made an "announcement". He said he was able to die now, because his important book was finished, and because he had found one person to whom he could give his accumulated life-learning. He pointed to Peters as that person. It caused dismay and some annoyance amongst the rest of the assembled company. Peters was even 'blamed' later for somehow causing this upset in everyone else's expectations!

One can see a kind of strategy in the Peters endorsement, in Gurdjieff's withholding such a bestowal on any of the other nominated group leaders. He gave none of them a reason for pre-eminence amongst the others. But his nomination of Peters was quite genuine. It is difficult to find anyone who could understand or accept that. Peters "embodied" the teaching better than any of the others. And he would not misuse such a bestowal. He didn't.

Peters only ever saw himself as "normal", and had no pretensions about his ability to understand and transmit Gurdjieff's teaching. He just gave as much as he had found of value in himself. But he was looked down on by the others, who didn't hesitate to "tell" him what he should or shouldn't do. They seemed to consider him almost a non-starter in the work.

A big problem here was, none of the others knew enough about the essences to see what Peters was. Somehow, they just didn't take him seriously. As I tried to pick his essence, from reading of his two earlier books, and then Balanced Man, the Saturn influence seemed most evident. That would've explained the tasks Gurdjieff gave him to perform, and the way he took on those obligations. Saturns are "doers" more than thinkers, who can't really compete with the more agile mental abilities of the Mercurys so attracted to the Gurdjieff teachings. But they are faithful, honest workers who will strive to fulfil their obligations.

In his further comments to me about Peters, Gurdjieff said there was no artifice or pretence there. He had understood the teaching subconsciously rather than consciously. (That's what we need!) And he was just "living it", while others talked about it but didn't live it. Peters had his problems in life, and much that he needed to work through. It wasn't easy for him. But he seemed to organise himself to fulfil his obligations as best he could.

**Praise for Saturn**

In Beelzebub Gurdjieff is unstinting of his praise for Saturns. (For example, see pages 92-3.) He said he liked them above the other essences, for their nearness to the Prime Creator. Saturns can be greatly undervalued in everyday life, because they're not exactly "star performers". But as trustworthy friends and conscientious workers, they can hardly be surpassed.

In essence terms, of course, all the essences are of equal worth and value. The various Gurdjieff 'groups', by their nature, tend to attract more Mercurys than any other essence. They can be kinds of "clubs for intellectuals". So it is important to see and value all the essences, not just the articulate and eloquent ones with interesting and rich thought-lives. What we devalue or put down in others, when it is a genuine part of their essence-expression, becomes a block in our perception of ourselves. But we need all those parts, finally, for our own completeness.

**Helping Saturns**

In the work of our first group of seven in 1984/5, Gurdjieff emphasised that it was an obligation on the more able essences – chiefly the three 'head' ones, Mercury, Moon and Jupiter – to "help" the other essences. Remember, from explanations earlier in this book, that the three 'head' essences weather 'shocks' easier and recover quicker. But Saturns, for instance, are subject to more body blows, with slower progress. They will labour on, with the best of intentions, so far as they are able. But their progress can be assisted by more understanding and help from the more able essences.

It was a pity that Fritz Peters' commitment to his essence wasn't recognised by the other "high flyers" in the work, and that they treated him as they did. Gurdjieff's "endorsement" of him helped to correct the effects of that on him. But then he had to endure the peeved reactions of those who thought they were more worthy than him to be named the master's "son" and "heir". And he got body blows all his life from those who thought he didn't appreciate the great opportunity he'd been given, and was "holding out" on passing on all he could have. But you don't go to a Saturn to have the finer points of Gurdjieff's teaching explained to you. Their best qualities are displayed in other ways.

**<u>Gurdjieff and "Interpreters'</u>**

The essence is an integral part of our inner "truth sense", and people in touch with their essence get a truer feeling-picture of the world than others. Fritz Peters was in touch with his essence. (He could have immediately started work in a "group of seven".) So, if you read his books carefully, you will find many interesting insights lurking there. He might not have understood everything that Ouspensky or J.G.Bennett - for example - talked about, but he was tuned-in enough to see and know when they were changing and 'interpreting' what Gurdjieff said. And he said so. So he recommended that people should read Gurdjieff's own writings, rather than those of his 'interpreters', to get the authentic flavour of the man and his teaching.

I have already given Gurdjieff's assessment of Ouspensky. One should by now then, be able to go back through his books and start to see where Ouspensky was adapting or misinterpreting what he was given. For example, he veers off into a rather intellectual understanding of that important component, "remembering oneself".

Instead of seeing how we 'remember' in order to maintain the feeling-sense of our inner selves <u>while</u> engaged in everyday activities, he put a different spin on it. He saw it as a 'splitting' of our attention, so that one was meant to be looking two ways at the same time. That is, he was trying to both look at his everyday reality and the part of him that was looking at that reality. He hadn't yet identified the self behind the self in himself. He therefore saw the 'remembering' practice as mental gymnastics. For him it was a kind of "remembering to do it". He didn't seem to see the home-coming sense of reassurance one can have of an inner self, separate from everything in the everyday world, while living in it.

The point of "remembering oneself" is that, one can thereby be "in the world" while inwardly knowing one is not "of it". One doesn't have to retire to a monastery to escape the coercive influence of everyday reality. The remembering of the different self, privately, within, even while going through the motions of playing the everyday game, is sufficient to separate oneself from it. This is an exercise 'busy' Westerners can use, while continuing to live otherwise active lives.

**And J.G.Bennett?**

Strangely, Bennett wasn't comfortable with everything Ouspensky said. But when I first mentioned Bennett to Gurdjieff, he also started to denounce the 'interpretation' there. Fritz Peters had been correct. At first, Gurdjieff called Bennett a "parasite" and an "opportunist". When I protested that I had got much from Bennett's books, he conceded they were "alright". But, he said, you have to "read between the lines of what Bennett wrote". It was just "Bennett's interpretation" of him. There was more in what Gurdjieff had told him than Bennett could grasp, and he had "missed a lot" of what he was told.

So I came to understand more of what Gurdjieff meant when he originally said to me that he'd been "misquoted". No-one he worked with had sufficiently grasped the range of elements integral to the teaching and its practice. While the work of Ouspensky and Bennett had provided a kind of bridge for Western thinkers to approach Gurdjieff, there was not enough there to properly fire the development process. There was more, which they couldn't or didn't provide.

Personally, I'm immensely grateful for the bridges Ouspensky and Bennett provided, which helped me to get where I am. But then I was given the opportunity to go further, which is what this book is about.

**Gurdjieff's Work with the Young Peters**

I think how much easier the whole task of transmitting his teaching would have been, if Gurdjieff had been able to train more young children in their essences as he did with Peters. Once we know what the essences are, and how they operate, it is a lot easier to identify them in children and guide their development intelligently. Before young people are locked into false personality roles by their 'upbringing', they naturally display more of their essence. They are "all essence" before they are subjected to those other influences.

It normally doesn't take long to identify a child's essence. One just needs to watch how they operate for a while. People can do this by acquainting themselves with all the essence characteristics and getting the "feel" of them. But I've had no children of my own, and limited access to others' children. (A notable exception is how I watched a young cousin develop as a Jupiter. I pointed out to the parents and grandmother – who were Saturn, Mars and Venus – what a great little "organiser" the child was. They were astonished as they saw it, and admired her abilities.) Of course, one needs to do this tactfully, without challenging the parents' right to know better what is more appropriate for their child than anyone else.

It is also by the 'upbringing' influences on children that karma and certain life experiences are set-up. (Parents are chosen for the life circumstances they will guide their children into.) So, one may not be altogether free to intervene in many cases with that. Or, one might try, but not get very far. You can't override a person's "reason for being here". If one has the opportunity however, to highlight a child's essence characteristics for them, it is surely a good thing to do what one can.

You will soon see how far you can proceed with it. In many cases, karma and life lessons can still be gone through with a helpful awareness of one's essence. And, Gurdjieff complains that many people are "slow learners", who could be pushed a bit to finish up their slow learning and get on with some real development.

Important essence assistance could be given by teachers in schools. It would involve the choice of tasks and activities that different children are given. Just as importantly, there will be a withholding of the regimenting, hypnotising influences which lock them into false personalities and 'sleep'. There would be far more freedom given for children to put together the world for themselves in their own way. This is not a freedom to distort or deny basic facts, but a tolerance of alternative "ways of seeing". It will be realised there are far more "forms of intelligence" amongst the human population than what is typically measured with IQ tests. We could say there are seven basic forms of intelligence. When a child has a "different way of seeing", one should not disrupt their confidence in that.

Gurdjieff gave me some pointers about this. He said that

> *what one does in a Masters or PhD (programme) is what one should be doing back, way down the ladder. ...this can be done with the youngest of learners, with the youngest of minds. ..(children) will go through the evolutionary stages of spirit much more quickly if information on history or life, or whatever, is done through that person's individual taste for it, at the time. .. And it comes down to allowing people a great deal more latitude in what they see subjectively as being correct.* (5/Feb/85)

He said that certain guiding rules could be used for managing children in this way, which could be employed by teachers who are sufficiently versed in the point of the exercise. They could be used with normal class sizes, because it needn't require one-to-one teaching.

**A Communicated Correction Over Peters**

As I said above, my impression just from limited reading of Fritz Peters books was that he was a Saturn essence. Gurdjieff has just intervened on this with more information. He told me Peters was a "rarer beast" than that – in fact, a Uranus essence. He added information I didn't have, and would probably have found it difficult to gain from published sources. Peters was regarded as a "lightweight" by the self-appointed elite in Gurdjieff circles. (That couldn't be said of a Saturn.) He had a habit of telling people what they didn't want to hear or know – which Gurdjieff was delighted with - and was sometimes erratic and would "blow up", or walk out of the room.

Those are typical Uranus characteristics, because that essence is intrinsically unstable and capricious. So you sometimes get brilliant interventions, and at other times it is childish or shallow. At last I could 'see' why the others reacted to and treated Peters as they did. (And, of course, while the stable, more capable essences would recoil from many of the unstable manifestations of a Uranus type, they would be reluctant to detail them in publications.) They had no idea about the manifestations of the Uranus essence. If Saturns need the "help" of the more able essences, then more so the Uranus essence. And most of what I said previously still stands.

There are reasons in this case why Peters could have been mistaken at first glance for a Saturn. Initially I wasn't alerted to the capricious elements, which are a dead give-away. But Gurdjieff had obviously "played Saturn" with Peters from the start to give him maximum stability. Uranus types benefit greatly from the stable, ordering energies of a Saturn, which enables them to present a more consistent everyday persona. They can also mirror or reflect any of the other essence characteristics on a short-term basis. So they can "present" as a Saturn at times.

Using the Saturn influence on Peters would have enabled

Gurdjieff to achieve most with him. Since Peters had told Gurdjieff he wanted to know "everything", he accommodated him as far as he could, and took him as far as he was able. Peters must have been an older soul to achieve as much as he did, and therefore quite strong in his essence.

(It becomes obvious then that Rachmilievitch as well as Peters – and Katherine Mansfield – were all Uranus essences. They were possibly the only ones at the Paris Institute. As I said in explaining the need to involve Uranus people in group activities with subsidiary reasons - in chapter 10 – they won't see the point of development work in the same way as the other essences. I believe Gurdjieff had to pay Rachmilievitch to attend the Institute. Peters was there as a youngster being provided with a home. And Katherine Mansfield was offered the possibility of healing for her medical condition. You do what you need to, to get the Uranus participation you require.)

**Impacting Those Who are Asleep**

Peters' development can be contrasted with Gurdjieff's other students. It is a lot easier to work with those still at the edge of childhood, compared to others who are older and carry a great burden through their socialisation into false personality roles. We're talking here too about the 1920s, in a Western society still very straight-jacketed with social expectations.

This is what Gurdjieff strove mightily to try to break down. It is fortunate that he was so "toughened" by his background and life experiences, that he could continually assault the 'bob-tailed' mentality of people. Few of us could maintain our vision and continually engage in such impacting behaviour on those around us.

It had to be "shocks" of course (for Gurdjieff) – berating and insulting people, and using every form of contrived acting and display to try to connect with the sleeping and disconnected subconscious of his students. That had to be balanced too, so he wasn't just outraging and abusing them all the time, but they could see there was wisdom and genuine concern for their well-being behind what he did.

**Two People**

Gurdjieff was almost like "two people". There was the inner, 'private' person that virtually no-one saw. And there was the outer teaching iconoclast, who laboured incessantly to destroy the false images in everyone's psyches. This is what he meant when he talked about his "artificial life".

He talked at times about taking oaths to do whatever was necessary to advance his teaching. There was, in fact, just the one oath, reviewed in chapter nine above. But in the final analysis, he apparently had little choice in having to live an artificial life to promote his cause. How else could he have conducted himself in those circumstances, especially when he needed to act as fast as possible to get things moving?

Inside himself, he knew there had only ever been one person in the world who intrinsically understood him - his grandmother. He had back-up from his father and Dean Borsch while growing up, and limited fellow-feeling in later years with de Hartmann and Orage. But no-one had touched his inner core since his grandmother. He had no-one to share his innermost life with. Thus his closeness to his guardian. In his life there was basically only his 'mission', and the need to get on with it. So he just kept "pushing on". He himself saw this as part of a person being "an adult", to carry the responsibility of what life dealt out and demanded of him.

He confided to me that occasionally, labouring under this regime, he could start to wonder if he was really the embodiment of all he sought to promote, or a charlatan. That would be normal in his circumstances. He only had himself to critically assess himself. The times when he took a "rest" to "indulge his vices" would have been important for recovering his equilibrium in the face of that.

However much he lacked any company for his personal self, it was also easier for him then to play the numerous roles that he did. He could move with less difficulty through the gamut of impacting roles, without 'investment' in any of them.

Then, he also had the inner assurance of his level

of development. When touching the energy of "the grasshopper" - most apparent around 1930/1 – it gave him great joy and buoyancy. When most involved in the great work of transmitting what he knew, as Beelzebub came together, his spirit soared. He pays tribute to this as the "aspiration" which is necessary in all our lives.

**The Place of Aspiration**

In his communicated teaching to me, and reviews of my progress, he continually underlined the importance of 'aspiration'. Nothing moves, or moves beneficially, without it. All genuine progress is fuelled by it. "What are we aspiring to, both in our present efforts, and in our life in general?"

When he resumed communication with me at the beginning of 2012, he asked me to write down what I expected from this book and working with him. I compiled a modest list, unsure about what was possible. When his response was communicated back to me, I was told he rolled around on the floor laughing. He said my hopes were "comical" and "as nothing". I wasn't aspiring to much, and that had to change.

So I set a more determined course, and committed myself to doing what was necessary to live and write the teaching. I wanted his important introductory teaching to be simplified and accessible. I wanted the result to be pleasing equally for him and me, and of substantial benefit to those who would read it. I learnt much through my writing, and came to see more of his genius, his game-plan, and the importance of his message and mission.

**Degrees of Aspiration**

The person submerged in their false personality has no real aspiration. Hopes and dreams are limited to what seems "possible" under the existing outer order of things, when they're either told or 'allowed' to pursue such things.

To Gurdjieff these people are "sheep". And we know what those are. They're weak and stupid animals who only move when they're pushed or led. "Sheep" is a good description of people in the everyday sleeping state. They wait for life to happen to them, and they have no real initiative to change anything for themselves. They wait to be told what to believe or do by the media or any of the established 'authorities'. Gurdjieff said to me (November 2012) that sheep have "no will, no risk, no life". They're people who have not yet imagined any desirable outcomes for themselves.

Yet the possibility lies with so many people to begin to change that for themselves. Where aspiration can be tapped, a person can start to project themselves positively to attain some real goals in life.

One published criticism of Gurdjieff is that, no student of his ever grasped what was expected of them. (See Anderson's The Unknowable Gurdjieff, p. 6.) But that is the problem with 'sheep'. They wait for someone else to direct and organise their life for them. ("Just tell me what you want me to do.") The real problem was that no student he had ever reached the stage of seeing that "it was up to them to do it for themselves". (Except Peters, of course. He just went on and did it.)

Some aspiration has to arise from within a person, and then be listened to and followed. Gurdjieff explained that as arising from a magnetic hub within oneself, which was still open to the influence of higher forces. He said this possibility was there for two kinds of people. Firstly, there were those in whom upbringing and education had not extinguished the sensing of inner longing. Secondly, there was what he called "simple" man.

The first are those who've become relatively proficient in everyday abilities, but still remain conscious inwardly of something missing from their lives. The second are those focused on more basic living, who've ignored or resisted most of the everyday socialising pressures. Gurdjieff regarded himself as a "simple man". This is not mental retardation. It is a more basic manner of living, where little sophistication has been allowed to develop in the false personality.

When, therefore, the presence and teaching of someone like Gurdjieff impacts these two kinds of people in life, they feel an unmistakable stirring within. A chord is struck. It speaks to and excites a hope in the heart. The aspiration is stirred. They feel, "Here is someone who knows something" and "This man has some real answers to the mystery of life".

The rest can be deduced from the explanations given in this book. It starts with the initial felt 'tug'. One realises a longing, and there is a desire to know more. Even when stalled by a threatening fear, we can still get glimpses of it, and work on moving past that. Finding the second self and the essence, are big breakthroughs. There is a parallel unfolding of what will give a new dimension and hope in our lives. There is the prospect of a different kind of life. We no longer have to feel confined within the parameters of the sociologically predictable.

## Aspiration and 'Work'

Gurdjieff constantly talks about "work", as in "working on oneself". If we didn't aspire to anything, we wouldn't see the point and meaning in such work. It is the prospect of "getting somewhere" and "achieving something" which motivates us in the work. We no longer want to stay where we are. Not when a new prospect presents itself.

Yet, work in this context is an unusual thing. Just "efforting" by itself isn't the reward. It is about what we can see ourselves reaching out for. Importantly, we set our intention. Gurdjieff once said that the attending to this, and keeping on, aren't as difficult (or decisive) as setting the original intention. (Views from the Real World, p. 214.) Once aspiration has led us to making the choice, we only need to "keep on" after that.

(Along the way, the "work" has more to do with battling the inertia of the everyday hypnotic/sleep state. Or it might be not succumbing to the disease of "tomorrow" (leaving things until 'tomorrow'), or resisting the illusory sense of "calm" we might imagine we had before involving ourselves in this quest. ("Maybe I was 'alright' before I got involved in all this.")

**Work and 'Play'**

This "work" is also a form of play. Gurdjieff worked very hard at writing Beelzebub, but it was also a very playful thing for him. All his role-play was a kind of play. If you look at the 1973 Seth channelling (referred to in the Preface), you will see Seth's claim that Gurdjieff told people to work because he really wanted them to play! Calling it "work" was a way of underlining the seriousness of the enterprise, and the need to stick at it. Many people in those days also would have felt guilty about playing. So Gurdjieff told them it was 'work', and they would embrace it with no sense of guilt.

For a Mercury essence especially, play can be a serious activity. Or, work is more purposeful, enjoyable and fulfilling if it can be seen as a game. When Sherlock Holmes found a genuine mystery or crime which grabbed his investigative interest, he would say: "The game in on!" There was a thrill in the chase.

**Work and 'Mastery'**

There is an intrinsic interest for Mercury essence people in persisting with a project or investigation until they have "gotten to the bottom" of whatever excited their initial interest or attention. They want to 'master' the problem. This quest for mastery was apparent in Gurdjieff's way of proceeding right from the start. So, whenever he found something worth doing, he "did a lot of it."

Then he found this was a key to switching the bodily/organic/instinctive part of us, to bring the final part of our "3-in-1" into place. He therefore recommended it for everyone, of whatever essence.

We see it in the practical tasks he asked people to perform. He wanted them to "do a lot of it", to aim for mastery in whatever they were doing. So, it might have been mowing the lawns, or peeling a sack of potatoes, or digging a hole. Whatever it was, he wanted them to stick at it, and do it properly. Mastering everyday physical tasks was the same in principle for him as going on to master spiritual abilities. (This worked with Peters.) We need to overcome any 'laziness', or struggle against the inertia which keeps us locked in hypnotic sleep, to make breakthroughs.

We might note here that Gurdjieff didn't favour the notion of 'enlightenment' as an end-goal. He said we become increasingly enlightened in stages along the way. So it accrued by degrees. But he said "mastery" was the thing to aim for. It was a far more down-to-earth and we could more easily identify our progress. We knew when we weren't getting it, and could adjust our efforts accordingly.

## Gurdjieff's Big Breakthrough

He told me he had realised at a certain point that it was "up to him, to DO". This was a "big breakthrough". He had, of course, travelled widely in his younger years to collect all the information he needed, as well as the techniques. But he then basically projected himself, by aspiration, and "sticking at it", into the role of Master. He didn't just say, "Well, I've collected everything I need now. So I'll just wait for mastery to appear, or unfold." No.

This can be seen as one of his "secrets". He said, "No waiting. Just do it." This is not to deny that there are times when we need to pause and take stock. Nor is he telling us to go for it when what we are doing is not clear. We need to grasp what we are doing, and what we hold in prospect should be evident to us. But then, it was for him at that stage a matter of just "pushing through".

Now, we are looking here, for the big breakthrough, at someone who has achieved or completed the 'meldings', and "has their own 'I'." He said then he "pushed and pushed" to activate the WILL and get it moving. (Remember, from earlier explanations, "will" comes into place, or on-line, with the achievement of the "3-in-1" melding.) It is there then to be used. But we must set out to deliberately use it.

Notice how the "remembering of oneself" has also been a "re-membering" of the parts of the self and psyche through the meldings. One is re-calling or re-collecting the fragmented parts or members of the intrinsic self. Three parts of outward expression are put back into one, along with seven aspects of the essence. When melded together again, we have the complete self. Its name is "I am".

With all the parts in place, Gurdjieff worked with his "I am" sense of himself "in the moment". He said it was then just a matter of "practising, practising". He affirmed his ableness, his wish and choice to be "able to do". We see at last what he was talking about in LIROT. He aspired to be "master", and then pushed until he got there. He said there was "risk" with this at first. But he ignored the temptation to stop until he got confirmatory feedback. And, when it started to come together then there was "no risk".

**Exhibiting it for Others**

As I said in chapter 1, we are fortunate in being close enough in time to someone who put it all together for themselves. Moreover, he explained how he got there, in contemporary terms. Different Masters can make their breakthroughs in slightly different ways, and it is worth reviewing any accounts left by them of how they did it. (Gurdjieff recommended this in his third salient point in Beelzebub.) In all cases, the crucial final choice was made ("I'm going for it!"), and then they followed their appropriate practices for longer or shorter periods of time until they got there.

For Gurdjieff it was very much a matter of continuing to "work at it". He got all the preliminaries in place, and then he worked at it. Of the few accounts I am aware of, where Masters made that final step into their Masterhood, no-one else has left us with such an immensely detailed list of the processes. But then again, it was precisely Gurdjieff's "mission" to give this information to the world – especially Westerners who had become so locked in an external reality they couldn't see the real world. He had to display the path to masterhood in steps and ways such people could see and follow.

# Index

## C



## D

## E

## F



## G

## N



## O



## P

## R



## S

## T



## U

## V



## W



## Y



## Z

Printed in the United States
By Bookmasters